The

THEOLOGY
of AUGUSTINE

The

THEOLOGY
of AUGUSTINE

An Introductory Guide to His Most Important Works

Matthew Levering

B
Baker Academic
a division of Baker Publishing Group
Grand Rapids, Michigan

© 2013 by Matthew Levering

Published by Baker Academic
a division of Baker Publishing Group
P.O. Box 6287, Grand Rapids, MI 49516-6287
www.bakeracademic.com

Printed in the United States of America

Library of Congress Cataloging-in-Publication Data

Levering, Matthew, 1971–
    The theology of Augustine : an introductory guide to his most important works / Matthew Levering.
        p.   cm.
    Includes bibliographical references and index.
    ISBN 978-0-8010-4848-7 (pbk.)
    1. Augustine, Saint, Bishop of Hippo. I. Title.
BR65.A9L48 2013
230'.14092—dc23   2012028425

13   14   15   16   17   18   19   7   6   5   4   3   2   1

To David Solomon

Contents

Acknowledgments

My first thanks go to my beloved wife, Joy! She is wonderful and she makes life fun. I thank God every day for her and for our children. This book was written as a spiritual exercise during a period when I was particularly in need of Augustine's wisdom. I sought out Lewis Ayres at an early stage of the project, and he graciously encouraged it. Gerald Boersma, my good friend and former student who has become an expert on Augustine under Lewis's tutelage, read the manuscript and made helpful suggestions, as did the Reformed theologian Michael Allen. Andrew Hofer, OP, a patristics scholar who has a mastery of all things theological, reviewed the manuscript twice, and without his help I don't think that the book could have come to fruition. At a crucial juncture, Scott Hahn pointed my attention to Augustine's *Answer to Faustus, a Manichean*. A version of chapter 2 appears as "Scriptural and Sacramental Signs: Augustine's *Answer to Faustus*," *Letter and Spirit* 7 (2011): 91–118. In November 2010 Joel Green invited me to speak to his Hermeneutics of Christian Scripture group at the Society of Biblical Literature, where I delivered an excerpt from what eventually became chapter 6. A version of this lecture was published as "Linear and Participatory History in Augustine's *City of God*," *Journal of Theological Interpretation* 5 (2011): 175–96, for which I am grateful. At Baker Academic, Rodney Clapp, Jim Kinney, and James Ernest generously took an interest in the manuscript, and Tim West guided it through production. Elizabeth Farnsworth, an excellent doctoral student in theology at the University of Dayton, skillfully compiled the indexes. In addition to these good friends, let me mention Hans Boersma, Michael Carter, Jason Heron, Reinhard Hütter, Bruce Marshall, Alan Mostrom, Michael Vanderburgh, and Thomas Joseph White, OP, who were among those whose friendship and mentoring meant so much to me during the period of writing. I dedicate the book to David Solomon, founder of the Center for Ethics and Culture at the University of Notre Dame, with gratitude and esteem.

Introduction

Augustine's friend and first biographer, Possidius, wrote that "so many things were dictated and published by him and so many things were discussed in the church, written down and amended, whether against various heretics or expounded from the canonical books for the edification of the holy sons of the Church, that scarcely any student would be able to read and know them all."[1] Augustine wrote over one hundred treatises, countless letters and sermons, and more than five million words in all. Although few scholars can become acquainted with all of his writings, there are certain pivotal works that one simply must know if one is interested in the development of Christian theology, biblical exegesis, and Western civilization.[2] This is especially the case because Augustine has always been, and remains today, a controversial thinker whose insights into the realities of God and salvation can be easily misunderstood.

Setting aside the longer exegetical works such as the *Literal Commentary on Genesis*, *On the Psalms*, and *Tractates on the Gospel of John*, which would burst the bounds of this book,[3] the list of Augustine's necessary works includes the following seven: *On Christian Doctrine* (396–97, 426); *Answer to Faustus, a Manichean* (397–98); *Homilies on the First Epistle of John* (407); *On the Predestination*

---

1. Possidius, *The Life of Saint Augustine* 18.9, trans. Herbert T. Weiskotten (Merchantville, NJ: Evolution, 2008), 27.

2. For Augustine's significance, see, for example, Jaroslav Pelikan, *The Christian Tradition: A History of the Development of Doctrine*, vol. 1, *The Emergence of the Catholic Tradition (100–600)* (Chicago: University of Chicago Press, 1971), 293.

3. For Augustine's exegesis and preaching, see, for example, John C. Cavadini, "Simplifying Augustine," in *Educating People of Faith: Exploring the History of Jewish and Christian Communities*, ed. John Van Engen (Grand Rapids: Eerdmans, 2004), 63–84; Jason Byassee, *Praise Seeking Understanding: Reading the Psalms with Augustine* (Grand Rapids: Eerdmans, 2007); Michael Fiedorowicz, *Psalmus Vox Totius Christi: Studien zu Augustins 'Enarrationes in Psalmos'* (Freiburg im Breisgau: Herder, 1997).

of the Saints (428–29); *Confessions* (397–401); *City of God* (413–26); and *On the Trinity* (399–419).[4] In order to engage later Catholic and Protestant theology—and in certain cases Eastern Orthodox theology[5]—one must know these works. Even more important, one must read these works to gain an appreciation for why such a great thinker gave his life to the realities proclaimed by Christian Scripture. And, lastly, it is by reading these works that one will be able to evaluate the development and present intellectual impasse of Western civilization. Augustine speaks as powerfully today as he did sixteen hundred years ago.

My task in this book is to present these seven pivotal works of Augustine. Here we find the themes that Augustine plumbed most deeply: how to interpret Christian Scripture, the relationship between the Old and New Testaments, the unity of the Church in charity, God's eternity and simplicity, grace and predestination, conversion, the meaning of history, the two "cities," the cross and resurrection of Jesus Christ, and the divine Trinity. The first two works, *On Christian Doctrine* and *Answer to Faustus, a Manichean*, set forth the central components of Augustine's theology of Scripture and of scriptural interpretation. The next two works, *Homilies on the First Epistle of John* and *On the Predestination of the Saints*, explore the grace of the Holy Spirit and the charity that unites the Body of Christ. The final three works, *Confessions*, *City of God*, and *On the Trinity*, form a triptych that shows how human life (individual and communal) is an ascent to full participation in the life of the Triune God, who descends in Christ and the Holy Spirit to make possible our sharing in the divine life.

Augustine wrote his longer works over a period of years. For example, *City of God* took around thirteen years to complete, and *On the Trinity* may have taken longer. Yet each of his works is a carefully orchestrated unity. It is therefore not enough simply to survey Augustine's central ideas. One needs to follow the argument of each work in its entirety in order to see how the great rhetorician weaves his ideas together in the service of Christian instruction. Many introductions to Augustine's theology treat his ideas on this and that topic, drawing upon a wide variety of his treatises, letters, and sermons. It seems to me more fruitful to introduce Augustine's major ideas by surveying his most important works in their entirety.[6]

---

4. These dates are standard approximations; most of these works cannot be dated with exactitude.

5. See A. G. Roeber, "Western, Eastern, or Global Orthodoxy? Some Reflections on St. Augustine of Hippo in Recent Literature," *Pro Ecclesia* 17 (2008): 210–23; Josef Lössl, "Augustine's *On the Trinity* in Gregory Palamas's *One Hundred and Fifty Chapters*," *Augustinian Studies* 30 (1999): 61–82.

6. William Harmless goes further and ensures that we listen to Augustine himself, albeit necessarily in short excerpts given the limitations of space: *Augustine in His Own Words*, ed. William Harmless, SJ (Washington, DC: Catholic University of America Press, 2010). For a topical introduction to Augustine's central ideas, see John M. Rist, *Augustine: Ancient Thought Baptized* (Cambridge: Cambridge University Press, 1994).

In preparing this book, I have had especially in mind the needs of students and educated readers who desire an introduction to Augustine. As a reader of Scripture, Augustine helps us to avoid historicism by constantly reminding us that true interpretation of Scripture requires learning both the historical meaning of the biblical "signs" and their salvific referent (*On Christian Doctrine* and *Answer to Faustus, a Manichean*). Since Christianity is a communion of persons rather than simply an interpretation of texts, we come to know Scripture rightly in the Church, where Scripture nourishes the love of God's people (*Homilies on the First Epistle of John*). This friendship with God and each other is not something that we can give ourselves, but is entirely God's gift in Christ and the Spirit (*On the Predestination of the Saints*). As individuals seeking true friendship (*Confessions*) and as communities seeking true peace (*City of God*), humans have been created for union with the Triune God, who draws us to himself by knowledge and by love (*On the Trinity*). Augustine offers a pattern of biblical reading, of living the Scriptures, that invites us to enjoy friendship with the Triune God who has created and redeemed us.

I include in this volume one work from each of Augustine's major disputations—namely, with the Manichees, Donatists, and Pelagians, respectively. Augustine's *Answer to Faustus, a Manichean* is particularly important for its defense of the Old Testament as Christian Scripture, especially through its insistence that words and deeds of the Old Testament often refer typologically to Christ and the Church. Augustine's *Homilies on the First Epistle of John* shows his exegetical effort to explore the requirements of charity and to end the fourth-century schism between Catholics and Donatists. Lastly, his *On the Predestination of the Saints*, which belongs to his anti-Pelagian writings, sets forth the biblical evidence in favor of the utter gratuity of the eternal God's gift of salvation.

The present book also attends to the variety of genres in which Augustine wrote. *Confessions* is autobiographical, even if it is far from autobiography in the modern sense given that it focuses on God, integrates Scripture heavily into its presentation, and ends with a meditation on time, eternity, and the origin and goal of creatures. *City of God* offers a view of Roman, biblical, and world history from creation to the eschatological new creation, and reflects on what makes for a true society of peace. *On the Trinity* investigates how we can learn to know, love, and praise the Triune God and thereby be transformed in our knowing and loving so as to share in the eternal Trinity. Although each of these three works is characterized by participatory ascent to God brought about by God's "descent" in Christ Jesus and the Holy Spirit, the fact that Augustine employs a different genre for each work helps him to engage readers from all walks of life.

On Christian Doctrine serves as a manual of instruction for Christian biblical interpretation, education, and preaching. Its genre is that of classical manuals on education and rhetoric. *Answer to Faustus, a Manichean* is a

polemical work, but it takes up one of the most important Christian tasks—
namely, accounting for the unity of the Old and New Testaments. *Homilies
on the First Epistle of John* exhibits Augustine the biblical interpreter, bishop,
and preacher, for whom the task of living out charity is paramount. Finally,
On the Predestination of the Saints draws from the whole of Scripture in order
to mount a biblical argument for our absolute dependence on God's grace for
salvation. We depend on God, who is perfect love.

Augustine's Life

Some remarks on Augustine's life are in order. He was born in Thagaste, which
now bears the name Souk Ahras, on November 13, 354 AD. Thagaste is sixty
miles south of Hippo (now Bône), where Augustine later served as bishop. Both
Thagaste and Hippo are in what is now Algeria, in North Africa.[7] The great
ancient city of Carthage was 160 miles from Thagaste. Originally founded as
a Punic colony, Carthage was conquered and destroyed by Rome in 146 BC
during the last Punic war. In the first century AD, Rome refounded Carthage
as a Roman colony and made it the capital of the province of Africa Procon-
sularis. By Augustine's day, it was among the Roman Empire's largest cities.
Augustine grew up, then, among Roman citizens who spoke Latin. He and his
family were "Papiria," a citizenship status coined in 89 BC to expand Roman
citizenship to Italian communities that had previously been in rebellion against
Rome. Like Carthage, Thagaste had been founded in the first century AD.

Augustine's mother, Monica, was a Catholic, and she ensured that the
household servants were as well. His father, Patricius, a middle-class landowner,
was a pagan. Worshipers of pagan gods remained common in Thagaste, as
throughout the Roman Empire. Indeed, Augustine was seven years old when
Emperor Julian began a concerted effort to turn the empire back to its traditional pagan worship, an effort that failed in part because of Julian's early
death.[8] Christians in North Africa were sharply divided between Catholics
and Donatists throughout most of Augustine's life.[9]

Some background to this division will be helpful. In 303, Emperor Diocletian
ordered that the Scriptures and the property of the Church be immediately

7. See the map provided in Wilhelm Gessel, "Die Stadt des Aurelius Augustinus," in *Collectanea Augustiniana: Mélanges T. J. van Bavel*, ed. B. Bruning, M. Lamberigts, and J. van Houtem
(Leuven: Leuven University Press, 1990), 73–94, at 86.

8. See Rowland Smith, *Julian's Gods: Religion and Philosophy in the Thought and Action
of Julian the Apostate* (London: Routledge, 1995).

9. See J. Kevin Coyle, "The Self-Identity of North African Christians in Augustine's Time,"
in *Augustinus Afer: Saint Augustin: Africanité et universalité*, ed. Pierre-Yves Fux, Jean-Michel
Roessli, and Otto Wermelinger (Fribourg: Éditions universitaires, 2003), 61–73. For a presentation of Donatism that is critical of Augustine's perspective, see Maureen A. Tilley, *The Bible in
Christian North Africa: The Donatist World* (Minneapolis: Fortress, 1997).

surrendered and that Christians offer worship to the gods. North African priests and bishops responded differently to this persecution. Some refused to hand over the Scriptures and were imprisoned and even martyred; others hid the Scriptures and placed false writings in their churches. Those who gave in to the persecution became known as *traditores*. After Emperor Constantine officially ended the persecution of Christianity (313),[10] tensions heated up in North Africa. In the election to succeed Bishop Mensurius of Carthage (who had been one of the *traditores*), his deacon Caecilian was elected. Shortly afterward, however, the lector Majorinus was elected amid charges that Caecilian had been consecrated by a *traditor*. When Majorinus died shortly thereafter, Donatus replaced him. The result was a schism, with two claimants to bishopric of Carthage. A council under the presidency of Pope Miltiades[11] ruled in favor of Caecilian and condemned Donatus for rebaptizing clergy who had been *traditores* (rebaptism having been advocated by the great third-century bishop of Carthage, Cyprian).[12] Donatus nonetheless held firmly to his claim until his death in 355. By the 390s, there were hundreds of Donatist bishops in North Africa, despite the fact that the Donatists experienced two significant schisms within their own ranks. In Hippo as in Thagaste, the majority of Christians were Donatists.

In keeping with the common practice of the day, Augustine was not baptized as an infant. Thanks to the ambition of his father, he was sent to school first in Thagaste and then, in his twelfth year, in nearby Madaura. After a break from school during his sixteenth year caused by financial troubles, he continued with his education, now in Carthage, where he prepared for a career as a rhetorician. During his first year at Carthage, his father died and Augustine took a mistress, with whom he soon had a son, Adeodatus.

At the age of eighteen, he began his teaching career in Thagaste and became a Manichee, a follower of the third-century Babylonian teacher Mani, who thought of himself as completing the teaching of Christ and taught a radical dualism, including the denial that Christ's body was real. Three years later Augustine moved to Carthage to teach rhetoric, and he later moved to Rome. In his thirtieth year he received an appointment as official orator in Milan. Abandoning his mistress and his career as a rhetorician, he was baptized at the age of thirty-two by Ambrose in Milan, and in that same year his mother,

---

10. For the significance of this event and its aftermath, see Peter Leithart, *Defending Constantine: The Twilight of an Empire and the Dawn of Christendom* (Downers Grove, IL: InterVarsity, 2010); Daniel H. Williams, "Constantine, Nicaea and the 'Fall' of the Church," in *Christian Origins: Theology, Rhetoric and Community*, ed. Lewis Ayres and Gareth Jones (London: Routledge, 1998), 117–36.

11. See J. E. Merdinger, *Rome and the African Church in the Time of Augustine* (New Haven: Yale University Press, 1997), 50–60.

12. See W. H. C. Frend, "The Donatist Church and St. Paul," in *Le epistole Paoline nei Manichei, i Donatisti e il primo Agostino* (Rome: Istituto Patristico Augustinianum, 1989), 85–123, at 86–93.

Monica, died. He returned to Thagaste, where he endured the death of his son, Adeodatus. He established a monastic community there and was ordained a priest in Hippo in 391. Around 395 he became coadjutor bishop of Hippo, and in 396 he became bishop of Hippo upon Bishop Valerius's death. The responsibilities of this position—including preaching, celebrating the Eucharist, administering and distributing Church property, settling legal disputes, and attending African episcopal councils—would occupy him until his death in 430.[13]

We will encounter much of this story in greater detail in Augustine's *Confessions*. The intellectual sources of Augustine's conversion included especially his reading of neo-Platonic thinkers,[14] Ambrose's sermons (which reconciled him to the Old Testament), and the writings of the apostle Paul. Even more important perhaps was the impact of his many close friendships, especially with his former student Alypius. It should also be noted that only a few years before Augustine's conversion, the Council of Constantinople (381) confirmed the Council of Nicaea's teaching on the divinity of the Son and affirmed the divinity of the Holy Spirit. During the years in which Augustine was studying Christianity with his friends in Carthage, Rome, and Milan, Arianizing views remained a live option. At the same time, worship of the traditional gods, astrology, divination, and other such practices were quite common.[15]

As a bishop, Augustine wrote in a wide variety of genres and participated in numerous ecclesial and theological debates, most notably against the Donatists

13. See Carol Harrison, *Augustine: Christian Truth and Fractured Humanity* (Oxford: Oxford University Press, 2000), 120–30; Michele Pellegrino, *The True Priest: The Priesthood as Preached and Practised by Saint Augustine*, trans. Arthur Gibson (New York: Palm, 1968). On Augustine's monastic rule, see Harrison, *Augustine*, 180–87; Thomas F. Martin, OSA, "Augustine and the Politics of Monasticism," in *Augustine and Politics*, ed. John Doody, Kevin L. Hughes, and Kim Paffenroth (Lanham, MD: Lexington Books, 2005), 165–86. See also Peter Iver Kaufman, "Augustine, Macedonius, and the Courts," *Augustinian Studies* 34 (2003): 67–82; Claude Lepelley, "Facing Wealth and Poverty: Defining Augustine's Social Doctrine," *Augustinian Studies* 38 (2007): 1–17.

14. The evolution of Augustine's relationship to neo-Platonic thought has been well summarized in Frederick Van Fleteren, "Interpretation, Assimilation, Appropriation: Recent Commentators on Augustine and His Tradition," in *Tradition and the Rule of Faith in the Early Church: Essays in Honor of Joseph T. Lienhard, S.J.*, ed. Ronnie J. Rombs and Alexander Y. Hwang (Washington, DC: Catholic University of America Press, 2010), 270–85, at 272–77.

15. For the "paganism" of Augustine's day, as well as imperial and local persecutions against pagans, see Pierre Chuvin, *A Chronicle of the Last Pagans*, trans. B. A. Archer (Cambridge, MA: Harvard University Press, 1990). On Christian relations with pagans in the fourth and fifth centuries, see Robert A. Markus, *The End of Ancient Christianity* (Cambridge: Cambridge University Press, 1990), 27–43, 97–135. In this book, Markus argues that Augustine defends "mediocre Christians" against the asceticism promoted as normative for all Christians by Jerome and Pelagius; for a similar argument, see George Lawless, OSA, "Augustine's Decentring of Asceticism," in *Augustine and His Critics: Essays in Honour of Gerald Bonner*, ed. Robert Dodaro and George Lawless (London: Routledge, 2000), 142–63. See also H. A. Drake, *Constantine and the Bishops: The Politics of Intolerance* (Baltimore, MD: Johns Hopkins University Press, 2000), 245–50; Gerald O'Daly, *Augustine's City of God: A Reader's Guide* (Oxford: Oxford University Press, 1999), 7–30.

and the Pelagians. Although his major works against the Donatists focused largely on the unity and holiness of the Church, he supported the imperial edicts in 405 and 412 that sought to suppress Donatism, ultimately by compelling Donatists to become Catholics.[16] He sided with those who called upon imperial soldiers to defend Catholics against Donatists. From 411 through the end of his life, Augustine found himself arguing most frequently against Pelagianism and its offshoots. Pelagius, a layman who lived in Rome, taught that we possess by means of our natural powers the ability to remain sinless.[17] The resulting debate over grace and election (predestination), an issue already well known to Origen, has recurred throughout the history of the Church.

Although his main reading after his conversion was the Bible, Augustine knew at least some of the works of certain fathers of the Church, including Origen, Hilary of Poitiers, Cyprian of Carthage, Basil of Caesarea, Gregory of Nazianzus, and of course Ambrose and Jerome.[18] He was not involved in the controversy between Cyril of Alexandria and Nestorius over whether the Virgin Mary was *Theotokos* (God-bearer) rather than merely the mother of the human nature of Jesus—a controversy that precipitated the Council of Ephesus in 431, the year after Augustine's death. As he lay dying, he recited penitential psalms.[19] He died while the Vandals were besieging Hippo, and he was buried in the local cemetery after a funeral Mass.

The Order of Chapters

A final note regarding the order of chapters. I begin with *On Christian Doctrine* because it gives a sense of Augustine's main preoccupations as an interpreter and preacher of Scripture. Especially important is his sense of how God, who is love, uses signs (words and deeds) to teach us to love God and each other. I next treat *Answer to Faustus, a Manichean* because here we encounter Augustine's insistence upon the unity of God's salvific teaching in Scripture: both the Old Testament and the New Testament teach us to love. Third, I

16. For discussion see Serge Lancel, *St. Augustine*, trans. Antonia Nevill (London: SCM, 2002), 162–73, 275–305; Peter Brown, *Augustine of Hippo: A Biography*, 2nd ed. (Berkeley: University of California Press, 2000), 229–39; Gerald W. Schlabach, *For the Joy Set before Us: Augustine and Self-Denying Love* (Notre Dame, IN: University of Notre Dame Press, 2001), 54–56, 119–42; Rist, *Augustine*, 239–45; John von Heyking, *Augustine and Politics as Longing in the World* (Columbia: University of Missouri Press, 2001), chap. 7.

17. For an overview and further bibliographical references, see Eugene TeSelle, "Pelagius, Pelagianism," in *Augustine through the Ages*, ed. Allan D. Fitzgerald, OSA (Grand Rapids: Eerdmans, 1999), 633–40.

18. For discussion see, for example, Joseph T. Lienhard, SJ, "Augustine of Hippo, Basil of Caesarea, and Gregory Nazianzen," in *Orthodox Readings of Augustine*, ed. George E. Demacopoulos and Aristotle Papanikolaou (Crestwood, NY: St. Vladimir's Seminary Press, 2008), 81–99; O'Daly, *Augustine's City of God*, chap. 3.

19. See Lancel, *St. Augustine*, 474–75.

survey the *Homilies on the First Epistle of John* because these homilies un-
derscore the christological, ecclesial, and eschatological context of Christian
love. The fourth work that I discuss is *On the Predestination of the Saints*,
where Augustine emphasizes that God loves and saves us not because we are
good but because he is.

These four works, each approaching love from a different angle, lay the
foundations for the exploration of Augustine's *Confessions*, *City of God*, and
On the Trinity. The *Confessions* explores how an individual person, aided by
friends, comes to know and love the living God. The *City of God* shows how
this individual participation in the Triune God (through knowing and loving
God) belongs within the broader participation of human history in God. *On
the Trinity* exhibits the life of true wisdom as an inquiry into the communion-
in-unity of God the Trinity, an inquiry that fosters our participation in the life
of the Triune God. All wisdom, all history, and every aspect of our life find
their fulfillment in God and his love.

Inevitably, my surveys of these pivotal works leave much out, and so my
footnotes point the reader to the relevant scholarly literature. As Augustine
would be the first to say, however, the main way to go further is to come to
know and love God the Trinity and one's neighbors, through the grace of
the Holy Spirit in the sacramental communion of Christ's Church. "May the
God of steadfastness and encouragement grant you to live in such harmony
with one another, in accord with Christ Jesus, that together you may with one
voice glorify the God and Father of our Lord Jesus Christ" (Rom. 15:5–6).

1

On Christian Doctrine

Augustine's first career as a rhetorician stands in the background of his *On Christian Doctrine*, the bulk of which was composed in 396–97 and which was completed in 426 by the addition of the final sections of Book 3 and the whole of Book 4.[1] In becoming a Christian, and then a priest and bishop, Augustine found himself still having much to do with words, both as an interpreter and as a preacher. The Christian preacher receives from the Church the sacred books of Scripture, which contain both the Law and the Prophets and the apostolic witness to Jesus Christ and the Church. The books that compose the New Testament assert that Jesus is the Messiah who fulfills the Law and the Prophets. The New Testament books thus not only require interpretation themselves, they also advance hermeneutical claims regarding the Scriptures of Israel. The words and deeds that Scripture reports must be interpreted if we are to understand their historical and theological significance. Moreover, the Christian preacher cannot undertake this task alone. Earlier Christians have interpreted Scripture in ways that the Church has received as authoritative and true, and debates over true interpretation have always been a feature of the Church's life.

In *On Christian Doctrine*, therefore, Augustine offers an account of biblical interpretation and preaching. He organizes his study around love. Scripture,

1. See Pamela Bright, "Biblical Ambiguity in African Exegesis," in *De doctrina christiana: A Classic of Western Culture*, ed. Duane W. H. Arnold and Pamela Bright (Notre Dame, IN: University of Notre Dame Press, 1995), 25–32, at 25. See also Brian Stock, *Augustine the Reader: Meditation, Self-Knowledge, and the Ethics of Interpretation* (Cambridge, MA: Harvard University Press, 1996), 199–206.

he argues, teaches us what and how to love. To become good interpreters, we must learn to recognize how the words of Scripture direct us to love of God and neighbor. In this task we can easily be led astray by biblical passages that seem to point in the opposite direction or that at least suggest that created goods, rather than God, can make us truly happy. We can also be led astray by lack of knowledge of the biblical languages or of other fields of learning, as well as by superstitions such as astrology.[2] Augustine is therefore interested in how interpreters of Scripture should be trained. He knows that by a proper use of speech, we can move others to love what we love, but we can also fall into pride on account of our learning or on account of our rhetorical eloquence. Despite this danger, biblical interpreters must be learned and rhetorically skilled.

Prologue

Augustine announces that he intends to offer certain rules for interpreting the Scriptures. He briefly addresses possible objections to his approach, foremost among them the view that erudition is not truly needed for understanding God's Word.[3] The Holy Spirit can illumine the meaning of biblical texts without any need for human instruction. While granting that this is so, Augustine points out that the usual way is for God to work through human teachers. Even St. Paul, after his encounter with the risen Lord on the Damascus road, had to go to the house of Ananias to be instructed, and even Moses learned from his father-in-law, Jethro. Likewise the centurion Cornelius, after being visited by an angel, had to go to St. Peter for instruction, and the Ethiopian eunuch learned from St. Philip. In general, therefore, God teaches humans through other humans.[4] God thereby ensures that the Church truly serves as an instrument of salvation, as it would not if God taught each individual everything directly, without mediation. If we could teach nothing to each other, how would relationships of love between fellow humans be fostered? So long as they recognize that every good gift comes from God, human teachers will not fall into pride at their own gifts or into envy when another teacher goes further. In offering his rules for interpretation, Augustine seeks not to explain the meaning of particular biblical texts but rather to show how to read biblical

2. François Dolbeau, "Le combat pastoral d'Augustin contre les astrologues, les devins et les guérisseurs," in *Augustinus Afer: Saint Augustin: Africanité et universalité*, ed. Pierre-Yves Fux, Jean-Michel Roessli, and Otto Wermelinger (Fribourg: Éditions universitaires, 2003), 167–82.

3. See Gerald A. Press, "The Subject and Structure of Augustine's *De doctrina christiana*," *Augustinian Studies* 11 (1980): 99–124, at 112–13; Eugene Kevane, "Paideia and Anti-Paideia: The *Prooemium* of St. Augustine's *De doctrina christiana*," *Augustinian Studies* 1 (1970): 153–80, at 160–76.

4. See Paul R. Kolbet, *Augustine and the Cure of Souls: Revising a Classical Ideal* (Notre Dame, IN: University of Notre Dame Press, 2010), 140–41, 152–53.

texts in general. The goal is to help the reader who encounters obscurities in Scripture, by showing how such obscurities should be handled.

Book 1

The two tasks that pertain to interpreting Scripture, Augustine notes, are discovering what there is to be learned and teaching what one has discovered.[5] He first explores how we discover what there is to be learned in Scripture.

He begins with a crucial distinction between things (*res*) and signs. By things, he means particular realities such as cattle, stones, trees, or water. In Scripture we learn about things through signs.[6] For example, Augustine mentions Genesis 28:11, "Taking one of the stones of the place, he [Jacob] put it under his head and lay down in that place to sleep." The stone that Jacob used for a pillow is a thing, and the word "stone" is a sign. Yet the matter is more complicated in Scripture, as Augustine immediately observes, because Jacob's stone also serves as a sign. The key to a right reading of Scripture is to realize that God can and does use things as signs. In this case, Jacob's stone is, in Augustine's view, a sign of Christ's humanity. All signs are signs of things; but not all things are signs. It should be noted that even God is a thing (*res*), although he is most certainly not a thing like other things and he is never a sign of another thing.

Treating things in themselves (and not as signs), Augustine inquires into what our attitude should be toward them. Because things are good, they attract us. On what thing or things should we set our hearts? The danger is that we will cleave to things that are passing away rather than to eternal things. But an equal danger is that we will reject created things as if we could get to our goal without the help of created things. Augustine therefore sets the following rule regarding things: "Some things are to be enjoyed, others to be used, and there are others which are to be enjoyed and used."[7] To enjoy a thing is

---

5. On the structure of the work, see Christoph Schäublin, "*De doctrina christiana*: A Classic of Western Culture?," in *De doctrina christiana: A Classic of Western Culture*, 47–67; G. A. Press, "The Subject and Structure of Augustine's *De doctrina christiana*," *Augustinian Studies* 11 (1980): 99–124.

6. See Frederick Van Fleteren, "Principles of Augustine's Hermeneutic: An Overview," in *Augustine: Biblical Exegete*, ed. Frederick Van Fleteren and Joseph C. Schnaubelt, OSA (New York: Peter Lang, 2001), 1–32, at 12–14.

7. Augustine, *On Christian Doctrine* 1.3.3, trans. D. W. Robertson Jr. (New York: Macmillan, 1958), 9. See Raymond Canning, *The Unity of Love for God and Neighbor in St. Augustine* (Heverlee, Belgium: Augustinian Historical Institute, 1993), chap. 3; Carol Harrison, *Beauty and Revelation in the Thought of Saint Augustine* (Oxford: Clarendon, 1992), 247–53; Rowan Williams, "Language, Reality and Desire in Augustine's *De Doctrina*," *Literature & Theology* 3 (1989): 138–50; William Riordan O'Connor, "The *Uti/Frui* Distinction in Augustine's Ethics," *Augustinian Studies* 14 (1983): 45–62; Oliver O'Donovan, "*Usus* and *Fruitio* in Augustine, *De doctrina christiana I*," *Journal of Theological Studies* 33 (1982): 361–97.

to cleave to it with all our heart. When we seek a thing in order to enjoy it, we make it our ultimate happiness and we consider it the resting point of our desire. If we can obtain the thing that we hope to enjoy, we think that we will be blessed and at rest, so that we will not wish to seek further things. Thus, something that is to be enjoyed must be loved strictly speaking for its own sake and not for the sake of any further good.[8] By contrast, to use a thing is to love something but not for its own sake. When our ultimate happiness rests in something, we love other things for the sake of the thing in which our ultimate happiness rests. Other things help us to obtain our goal, and we love them in reference to that ultimate goal. When we love something but do not rest in it because it cannot make us fully happy and blessed, we love the thing in its reference to what we hope to enjoy. In other words, we use the thing on our path toward the happiness that we hope to enjoy.

It is important, therefore, to know what things to enjoy and what to use. All too frequently we seek to enjoy, or place our ultimate happiness in, things that cannot bear this weight. We must learn instead to use these things rather than to cleave to them for their own sake. Otherwise we will find ourselves loving created things above God. In our journey back to our Creator God, we need the help of many things in order to reach our true goal. Augustine compares the human person to a wanderer who is attempting to return to his homeland. The wanderer needs carriages and ships to return home, but if the wanderer got attached to the journey with its carriages and ships and began to love these things more than his homeland, he would no longer want to return home. This is the situation in which many of us find ourselves; we are alienated from the homeland that would give us true happiness, because we have become attached to this world. This world is good, but it is not the infinite good for which we were made, and so it cannot give us happiness. God made it so that we, and others, can use the things in it to journey to him. By means of "the things that have been made," we should strive for union with God's "invisible nature, namely, his eternal power and deity" (Rom. 1:20).

The Father, Son, and Holy Spirit are the "things" (res) that we were created to enjoy. These three are one in divinity, but they are distinct in relation to each other. Our human concepts of God fall infinitely short of God. But even though our words about God are inadequate, nonetheless we can speak truth about God. Augustine explores the various ways in which people conceive of God. Some conceive of God as the sun or as the entire cosmos; some conceive of gods among which one is primary. But we do not conceive of God truthfully in these ways. We begin to speak truth about God when we recognize that God is greater than all finite things. God could not be less than the most perfect

---

8. See Gerard J. P. O'Daly, "Hierarchies in Augustine's Thought," in *From Augustine to Eriugena: Essays on Neoplatonism and Christianity in Honor of John O'Meara*, ed. F. X. Martin, OSA, and J. A. Richmond (Washington, DC: Catholic University of America Press, 1991), 143–54.

finite thing. Therefore he must be living, and indeed he must be simply the perfection of life itself. He must be intelligent, and not in a mutable way but supremely so, since it is better to be unchangeably wise than to be threatened with a return to foolishness. When we imagine God as a finite thing, we show that our minds need purification so as to see the divine light. This purification is the first step of our journey to our homeland, God himself. Since God is infinite spirit, we travel toward God not by spatial movement but by holy love. By our own strength, we cannot supply ourselves with such love; to suppose that we can is the sin of pride. The incarnate Son of God, however, has shown us the path of humility by which we should travel.

Still speaking of things we should enjoy, Augustine offers a brief account of Jesus Christ. He quotes John 1:14, "the Word became flesh and dwelt among us." The divine Word becoming flesh can be conceived along the lines of our thought becoming speech. Our thought does not itself change, but it assumes the form of vocal words so that others can hear it. Likewise, the divine Word, while remaining unchanged in itself, assumed a human nature so that we could see, hear, and touch him. Christ is both physician and medicine to our wound of sin.[9] He applies the cure of humility to our disease of pride. His death pays the penalty owed by sin and frees us from eternal death. Having undergone death, he had the power to rise from the dead, so we can trust him to raise us from the dead and to glorify our bodies so that they will no longer be subject to death. Since he has loved us so much, we should rejoice to have him as our judge. He has given us his Holy Spirit so that we might love each other and receive our eternal reward. In the Church, which is his "body" (Eph. 1:23), he unites us in charity with him and with each other. Those who love him are liberated from the slavery of sin and will live in glorious union with him forever. Christ calls us to enjoy him now and eternally.

Given his many friendships, Augustine is aware that it seems harsh to speak of using, rather than enjoying, our fellow humans and ourselves. True friends do not use each other for gain, but rather they share interests with each other and enjoy spending time with each other. Yet the distinction that he wants to highlight has to do with how much more we should love God than we love any created reality. Strictly speaking, the only way to love another person for his or her own sake, or to love ourselves for our own sake, would be to turn another person or ourselves into an idol. We cannot rest in other humans or ourselves in the sense of finding our ultimate happiness in them. Neither other humans nor we ourselves have the resources to give us enduring blessedness. If in this technical sense we tried to "enjoy" each other or ourselves, we would already fail to love each other or ourselves as we ought. This is so because

---

9. See Thomas F. Martin, OSA, "Paul the Patient: *Christus Medicus* and the 'Stimulus Carnis' (2 Cor. 12:7): A Consideration of Augustine's Medicinal Christology," *Augustinian Studies* 32 (2001): 219–56; Harrison, *Beauty and Revelation*, 221–24; R. Arbresmann, "The Concept of 'Christus Medicus' in Saint Augustine," *Traditio* 10 (1954): 1–28.

the dignity and goodness of human existence is enhanced by our connection to the eternal God. Seen in light of our connection to God, we are more than merely transient creatures; we have enduring existence and value. Without this connection to God, we would lack enduring existence and value. If we try to enjoy others or ourselves as if we were God, we paradoxically find ourselves much less worthy of love.

When we love others and ourselves on account of God, we "use" ourselves and others rather than "enjoy" ourselves and others. In other words, God is our goal. All our other relationships find their fullness in relation to our enjoyment of God. God gives us our ultimate happiness, in which all our other relationships will be fulfilled. God alone is lovable and enjoyable with our whole hearts, and other relationships are true friendships insofar as they are ordered to our friendship with God. If they draw us away from God, they are false friendships, since they would not then be ordered to our true good.[10] Put another way, in loving our neighbors and ourselves, we should do nothing that is not also fully and truly love of God. If we were to act against the love of God, we would thereby fail also to be true lovers of our neighbors and ourselves. With regard to our neighbors and ourselves, "use" therefore signifies rightly ordered love rather than manipulation or instrumentalization. When we "use" nonrational things rightly, we are not in a relationship of love with them, since love is an interpersonal communion—although we love our bodies, since they belong to ourselves. Those who seem to hate their bodies in fact hate the limitations and defects of their bodies rather than their bodies per se.

This discussion of the distinction between using and enjoying prepares Augustine to interpret Jesus's teaching, "You shall love the Lord your God with all your heart, and with all your soul, and with all your mind. This is the great and first commandment. And a second is like it, You shall love your neighbor as yourself. On these two commandments depend all the law and the prophets" (Matt. 22:37–40). To love rightly, we must love God above all, and all things in relation to God. We must love others as we love ourselves; and we must love ourselves while being willing to sacrifice our bodily lives out of love for others. Although we should love all others equally, we cannot distribute our acts of love equally among all humans on earth. Those closest to us have first claim to our acts of love.

Just as theatergoers who love a certain actor love each other on account of that actor, says Augustine, so it is for those who share a love for God. Like theatergoers who spread the word about the great actor, so those who love God spread the word about God. If any hate the great actor—or hate God—the

10. For Augustine on friendship, with attention to the influence of the neo-Platonists and Cicero, see Kim Paffenroth, "Friendship as Personal, Social, and Theological Virtue in Augustine," in *Augustine and Politics*, ed. John Doody, Kevin L. Hughes, and Kim Paffenroth (Lanham, MD: Lexington Books, 2005), 53–65. See also Donald X. Burt, OSA, *Friendship and Society: An Introduction to Augustine's Practical Philosophy* (Grand Rapids: Eerdmans, 1999), 59–68.

lovers hate this hatred and strive to change it. If those who hate God really knew him, they would love him. God has no need for our love; he desires our love not for his sake but for ours, so that he can reward us eternally. In a similar way, we have no need for the love of our enemies, since we do not fear that they can take away what we love. Rather, we are sorry for them since they are missing out on so great a good, and we wish for them to be able to share it with us in the communion of love. In the parable of the good Samaritan, Jesus makes clear that all humans, including our enemies, are our neighbors and are to be loved. We owe benevolence and mercy to all (see also Matt. 5:44; Rom. 13:9–10), so that we may enjoy God.

The distinction between "enjoy" and "use," as the two modes of love, causes some difficulties when it comes to God's love for us. God does not love us as his ultimate happiness. If we were God's ultimate happiness, he would be needy in relation to us, and his love would be demanding of gift rather than the source of all gift. He must, then, "use" us; but Augustine immediately adds that he doesn't "use" as we do. When we use a thing, we love it in reference to God. Our goal is to enjoy God for his own sake, and so we do not love other things as our ultimate end, but instead we love them with reference to that end. God loves his own good, and in loving his own good, he loves us as ordered to that good. God's love of us can be called "use" because he loves us not as his ultimate good but as ordered to that good. He is the divine good, and he wills to share it with us; in this regard he can be said to "use" us, by ordering us to the good that he is. The difference between his "use" of things and our "use" of things, therefore, is that we use things as part of our journey to attain our end, whereas he already is his end and he uses things to give them their end. His use is useful not to him but to us. Certainly, when we imitate God's love, we serve others mercifully in order to be useful to them rather than to advance our own purposes; but precisely such mercy actually does advance our own purposes, by configuring us to Christ. The reward that God gives us consists in our enjoyment of God, through which we enjoy each other in God.

If we "enjoy" ourselves, then we rely upon a created thing for our ultimate happiness. It is this pride, ridiculous when viewed objectively, that constituted the fall of the angels and the fall of humankind. Holy persons show us the goodness of created things, but they do not allow us to stop there. They guide us toward the source of all goodness, God. In this manner Paul refuses to permit his flock to find their good in him: "Was Paul crucified for you? Or were you baptized in the name of Paul?" (1 Cor. 1:13); "Neither he who plants nor he who waters is anything, but only God who gives the growth" (1 Cor. 3:7). The key is to refuse to place our hope for happiness in anything but God. If we cleave to created things, we turn ourselves away from their source. Even our delight in the beloved cannot be our goal. If we focus on *our* delight, we will lose the beloved. Even Christ, if we know him solely in his humanity, cannot lead us to our goal (see 2 Cor. 5:16). When we know the human Christ in his divinity, we come to know the Father in the Holy Spirit, and we can enjoy him. The Word dwells with us in time and dies for us, but he does so not to enclose us in temporal things but to lead us, in the flesh, to enjoy eternal things at the right hand of the Father.[11]

Scripture, then, teaches about temporal and eternal things. The purpose of the whole of Scripture is that we come to love rightly, to "enjoy," the eternal Trinity in the fellowship of the saints. This purpose is at the heart of the providentially ordered course of temporal things recorded in Scripture. These temporal things direct us to our goal without being themselves our goal. With regard to the temporal things of salvation history, Augustine states that we should "love those things by which we are carried along for the sake of that toward which we are carried."[12] He goes on to say that Scripture is only understood rightly when it is understood, in all its parts, to be about the love of God and neighbor. If, in trying to understand a biblical text, we interpret it in a manner that builds up charity but that turns out not to be the meaning intended by the author, we can be sure that we have not distorted the fundamental meaning of the text. Granted that it is best to seek the meaning intended by the author, we should not forget that Scripture is about love. We must approach Scripture in faith, hope, and love, and not place our trust in our own interpretations, which can lead us astray. Not erudition, but faith, hope, and love lead us to our goal of the vision of God. Many will attain this goal without studying even the books of Scripture. Indeed, biblical erudition is of no value unless it serves a life of faith, hope, and love; Scripture will not endure eternally, but love will. Since God gave us Scripture not so that we might rest in it but in order that we might come to enjoy him forever in love, we cannot read Scripture rightly unless by faith we know what is to be hoped for and loved, and unless by hope and charity we live accordingly.

Book 2

Just as the subject of Book 1 was things, the subject of Book 2 is signs.[13] As examples of signs, Augustine gives the footprints of an animal or the smoke of a fire. Signs are things that signify not themselves but something else. Footprints

---

11. See Lewis Ayres, "Augustine on the Rule of Faith: Rhetoric, Christology, and the Foundation of Christian Thinking," *Augustinian Studies* 36 (2005): 33–49. See also Mark D. Jordan, "Words and Word: Incarnation and Signification in Augustine's *De doctrina christiana*," *Augustinian Studies* 11 (1980): 177–96, at 192–96.

12. Augustine, *On Christian Doctrine* 1.35.39, p. 30.

13. For discussion see Robert A. Markus, *Signs and Meanings: World and Text in Ancient Christianity* (Liverpool: Liverpool University Press, 1996), especially chaps. 1 and 3; John M. Rist, *Augustine: Ancient Thought Baptized* (Cambridge: Cambridge University Press, 1994), chap. 2; Robert William Bernard, "In Figura: Terminology Pertaining to Figurative Exegesis in the Works of Augustine of Hippo" (PhD diss., Princeton University, 1984), 33–91.

or smoke are natural signs, but Augustine focuses on conventional signs. A conventional sign is one that living creatures make in order to convey an emotion, sensation, or idea. This kind of sign could be signified otherwise, unlike a footprint. Instances of this kind of sign include when we nod in agreement, a military flag, and words. Human language in the form of words can be articulated vocally or written down. Because of human dissension, humans have not one language but many (see Gen. 11:1–9).[14] Scripture is written in Hebrew and Greek, and then translated into other languages so that the truth of salvation might spread.

If Scripture is an instrument of salvation, then why does it need interpretation? Augustine argues that God allowed obscurities and ambiguities to be present in Scripture so that those who are intellectually proud might be humbled by the labor of interpretation, and so that the message of Scripture might not be disdained because it seemed too simple.[15] Regarding the latter point, Augustine recognizes the delight that humans take in similitudes or figures. He gives an example of this by using a passage from the Song of Songs to describe the Church's ability to conquer idolatry and to bring about the love of God and neighbor. Similitudes help our minds to grasp truth more easily, and we value insights more when they are achieved through difficult labor. Scripture contains both clear passages and obscure passages in order that people neither give up nor become complacent. What is taught obscurely in one place is taught clearly in another.

The first step in the interpretation of Scripture, says Augustine, is to be moved by the holy fear of God, by which we seek to do his will. Fear of God reminds us that we are mortal and thereby curtails our foolish pride. The second step is to attain piety. Piety makes us meek readers of Scripture. Otherwise we tend to defend our vices against Scripture's condemnation or to place ourselves above Scripture in other ways. To learn from Scripture, we must be docile to God speaking through it. The third step in the interpretation of Scripture consists in knowledge. The reader of Scripture comes to know that we must love God for his own sake, and we must love our neighbor and ourselves in reference to God. This knowledge challenges us to realize that our loves have not been well ordered; we have loved creatures to the contempt of the Creator. In fear of God and piety, the interpreter of Scripture must begin, therefore, by lamenting his sins. The fourth step is to gain fortitude. Such fortitude enables us to seek justice and extract ourselves from the love of the world, so as to learn to love eternal things—the Trinity—as we should. The

14. See David Dawson, "Sign Theory, Allegorical Reading, and the Motions of the Soul in *De doctrina Christiana*," in *De doctrina christiana: A Classic of Western Culture*, 123–41, at 130–31.

15. On this point, see J. Patout Burns, "Delighting the Spirit: Augustine's Practice of Figurative Interpretation," in *De doctrina christiana: A Classic of Western Culture*, 182–94; Jason Byassee, *Praise Seeking Understanding: Reading the Psalms with Augustine* (Grand Rapids: Eerdmans, 2007), 100–101, 178–80, and elsewhere.

fifth step is mercy. Loving our neighbor purifies our minds and hearts so that we can love the Trinity. When we love our enemy, we have arrived at the sixth step, purity of heart. This step involves dying to the world, so that our joy comes from the light of the Trinity and we do not allow the desire to please others and avoid adversity to cause us to turn from the truth that challenges us. The seventh and final step in the interpretation of Scripture is the peace of wisdom.

To interpret Scripture, then, is a work of virtue above all, and its goal is the transformation of the interpreter in the love of God and neighbor. The steps of fear of God, piety, knowledge, fortitude, mercy, purity of heart, and wisdom make clear that one reads Scripture so as to encounter the reality of God and to be changed into a lover of God and neighbor, not merely to become learned in words. On this foundation, Augustine turns his attention to the third step, the knowledge of Scripture. To be knowledgeable in Scripture, one must have read the canonical books of Scripture. Those books are canonical that are accepted by the great majority of the most important churches.[16] He lists these books, including (among books that were later contested) Judith, 1 and 2 Maccabees, Tobit, Wisdom of Solomon, and Sirach. Having become familiar with these books by reading them, the biblical interpreter should focus first on those things that are clearly said in Scripture, so as to understand the contours of faith, hope, and love. Only then should the obscure passages of Scripture be studied, and the interpretation of the obscure passages should be guided by the meaning of the clear passages.

With regard to obscure passages, Augustine notes that words, as signs, can be either literal or figurative in their designation. Words intended literally can be obscure because their meaning is not known. In this regard he urges the study of Hebrew and Greek, because otherwise one has to rely on the multiplicity of translations, without knowing which if any of them are accurate as regards the passage in question (although comparing translations can also be of use). He warns against being offended by Latin barbarisms in the translations of Scripture, and he also warns against an overly literal translation that will not be comprehensible to its readers. He defends the authority and inspiration of the Septuagint, even in cases where it differs from the Hebrew manuscripts. Words intended figuratively, when obscure, have to be studied in two ways: through the knowledge of languages and through the knowledge of things. Knowing the literal Hebrew meaning of names and places (such as Adam or Jerusalem) can help us to discern the figure. So can knowing about things; for example, when we know how serpents defend their head by exposing their body, we gain insight into what it means to be "wise as serpents" (Matt. 10:16).

---

16. See Anne-Marie La Bonnardière, "The Canon of Sacred Scripture," in *Augustine and the Bible*, ed. and trans. Pamela Bright (Notre Dame, IN: University of Notre Dame Press, 1999), 26–41.

His favorite example is knowledge of numbers, for instance the number forty, which reduces to four and ten and leads to quite a few figurative meanings for Augustine. He also extols the value of musical knowledge, despite the myth of the nine muses.

To understand what pagan knowledge should be studied, we need to know how to separate what is superstitious from what is not superstitious in pagan modes of signification. The making and worshiping of idols, the practice of magic and enchantments (including for supposed medical purposes), superstitious customs such as kicking a stone to preserve friendship, and astrological prognostications are deeply deleterious nonsense.[17] Scripture condemns these attempts at signifying as demonic productions and snares. Other pagan modes of signification, however, are rooted not in the conjunction of demons and humans but in the development of institutions that serve human well-being.[18] These include human institutions such as customs of dress, weights and measures, coinage, the forms of letters and languages, and so forth. He is less sanguine about paintings, statues, and poetic tales; these he considers superfluous because of their tendency toward falsehood.[19] Among institutions that have their source not in human ingenuity but in the order of things, Augustine especially values history; knowledge of the Roman consuls, for instance, can help to identify the age at which Christ died on the cross. He mentions that the study of history suggested to Ambrose that during Plato's travels in Egypt, Plato may have learned from Jewish books. Augustine praises geography, studies of plants and animals, and astronomy, although he warns that the latter is of little use for interpreting Scripture. He commends the practical arts and mathematics. Dialectical disputation and rhetoric are helpful but only in certain forms.[20] The rules of valid inference, definition, and judgment likewise serve biblical interpretation.[21]

17. See Markus, *Signs and Meanings*, 134–40.

18. See William S. Babcock, "*Caritas* and Signification in *De doctrina christiana* 1–3," in *De doctrina christiana: A Classic of Western Culture*, 145–63, at 152–57; William E. Klingshirn, "Divination and the Disciplines of Knowledge according to Augustine," in *Augustine and the Disciplines: From Cassiacum to Confessions*, ed. Karla Pollmann and Mark Vessey (Oxford: Oxford University Press, 2005), 113–40.

19. See Haijo J. Westra, "Augustine and Poetic Exegesis," in *Poetry and Exegesis in Premodern Latin Christianity: The Encounter between Classical and Christian Strategies of Interpretation*, ed. Willemien Otten and Karla Pollmann (Leiden: Brill, 2007), 11–28.

20. See Joseph Lienhard, SJ, "Reading the Bible and Learning to Read: The Influence of Education on St. Augustine's Exegesis," *Augustinian Studies* 27 (1996): 7–25; Stefan Hessbrüggen-Walter, "Augustine's Critique of Dialectic: Between Ambrose and the Arians," in *Augustine and the Disciplines*, 184–205; Lewis Ayres, *Augustine and the Trinity* (Cambridge: Cambridge University Press, 2010), 123–28, 132.

21. For the argument that Augustine's program for the liberal arts should be seen within the broader context of his response to Porphyry, see Frederick Van Fleteren, "St. Augustine, Neoplatonism, and the Liberal Arts: The Background to *De doctrina christiana*," in *De doctrina christiana: A Classic of Western Culture*, 15–24.

None of these forms of knowledge can lead to the blessed life, and so Augustine cautions that Christian students should not be carried away by them. Using the image of despoiling the Egyptians (Exod. 11:2), he argues that Christians should appropriate the best aspects of pagan philosophy, just as Cyprian, Hilary, and many Greek Christian writers have done. When they gain knowledge from the pagans, Christians should not become puffed up with pride. Only knowledge joined with charity and humility is useful unto salvation (see 1 Cor. 8:1). Making the sign of the cross reminds us that our salvation consists in doing good deeds in Christ, clinging to him in love, hoping to share in his eternal reward, and reverencing the sacraments. Since our salvation comes from Christ, pride in our knowledge is deadly. Our goal is "to know the love of Christ which surpasses knowledge, that you may be filled with all the fullness of God" (Eph. 3:19). Indeed, the knowledge that humble and charitable readers can gain from the Scriptures far surpasses the knowledge that can be obtained from pagan learning.

Book 3

Augustine inquires further into how to interpret ambiguous words or signs in Scripture. In matters of punctuation, for example, we should follow the construction that best fits with the rule of faith and the context of the words. At times two constructions of a difficult sentence will be equally permissible. It is crucial not to interpret figurative signs literally. Although some of the Jewish people did so, they had the excuse that their signs were commanded by God and were ordered to true worship. Their signs were useful because they truly prepared the Jewish people for Christ's coming, as shown by the notable zeal of the first church in Jerusalem. The first churches of the Jews discovered with joy the full meaning of the signs of the Old Testament. Even during the period of the Old Testament, some Jews knew in faith the meaning of the signs rather than being "enslaved" to them (through not knowing their meaning). These Jews, among whom Augustine includes the patriarchs and the prophets, were already "spiritual and free."[22] By contrast, due to the influence of generations of paganism, the first churches in pagan cities were not as zealous. The pagan idols, as useless signs, could only symbolize other creatures.[23]

22. Augustine, *On Christian Doctrine* 3.9.13, p. 87. See Rowan Williams, "Language, Reality and Desire," 146–47; Michael A. Signer, "From Theory to Practice: The *De doctrina christiana* and the Exegesis of Andrew of St. Victor," in *Reading and Wisdom: The* De doctrina christiana *of Augustine in the Middle Ages*, ed. Edward D. English (Notre Dame, IN: University of Notre Dame Press, 1995), 84–98, at 85–89.

23. See Kolbet, *Augustine and the Cure of Souls*, 146–47; Robert A. Markus, "Signs, Communication, and Communities in Augustine's *De doctrina Christiana*," in *De doctrina christiana: A Classic of Western Culture*, 97–108, at 103–6.

Augustine adds that taking literal signs as though they were figurative must also be avoided. To distinguish between literal and figurative (metaphorical and allegorical) signs, he offers this rule: signs can be literal only if they accord with the truth of faith and foster love of God and neighbor.[24] With regard to the truth of faith, Scripture refuses to allow us to rest in our own opinions. It presents us instead with the Catholic faith in three modes: past, present, and future. With regard to love of God and neighbor, Scripture challenges our tendency to suppose that our local customs must be right. It challenges our cupidity, our cleaving to the creature rather than to the Creator, by teaching charity. When Scripture attributes any bitterness or anger in word or deed to God or to his saints, the meaning of this has to do with the destruction of the reign of cupidity; otherwise it is figurative. Cupidity needs to be destroyed because it destroys those in whom it reigns. By being liberated from cupidity, we are enabled to love God and neighbor.[25]

Augustine takes as an example the patriarchs' having several wives. Since this was done by reason of the legitimate need for more children rather than by reason of lust, this practice was not in itself sinful, although it should no longer be practiced today. It should be read figuratively as well as literally, however, because it is most clearly useful for destroying cupidity and fostering charity when it is read figuratively. He emphasizes that the fact that having many wives once was acceptable, and now is not, does not mean that there is no absolute standard of justice. On the contrary, the absolute standard is the golden rule: "Whatever you wish that men would do to you, do so to them" (Matt. 7:12). This rule of charity stands as a fundamental rule for interpreting Scripture. The literal and figurative meanings of Scripture cannot be opposed to the reign of charity. If one interprets Scripture to say something opposed to charity, one has misinterpreted Scripture. Thus if a biblical passage seems to commend vice, its true sense is figurative. For instance, when Romans 12:20 urges us to care for our enemies because "by so doing you will heap burning coals upon his head," the meaning is not that we will thereby take vengeance on our enemies but rather that we will instill penitence in our enemies and turn them into our friends.

To his rule for distinguishing between literal and figurative passages in Scripture, Augustine adds the point that some teachings in Scripture are meant for everyone, while other teachings are meant only for some. His concern here is particularly with those who, in encouraging celibacy, take as figurative the

24. See Roland J. Teske, "Criteria for Figurative Interpretation in St. Augustine," in *De doctrina christiana: A Classic of Western Culture*, 109–22.

25. See William S. Babcock, "*Cupiditas* and *Caritas*: The Early Augustine on Love and Fulfillment," in *Augustine Today*, ed. Richard John Neuhaus (Grand Rapids: Eerdmans, 1993), 1–34, at 31–33; A. N. Williams, *The Divine Sense: The Intellect in Patristic Theology* (Cambridge: Cambridge University Press, 2007), 157–62; Ernest L. Fortin, "Augustine and the Hermeneutics of Love: Some Preliminary Considerations," in *Augustine Today*, 35–59, at 51.

statements in Scripture in favor of marriage. These statements should be taken literally, but they need not apply to everyone, as other statements of Scripture show. Equally, the biblical warrant for having many wives applied only when the time, place, and circumstances required having more children, something that is not the case now. Augustine argues that the patriarchs did not have many wives on grounds of lust, with the notable exception of Solomon. The sins of the patriarchs are both figurative and, in the sense that they caution us against pride, literal.

Words that are figurative in Scripture are so by some likeness or relation to another thing. The figure can be positive or negative. For example, Jesus at one time warns against "the leaven of the Pharisees" (Matt. 16:11) and at another compares the kingdom of God to "leaven" (Luke 13:20–21). In the same way, figurative use of "lion" and "serpent" is sometimes positive and sometimes negative. "Water" has a wide variety of diverse, though not contrary, figurative meanings. If a single passage of Scripture can be interpreted in two or more ways and the intended meaning of the author cannot be known, this is okay so long as none of the meanings contradicts the truth taught elsewhere in Scripture. In working through the human author of the biblical passage, the Holy Spirit knew what other true meanings could and would be elucidated by interpreters. When comparison with similar biblical passages leaves an ambiguity about meaning, in such cases we must use our reason with utmost caution. Augustine adds that knowledge about Scripture's figurative meaning is aided by grammatical knowledge of the various kinds of tropes.

Book 3 concludes with a discussion of the seven rules for biblical interpretation proposed by the Donatist author Tyconius.[26] Although Augustine points out that there are numerous passages in Scripture whose meaning cannot be found by following these rules, he nonetheless considers the rules to be generally helpful for determining the figurative meaning of biblical passages. The first rule is that Christ and the Church can both be indicated in one passage. The second rule is that the Church here and now contains true members and false members. The third has to do with the relationship between the promises (faith) and the law (works), although Tyconius imagines that we ourselves, rather than God, are the origin of our faith. The fourth rule consists in the relationship of a part to the whole, for example when something is said of "Jerusalem" or "Babylon" that in fact applies to all peoples, or when something is said of the nation of Israel that applies to the Israel that is constituted by faith. The fifth rule has to do with Scripture's way of accounting for time, especially the use of symbolic numbers. The sixth rule handles seeming contradictions in

26. See Pamela Bright, "'The Preponderating Influence of Augustine': A Study of the Epitomes of the *Book of Rules* of the Donatist Tyconius," in *Augustine and the Bible*, 109–28; Robert A. Kugler, "Tyconius's *Mystic Rules* and the Rules of Augustine," in *Augustine and the Bible*, 129–48; Charles Kannengiesser, "Augustine and Tyconius: A Conflict of Christian Hermeneutics in Roman Africa," in *Augustine and the Bible*, 149–77.

Scripture's historical timeline, for example with respect to the emergence of
the diversity of languages, by proposing that certain passages recapitulate and
illumine earlier ones. The seventh rule observes that some passages regarding
the devil in fact have to do with his "body," that is to say those who follow
him. In the context of piety, prayer, and study, these rules will aid those who
seek Scripture's figurative meanings.

Book 4

The first three books have to do with understanding the meaning of the signs
of Scripture. In this fourth book, composed some years after the earlier parts,
Augustine makes good on his promise in the prologue to say something about
the teaching of Scripture. He notes that he does not wish to repeat here the
rules of rhetoric that he taught for many years as a young man, because
rhetoric can be used in favor of both truth and lies. Even so, rhetoric should
be learned, if one can do so quickly and by imitating the example of others,
since eloquence helps one in the labor of conciliating, inspiring, reproving,
and instructing an audience.[27] In order to speak wisely, however, the crucial
thing is to have understood the Scriptures oneself, or at least to retain in
memory many wise biblical passages that one can quote to good effect. One
will also be well served by reading and remembering the works of those who
have written wisely (and eloquently) about Scripture.

Augustine singles out St. Paul for particular eloquence of speech.[28] Lest he
seem to be admitting that of the biblical authors Paul alone is eloquent, he
also gives the example of the prophet Amos, as translated by Jerome. In both
cases he examines passages from their writings in light of the rules of rhetoric.
If the biblical authors were eloquent, why were they sometimes obscure? They
thereby inspired the labor of interpreters and made clear the importance of
piety for interpretation. But their expositors should seek clarity rather than
imitating their occasional obscurity. Preachers of Scripture should attend to
their audience's cues, so that once the audience has understood a point, the
preacher should move to another point. Once the audience has heard the truth
and understood it, the goal of preaching has been attained. Until the audience
has understood, the preacher has not really "spoken." The best preaching will

27. See John C. Cavadini, "The Sweetness of the Word: Salvation and Rhetoric in Augustine's
De doctrina christiana," in *De doctrina christiana: A Classic of Western Culture*, 164–81; Carol
Harrison, "The Rhetoric of Scripture and Preaching: Classical Decadence or Christian Aes-
thetic?," in *Augustine and His Critics: Essays in Honour of Gerald Bonner*, ed. Robert Dodaro
and George Lawless (London: Routledge, 2000), 214–30; Ernest L. Fortin, AA, "Augustine and
the Problem of Christian Rhetoric," *Augustinian Studies* 5 (1974): 85–100.
28. See Thomas F. Martin, OSA, "*Vox Pauli*: Augustine and the Claims to Speak for Paul,
an Exploration of Rhetoric at the Service of Exegesis," *Journal of Early Christian Studies* 8
(2000): 237–72, at 249–54.

be not only direct but also eloquent, because a preacher should teach, delight, and move the audience. The preacher who delights the audience will be able to hold the audience's attention. The audience should be moved to love what the preacher says is lovable and to sorrow at what the preacher says is sorrowful. Although instruction is primary, nonetheless the gift of moving an audience should not be scorned, since the goal of preaching is that the audience assent wholeheartedly to what it learns. Augustine warns, however, against overly florid eloquence.

What about Jesus's command, "Do not be anxious how you are to speak or what you are to say; for what you are to say will be given to you in that hour" (Matt. 10:19)? Augustine emphasizes that prayer before speaking is primary, but he also points out that St. Paul taught Timothy and Titus what they should teach others. Although the Holy Spirit raises up Christian teachers, nonetheless these teachers cannot suppose that they do not need to learn the content of faith from others.

In striving to teach, delight, and move their audience, Christian teachers will also need to reflect upon Cicero's dictum that we should speak about the thing in accord with its significance, so that we speak about minor matters in a subdued way and about grand matters in a grand way.[29] Matters of justice that might have seemed minor to Cicero will not seem minor to Christians. A charitable action that might seem to be of little note is great in God's eyes. The use of the grand manner of speech should be reserved for moving one's audience to a deeper conversion and love of God. As an example of subdued rhetorical style, he examines a passage from Galatians and considers especially Paul's manner of raising and answering objections to his own position. In Romans, he finds examples of the moderate and the grand rhetorical style. From Cyprian and Ambrose he gives examples of the subdued, moderate, and grand rhetorical styles. He cautions against overuse of the grand rhetorical style, because even though it is powerful for moving an audience, the audience also tires of it quickly. He also explores how to mix the styles and the effects of each style. He adds that the life of the speaker, even more than the speaker's eloquence, will influence whether the speaker's words are persuasive, although even hypocritical speakers can persuade others to do good.

Conclusion

In the Prologue of On Christian Doctrine, Augustine responds to "Christians who rejoice to know the Sacred Scriptures without human instruction."[30] God could have revealed things directly to each individual human, and in some cases

29. See Adolf Primmer, "The Function of the genera dicendi in De doctrina christiana 4," in De doctrina christiana: A Classic of Western Culture, 68–86.

30. Augustine, On Christian Doctrine, Prologue.5, p. 4.

God has revealed himself directly. But in almost every case, God has required that we learn from others. Even in speaking to us directly in Jesus Christ, God ensured that we would learn Jesus's words and deeds from others, who would have to interpret them. The divinity of Jesus Christ is mediated through his humanity, and the biblical signs that testify to him are mediated to us through Israel and the Church. The guidance of the Holy Spirit does not take away from the profound presence of human mediation and interpretation at the heart of God's work of salvation. Why did God choose this way to reveal himself?

Augustine's answer is that given the needs and capacities of fallen human nature, God reveals himself through signs so as to train us in love. Since we must learn about God through signs that have been given in history, we can come to God only within the community of wisdom and love built up by Christ and the Holy Spirit. To learn from Christ in the Church means to learn how to move from sign to thing, so as to cleave in love to the unseen God who is revealed through signs. Those whose task it is to interpret Scripture for others must employ its signs for the purpose of leading others to love of God and neighbor. This purpose does not mean abandoning the liberal arts or the methods of persuasive public speaking. But it does mean redirecting such learning toward the goal of Christian wisdom. If such a redirection is to succeed, Christian interpreters must not become puffed up by their learning and must practice what they preach. In the school that is the Church, the labor of learning and teaching is at the service of love of God and neighbor.

2

Answer to Faustus, a Manichean

I n exile during the mid-380s, the Manichean bishop Faustus wrote a work titled *The Chapters*, in which he defends Manichean doctrine against Catholic criticisms.[1] Almost half of these chapters defend some aspect of Manichean rejection of the Old Testament, while most of the other chapters take up the Manichean denial that Jesus was born. Augustine's *Answer to Faustus, a Manichean*, composed in 397–98 on the heels of *On Christian Doctrine*, takes up each of Faustus's thirty-three chapters in turn. I will focus my attention on those chapters that have particularly to do with the Old Testament: thus, in Augustine's work, Books 4, 6, 9, 10, 12–19, 22, and 30–32. Although these books inevitably contain some repetition, nonetheless they constitute an extraordinary Christian theology of the Old Testament and its relation to the New. Having developed his theology of scriptural signs in *On Christian Doctrine*, he here enriches it through careful reflection on Scripture's two Testaments as a unified witness to God's love.[2] For each book

1. See Augustine, *Answer to Faustus, a Manichean*, trans. Roland Teske, SJ (Hyde Park, NY: New City, 2007). For discussion of Manichean doctrine and its influence on Augustine, see Johannes Van Oort, "Augustine and Manichaeism in Roman North Africa: Remarks on an African Debate and Its Universal Consequences," in *Augustinus Afer: Saint Augustin: Africanité et universalité*, ed. Pierre-Yves Fux, Jean-Michel Roessli, and Otto Wermelinger (Fribourg: Éditions universitaires, 2003), 199–210; Jason David BeDuhn, *Augustine's Manichaean Dilemma*, vol. 1, *Conversion and Apostasy, 373–388 C.E.* (Philadelphia: University of Pennsylvania Press, 2009).

2. See Paula Fredriksen, *Augustine and the Jews: A Christian Defense of Jews and Judaism* (New York: Doubleday, 2008), 240. For discussion of Faustus's critique of the Old Testament in the context of the anti-Judaism of earlier Catholic authors (and of Augustine's own earlier anti-Manichean works), see Fredriksen, *Augustine and the Jews*, 213–23, 232–34; Kari Kloos,

I first review Faustus's critique of the Catholic position and then examine in detail Augustine's reply.[3]

Books 4, 6, 9, 10

In Book 4, Faustus responds to the question, "Do you accept the Old Testament?"[4] His reply is that he could only accept it if it contained his inheritance. He argues that the Old Testament speaks only of the inheritance of the Jews—namely, the land of Canaan. Only those who obey the laws of Israel—circumcision, the food laws, and so forth—will receive this land. Since Faustus does not obey these laws, and is not among those who will inherit the land of Canaan, he finds that the Old Testament has nothing to offer him.

Augustine answers Faustus by conceding that the laws and promises of the Old Testament refer literally to the people of Israel alone, but he argues that these laws and promises prefigure something greater. Since the Manicheans accept St. Paul as an authority, Augustine seeks to ground his theology of the Old Testament in the teachings of Paul. Paul makes clear that the Old Testament has a strongly figural meaning: "All these were symbols of us. . . . All these things happened to them as symbols, but they were written down on account of us, upon whom the end of the ages has come" (1 Cor. 10:6, 11).[5] The Greek words are *typoi* (v. 6) and *typikōs* (v. 11), from which the English word "typology" derives. The "symbols" that Paul has in view have to do with the exodus of the people of Israel from Egypt, especially God's guiding the people in a "pillar of cloud" (Exod. 13:21), leading the people

---

"History as Witness: Augustine's Interpretation of the History of Israel in *Contra Faustum* and *De trinitate*," in *Augustine and History*, ed. Christopher T. Daly, John Doody, and Kim Paffenroth (Lanham, MD: Lexington Books, 2008), 31–51, especially 38–43. See also Jeremy Cohen, "'Slay Them Not': Augustine and the Jews in Modern Scholarship," *Medieval Encounters* 4 (1998): 78–92.

3. Few theologians today are aware of the contribution that *Answer to Faustus* makes to later theology of Scripture. As Peter Leithart remarks, therefore, "We need a brief overview of the treatise, and it would not hurt to have a monograph on it." See Leithart, "More Than a Dainty Sip: Old and New in Augustine's *Contra Faustum*," unpublished essay, 3n7. See also Leithart's "Conjugating the Rites: Old and New in Augustine's Theory of Signs," *Calvin Theological Journal* 34 (1999): 136–47. In what follows, I cannot offer a monograph but I do hope to provide a "brief overview" focused on the portions of *Answer to Faustus* relevant to the relationship of the Old and New Testaments.

4. For background see Hans-Joachim Klimkeit, "The Use of Scripture in Manichaeism," in Manfred Heuser and Hans-Joachim Klimkeit, *Studies in Manichaean Literature and Art* (Leiden: Brill, 1998), 111–22; C. P. Bammel, "Pauline Exegesis, Manichaeism and Philosophy in the Early Augustine," in *Christian Faith and Greek Philosophy in Late Antiquity: Essays in Tribute to George Christopher Stead*, ed. Lionel R. Wickham and Caroline P. Bammel (Leiden: Brill, 1993), 1–25.

5. I employ here Augustine's Latin version of 1 Cor. 10:6, 11 as rendered in Teske's translation of Augustine, *Answer to Faustus, a Manichean*, 82.

across the sea on dry land (Exod. 14:22), feeding the people with "bread from heaven" (Exod. 16:4), and giving the people water from a rock (Exod. 17:6). Paul holds that these events from Israel's history prefigure Christ and the Church: "I want you to know, brethren, that our fathers were all under the cloud, and all passed through the sea, and all were baptized into Moses in the cloud and in the sea, and all ate the same supernatural food and all drank the same supernatural drink. For they drank from the supernatural Rock which followed them, and the Rock was Christ" (1 Cor. 10:1–4). For Paul, this typological interpretation of Israel's exodus serves as a warning to Christians, since God punished the murmuring of the Israelites and their desire to return to Egypt by allowing them to die in the wilderness rather than to reach the promised land.

Augustine argues that Paul here instructs the Church on how to understand the covenantal promises and laws that God gave the people of Israel. These covenantal promises and laws prefigure their fulfillment in Christ. The Israelites who received these promises and laws in expectation of their fulfillment were already united by faith with Christ. On this view, the Church of Christ was already present in Israel, although Israel knew Christ only through figures rather than in the way that we now know him. Augustine quotes the risen Jesus: "Everything written about me in the law of Moses and the prophets and the psalms must be fulfilled" (Luke 24:44). It thus cannot be that the Old Testament, as Faustus supposes, teaches only about the promise of the land of Canaan to the Jews who follow circumcision, the food laws, and so forth. It must be that the Old Testament teaches about the saving power of Jesus, including his crucifixion and resurrection. The fact that Jesus is not raised to a renewed earthly life, but rather is glorified, shows that the promises of God to Israel are about more than long life for the Jews in the land of Canaan. The promises of God pertain ultimately to the glory that has been revealed in the risen Lord.

On this basis, Augustine holds that the authors of the Old Testament were guided by God, both in their words and in their deeds, to signify prophetically through material images the glorious fulfillment that was to come. The whole history of the people of Israel was prophetic. God used even the sins of the people to show his intention to fulfill his covenants with Israel in a manner that would go well beyond the literal sense of dwelling peacefully in the land of Canaan.

Whereas Book 4 focuses on the promises, Book 6 takes up the law. Recall that Faustus thinks that he must reject the Old Testament not only because he does not want (nor is he included in) the reward of dwelling forever in Canaan, but also because he does not observe circumcision, the food laws, and so forth. Faustus argues that Catholics too reject the law as useless, and he criticizes Catholics as dissemblers for their attempt to praise the Old Testament while rejecting its core practices.

Augustine replies that God in fact gave Israel two kinds of laws: laws that are intended to regulate behavior and laws that are intended to symbolize something with respect to the relationship of Israel to God. Circumcision and the food laws are the latter kind. They are symbolic indicators of the people's relationship to God. Because they cannot achieve the intimacy that they symbolize, they foreshadow their own fulfillment. They do not serve any other necessary purpose, by contrast to laws that regulate behavior in a necessary way, such as we find in the Decalogue. Now that the fulfillment has come, Christians do not observe the laws that have a symbolic function in the Old Testament, since Christians observe the realities that these laws symbolized. An example is circumcision: Christians observe the circumcision of the heart prefigured by the circumcision of the flesh (cf. Deut. 30:6; Rom. 4:11). Faustus holds that holiness could not be signified by the circumcision of the male sexual organ, but Augustine points out that sexual generation is not despised by God. To become children of God, we must first become children through sexual generation. If God wishes, God can symbolize spiritual begetting by means of the circumcision of an organ involved in physical begetting.[6]

The strict Sabbath rest of the Old Testament provides Augustine with an example of why Christians should continue to care about the Old Testament's symbolic laws, even though we no longer practice them.[7] The law regarding the Sabbath rest symbolizes the eternal rest to which Jesus, at the right hand of the Father, is leading his people. By reading about this reality as prefigured by the deeds and words of the people of Israel, we are helpfully taught to make this reality the center of our lives. Similarly, reading about the various animal sacrifices guides the Christian to reflect upon the sacrifice of Christ, symbolized by all the animal sacrifices. Since the laws about animal sacrifices symbolize Israel's intimacy with God in worship, without being able in themselves to accomplish this reality, the meaning of the animal sacrifices is fulfilled, not evacuated, by Jesus's death on the cross and our participation in this sacrifice in eucharistic worship.[8] In the same vein, the food laws forbid eating certain things on symbolic grounds. Thus an animal that does not ruminate is "unclean" because it symbolizes humans who do not recall and meditate upon the words of wisdom that they have heard (cf. Prov. 21:20). By abstaining from

6. As Fredriksen shows, Augustine's positive interpretation of circumcision contrasts sharply with earlier pagan and Catholic critiques of circumcision; see Fredriksen, *Augustine and the Jews*, 250–54; cf. 316–19. Fredriksen's thesis is that by affirming that the Jews had been right to observe God's commandments literally and that these commandments were good (even though now fulfilled), Augustine "stood centuries of traditional anti-Jewish polemic, both orthodox and heterodox, on its head" (244).

7. See Kloos, "History as Witness," 40–41.

8. On the Eucharist, see Joanne McWilliam, "Weaving the Strands Together: A Decade in Augustine's Eucharistic Theology," *Augustiniana* 41 (1991): 497–506; Jaroslav Pelikan, *The Christian Tradition: A History of the Development of Doctrine*, vol. 1, *The Emergence of the Catholic Tradition (100–600)* (Chicago: University of Chicago Press, 1971), 304–6.

eating this kind of animal, people are guided in avoiding this defect. Again, the laws regarding the feast of tabernacles or regarding wearing a garment woven of wool and linen (Deut. 22:11) have symbolic rather than regulative value. Now that Jesus has shown us the path of life, the symbolism of these laws is no longer necessary and his followers no longer need to observe the laws.

Even so, we can still benefit from the prophetic authority of these laws. As Augustine says, "The scripture that then required symbolic actions is therefore now a witness to the realities that were symbolized, and those practices that were then observed for the purpose of foretelling events are now read out for the purpose of confirming them."[9] He finds confirmation of this in 1 Corinthians 9:9–10, "For it is written in the law of Moses, 'You shall not muzzle an ox when it is treading out the grain.' Is it for oxen that God is concerned? Does he not speak entirely for our sake? It was written for our sake." Throughout Book 6, Augustine pauses frequently to show that the practices and beliefs of the Manicheans are rooted in profound contradiction and absurdity, by contrast to the meaningfulness of the Jewish and Catholic practices and beliefs.

In Book 9, Faustus notes that the apostles who were born Jews were permitted to abandon the laws of the Old Testament. He argues therefore that as a gentile he is justified in ignoring the Old Testament completely. He compares the Old Testament to a bitter tree and the New Testament to a sweet tree. Augustine points out in reply that Paul thinks of the gentiles as grafted onto the root of Israel (see Rom. 11). To be a Christian means to be joined to that root, rather than to do as Faustus has done and reject the root. Book 10 records a similar argument on Faustus's part. He urges that the Old Testament and its promises regarding long life in Canaan are the property of the Jews, and in obedience to the Decalogue (as recorded also in Jesus's teaching) he must not covet the Jews' property. Augustine repeats the distinction between regulative and prophetic laws. Christians do not need to obey the prophetic laws, but neither can these laws be ignored. Rather, these laws now bear testimony to their fulfillment by Christ. The arrival of the reality does not displace the figure, because the figure continues to instruct us about the reality. Augustine again appeals to 1 Corinthians 10:11 to make clear that the Old Testament was written for Christians as well as for the Jewish people, even though the Jews were specially chosen by God to receive and obey the laws in a literal way prior to Christ's coming.

Books 12–19

In Book 12 Faustus argues that there is no need for prophetic testimony to Christ, because God testifies to Christ at his baptism by John (Matt. 3:17), and

---

9. Augustine, *Answer to Faustus, a Manichean* 6.9, p. 104.

because Jesus also testifies that he has come forth from the Father (John 8:18; 16:28). Augustine replies that the Jewish prophets foretold Christ and that their prophecies remain important for Christian faith. Since, as has already been noted, Faustus accepts the authority of Paul, Augustine uses Paul's authority to make the case regarding the testimony of the prophets to Christ and the value of their testimony for Christians. Romans 1:2, for instance, teaches that the gospel of Jesus Christ was promised through the prophets; Galatians 3:16 speaks of the promises made to Abraham and to his offspring (Christ) in whom all nations will be blessed. Elsewhere Paul praises the advantages that God has given to the Jewish people. By listening to the prophets' testimony, we avoid inventing a false understanding of Christ like the one into which the Manicheans have fallen. Augustine goes through the Old Testament and finds numerous prophecies, including the creation of man in the image of God (perfected in Christ as the new Adam), the creation of Eve from the rib of Adam (fulfilled by the Church being formed through the blood that flowed from Christ's wounded side), the marriage of man and woman being an image of Christ and the Church (Eph. 5:32), the death of Abel as a figure of the death of Christ, the mark of Cain as foreshadowing the mark (and bodily protection) of the Jewish people after the crucifixion of Christ and the destruction of the temple,[10] Noah's ark as a figure of the Church, Joseph's suffering at the hands of his brothers and being honored by the Egyptians (gentiles) as a figure of Christ, the symbolism of the Passover lamb, the royal and priestly power of David, Isaiah's prophecy of the Suffering Servant, Daniel's prophecy of the Son of Man, and many others. Faustus claims that no Jewish witnesses are needed, but Paul himself quotes Isaiah in Romans 10 precisely to show that the testimony of the Jewish prophets is needed in the proclamation of the gospel to whose truth the prophets attest.[11] It is not for nothing that Abraham is "the father of all who believe" (Rom. 4:11).

Book 13 continues the same debate. Faustus argues that even if the Jewish prophets foretold Christ, it should not matter to gentile Christians. Gentile Christians owe nothing to the Jewish prophets, but rather owe all to Christ himself. The indirect testimony of the prophets may be of value to Jews, but not to non-Jews to whom the prophets never preached. Christ's direct word and example convert the gentiles, and so they do not need the prophets.

Augustine replies by taking another angle, this time focused on the term "Christ." Where, he asks, did Faustus learn the name "Christ"? It has its meaning from the Old Testament. The people of Israel were expecting a "Christ,"

10. For discussion see Fredriksen, *Augustine and the Jews*, 263–77, 319; Jason Byassee, *Praise Seeking Understanding: Reading the Psalms with Augustine* (Grand Rapids: Eerdmans, 2007), 172–73.
11. See Fredriksen, *Augustine and the Jews*, 320–24; Lewis Ayres, "Augustine on the Rule of Faith: Rhetoric, Christology, and the Foundation of Christian Thinking," *Augustinian Studies* 36 (2005): 33–49, at 38–40.

an anointed one, to come and fulfill the role of priest and king in Israel. Paul and the Gospels introduce Jesus Christ in terms of the expectations of the prophets of Israel. Here Augustine has recourse again to Paul's affirmation that God had promised the gospel of Jesus Christ "through his prophets in the holy scriptures" (Rom. 1:2), and Augustine also appeals to Matthew's use of Isaiah 7:14 in announcing the birth of Jesus Christ. Against Faustus's claim that no witnesses other than Christ are needed, Augustine points to the role that Mani plays for Faustus, since Mani styled himself in his letters "an apostle of Jesus Christ." Mani's errors show Augustine how important it is to understand what "Christ" means through the Jewish people, whom God had instructed on this matter. Whether Jesus is the Christ becomes apparent in light of the Jewish testimonies to the coming of the Christ. Not only do Paul and Matthew make precisely this point, so does Jesus in the Gospel of John: "You search the scriptures, because you think that in them you have eternal life; and it is they that bear witness to me. . . . If you believed Moses, you would believe me, for he wrote of me" (John 5:39, 46). Believing truly about Christ requires learning from trustworthy witnesses, and the very witnesses that Christ himself commends (the Old Testament prophets) are rejected by Faustus in favor of Mani.

In addition, Augustine argues that the prophets bear witness to events that have occurred since the coming of Christ and thus have to do with the gentiles rather than strictly with the Jews. Regarding the Roman persecution of the Church of Christ, and of the Church's universal extension, he quotes Psalm 2:2, "The kings of the earth set themselves, and the rulers take counsel together, against the LORD and his anointed," and Psalm 2:8, "I will make the nations your heritage, and the ends of the earth your possession." He also quotes various passages from Isaiah and Jeremiah, and from Paul quoting Isaiah, that prophesy the destruction of the idols and the rise of faith among the gentile nations. The Old Testament also assists in understanding why some members of the Church of Christ fall away from holiness and produce divisions. As Paul says, "Whatever was written in former days was written for our instruction, that by steadfastness and by the encouragement of the scriptures we might have hope" (Rom. 15:4).

According to Faustus, Moses is anathema because he cursed Christ in Deuteronomy 21:23: "His body shall not remain all night upon the tree, but you shall bury him the same day, for a hanged man is accursed by God." This is the topic of Book 14. Augustine first points out that the Manicheans deny that Christ had a mortal body, so that the curse would not, therefore, apply to their Christ. He goes on to connect Moses's curse in Deuteronomy with the curse that God applied to eating of the tree of the knowledge of good and evil. When the first humans ate of that tree, human nature was disordered and they suffered the curse of death. When the innocent Christ hung on the tree, he bore the curse for us. In this regard Augustine quotes Paul extensively: "Christ redeemed us from the curse of the law, having become a curse for us"

(Gal. 3:13); ". . . sending his own Son in the likeness of sinful flesh and for sin, he condemned sin in the flesh" (Rom. 8:3); "For our sake he made him to be sin who knew no sin, so that in him we might become the righteousness of God" (2 Cor. 5:21). On the wood of the cross, Christ bore the curse of sin and death for us and redeemed us from this curse. Augustine expresses his gratitude for being rescued both from the curse and from the false teaching of the Manicheans, whose doctrine had captivated him for many years. The death that we must avoid is the death of the soul. Christ's death, which bears the curse, frees our souls from condemnation.

Book 15 contains yet another argument from Faustus for rejecting the Old Testament. He proposes that one can be fully nourished by the Old Testament (as the Jews were and are today), or fully nourished by the New Testament, or half-nourished by both. To accept both Testaments means to be only half-nourished by the New Testament; it is like diluting honey with a half portion of vinegar. To change the metaphor, the Church should receive only Christ's Testament. The Testament of the Jews, with its promises of long life in Canaan, has no place in the Church, because the Church is already fully enriched by the bridal gift of Christ's own Testament. Indeed, Faustus holds that the God of the Jews has proven himself unable to fulfill his promises to the Jews, whereas the risen Christ has shown that he can fulfill his promises. Again changing the metaphor, Faustus argues that to accept both Testaments is to turn the Christian faith into a monstrous entity, like a centaur that is half horse and half man but fully neither. In defense of his position, he quotes Romans 7:2–3, where Paul suggests that continuing in the observance of the law, now that the law is dead and we have been united to Christ, is like adultery. We must now worship only the God of the New Testament.

Augustine's response begins with the metaphor of diluting the honey with vinegar. If Faustus is right, then Paul himself must be guilty of diluting the gospel, because Paul begins by calling himself "a servant of Christ Jesus, called to be an apostle" (Rom. 1:1) and in the same sentence brings in God's promises "through his prophets in the holy scriptures, the gospel concerning his Son, who was descended from David according to the flesh" (Rom. 1:2–3). If employing the Old Testament necessarily dilutes the New, then Paul has done it and should be rejected. But as Jesus suggests, the proper way to understand the two Testaments is to think of the householder "who brings out of his treasure what is new and what is old" (Matt. 13:52). Augustine argues that the Old and New Testaments are not two completely different things, laid side by side as it were. Rather, since the words and deeds of the Old Testament prefigure the deeds of the New, the Old Testament is interiorly related to the New.[12] The

12. For discussion see Michael Cameron, "The Christological Substructure of Augustine's Figurative Exegesis," in *Augustine and the Bible*, ed. and trans. Pamela Bright (Notre Dame, IN: University of Notre Dame Press, 1999), 74–103, at 94–96.

patriarchs and prophets of the Old Testament looked forward in faith to a future fulfillment that goes beyond anything that they had experienced. They desired an intimacy with God far greater than could be accomplished simply by long life in Canaan. In figures, they spoke of the messianic fulfillment that they loved. Their writings, as prophetic, relate interiorly to the reality revealed in the New Testament. Failure to appreciate this interior relationship of figure and reality leads to imagining that the Old and New Testaments are related like two separate substances, honey and vinegar, so that one has the law on this side and Christ on the other. Augustine's point is that this is a false separation. Thus for example the conversion of the gentiles is not solely a New Testament reality; it is prophesied and prefigured in the Old Testament. The Old Testament cannot be put to the side like an alien substance that competes for space with the New.

In this vein Augustine observes that a favorite Manichean text, in which Paul teaches that the Corinthians are "a letter from Christ delivered by us, written not with ink but with the Spirit of the living God, not on tablets of stone but on tablets of human hearts" (2 Cor. 3:3), in fact builds upon Jeremiah 31:33 and Ezekiel 11:19. The Decalogue is not foreign to Christians, but rather describes the loving relationship to God and neighbor that the grace of the Holy Spirit enables us to fulfill. Augustine answers Faustus's charge of adultery with another god by quoting Deuteronomy 6:4, which teaches the one God in whom Christians believe, and by contrasting this faith with Manichean belief in many spirit-beings who are begotten of God's own substance and in Mani as the perfect teacher of divine realities. Going through the list of the ten commandments, Augustine shows how Manichean doctrine undermines each one of them. With respect to 2 Corinthians 3:6, "The written code kills, but the Spirit gives life," he argues that Paul here no more intends to condemn the law than Paul intends to condemn knowledge when he writes, "Knowledge puffs up, but love builds up" (1 Cor. 8:1). The problem is not with the letter of the law, or with knowledge, but with the pride of sinners. "The law is good, if any one uses it lawfully" (1 Tim. 1:8), but as Paul also says, "It was sin, working death in me through what is good, in order that sin might be shown to be sin, and through the commandment might become sinful beyond measure" (Rom. 7:13). Even the Manicheans, Augustine notes at the end of Book 15, have been expressly foretold in Scripture. Thus Paul warns that "in later times some will depart from the faith by giving heed to deceitful spirits and doctrines of demons, through the pretensions of liars whose consciences are seared, who forbid marriage and enjoin abstinence from foods which God created to be received with thanksgiving by those who believe and know the truth. For everything created by God is good" (1 Tim. 4:1–4).

In Book 16 Faustus turns to the claim of Jesus in John 5:46, "If you believed Moses, you would believe me, for he wrote of me." Faustus notes that it would be possible to affirm that Moses wrote of Christ without thereby receiving the

Old Testament. Moses might have inadvertently written about Christ. After all, even the demons testified to Christ. Yet, not finding any evidence that Moses wrote of Christ, Faustus prefers to think that this passage was not really said by Jesus but instead is a later interpolation. The evidence that is often adduced in favor of Moses writing about Christ—for instance, Deuteronomy 18:18, "I will raise up for them a prophet like you from among their brethren"—Faustus finds to be unpersuasive, since Christ was God rather than being a sinful prophet like Moses. Faustus denies that believing Moses would lead to believing Christ, because the two teach quite opposite things (for example, about the Sabbath and food laws). Even had Moses written of Christ, Christians should avoid the Old Testament because the law of Moses would only enslave Christians.

Augustine responds by insisting that everything that Moses wrote prefigures Christ or praises Christ's grace and glory. For example, the temple, animal sacrifice, the altar, and the Mosaic priesthood are all mentioned positively by Christ in the Gospels,[13] and their figurative meaning is shown when Christ compares his body to the temple (John 2:19) and when Paul calls believers the temple of God (1 Cor. 3:17). Augustine challenges Faustus's claim that Jesus did not say the words attributed to him in John 5:46. There is no basis for denying the authenticity of the verses that contradict one's position, especially if one then builds one's case on other seemingly more amenable verses. He then takes up the verse mentioned by Faustus, Deuteronomy 18:18. The differences between Christ and Moses are obvious, but these differences do not mean that Christ is not a prophet like Moses. Christ does not need to be like Moses in every way in order to be like him. After all, Christ is described as like a "lamb" and a "rock" in the New Testament. Likeness does not require equivalence. Because Christ is God, Christ is not like Moses; but at the same time because Christ is a man, Christ is like Moses. Christ is not a sinner, but he is like a sinner in the sense that God sent him "in the likeness of sinful flesh" (Rom. 8:3). Jesus speaks of himself as a prophet in Matthew 13:57. Jesus leads us into the kingdom of heaven, just as Moses was called to lead the people of Israel into the promised land. Moses's literal successor was named Jesus (Joshua), thereby prefiguring his true successor.

Furthermore, Moses is hardly as bad as Faustus suggests. At the transfiguration, after all, Moses and Elijah merited to stand with Jesus. Jesus makes clear that the God proclaimed by Moses—the God of Abraham, Isaac, and Jacob (cf. Matt. 8:11; 22:32)—is the true God, despite Manichean claims to the contrary. Jesus was not a prophet who sought to lead the Jews away from their God in violation of Deuteronomy 13:1–2.[14] Indeed, this very passage

13. On Augustine's positive reading of the temple sacrifices, see Fredriksen, *Augustine and the Jews*, 246–50.

14. On the development in Augustine's thought on this point, see Fredriksen, *Augustine and the Jews*, 255. In his *Commentary on Galatians* and *On Christian Doctrine*, Augustine held that Jesus violated the Jewish law, whereas Augustine denies this in *Answer to Faustus, a Manichean*.

from Moses foreshadows Mani's leading people away from Christ. Insofar as they teach Moses's law, Jesus honors those who "sit on Moses' seat" (Matt. 23:2), although he warns against their hypocrisy.

Augustine's point is that there is plenty of reason to believe that Deuteronomy 18:18 applies to Christ. Once this is recognized, one comes to appreciate why Jesus taught that Moses, in all his writings, "wrote of me" (John 5:46). Moses and his writings signify Christ in diverse ways. For instance, when Moses, striking the rock that according to Paul signifies Christ, doubts the power of God, Moses foreshadows those who nailed Christ to the cross (and the water that flows from the rock foreshadows the grace that flows from the cross). Moses's death on the mountain, similarly, signifies the death of pride that occurs when Christ's glory is recognized. Moreover, even wicked men in the Old Testament, as in the New, are able to speak symbolically of Jesus. As regards Moses's teachings about the Sabbath and unclean foods, Faustus does not take into account the difference in times. The literal observance of the Sabbath foreshadowed the eternal Sabbath into which the risen Christ leads us. Circumcision of the flesh foreshadowed the circumcision of the heart won by Christ's cross. The commandment that circumcision be undertaken on the eighth day corresponds to Christ's rising on the eighth day after the Sabbath. The clean and unclean animals symbolize behaviors that place us within or outside the Church. In each case, the figure taken literally cannot accomplish intimacy with God, but the figure promotes faith that God will accomplish this reality for us through Christ. Catholics receive Moses's commandments by observing "them all no longer in figures but in the realities that those figures foretold by their signification."[15]

Book 17 addresses Faustus's claim that Matthew 5:17, "Think not that I have come to abolish the law and the prophets; I have come not to abolish them but to fulfill them," was invented by Matthew or interpolated into the Gospel by a later writer. Faustus emphasizes that the reason why many Jews of Jesus's time thought that he was abolishing the Law and the Prophets is because he was indeed doing so, as can be seen by his numerous additions to and subtractions from the law of Moses. On this view, Jesus deliberately violated the warning of Deuteronomy 5:32, where Moses says, "You shall be careful to do therefore as the LORD your God has commanded you; you shall not turn aside to the right hand or to the left."

Since one of Faustus's arguments is that Matthew was not actually present on the mountain when Jesus gave this sermon, Augustine points out that neither were Mani and Faustus. If Matthew is not to be believed for this reason, then neither are Mani and Faustus. But Augustine gladly grants that Jesus did indeed seem to be a destroyer of the Law and the Prophets to those Jews who did not understand him. Quoting Paul, Augustine notes that "love is the

---

15. Augustine, *Answer to Faustus, a Manichean* 16.32, p. 225.

fulfilling of the law" (Rom. 13:10). Jesus fulfills the law in two ways: by loving
God and neighbor, and by bringing about what the law had prefigured. He
thereby fulfills the law, as John says, in "grace and truth" (John 1:17). He does
not add or subtract from the law, but instead he carries out the law through
the grace of charity and the truth of fulfilled prophecy.

Matthew 5:17 is also the subject of Book 18, where Faustus again presses
his claim that both Manicheans and Christians obviously reject Moses's commandments by refusing to circumcise, to obey the laws about unclean foods,
and to sacrifice animals. Augustine replies by directing Faustus's attention to
Jeremiah 31:31–33:

> Behold, the days are coming, says the LORD, when I will make a new covenant
> with the house of Israel and the house of Judah, not like the covenant which
> I made with their fathers when I took them by the hand to bring them out of
> the land of Egypt, my covenant which they broke, though I was their husband,
> says the LORD. But this is the covenant which I will make with the house of
> Israel after those days, says the LORD: I will put my law within them, and I will
> write it upon their hearts; and I will be their God, and they shall be my people.

Augustine's point is that the Old Testament explicitly looks forward to a New
Testament. As such, it is to be expected that the Old Testament is not yet God's
final word for his people, but rather contains symbolic words and deeds that
prepare the people for God's final word. When God gives his new covenant,
the reality toward which the symbols pointed will be revealed, and the full
meaning of the symbols will also thereby be revealed. This has happened in
Jesus Christ, just as Paul shows in 2 Corinthians 3. Christians now observe
the symbols in the reality, which is different from supposing that the symbols
themselves have been rejected. By contrast, the pagan rites were rejected by the
Jewish people and are rejected by Christians. The Jewish Sabbath took place
on the same day that pagans dedicated to Saturn, but the Sabbath's purpose,
far from being similar to pagan worship of creatures, was to foreshadow our
rest in the risen Christ. As Paul says of the Sabbath and other Jewish festivals,
"These are only a shadow of what is to come; but the substance belongs to
Christ" (Col. 2:17). The Jewish animal sacrifices did not imagine that God is
placated for sin by the blood of animals; instead they prefigured our redemption
by Christ's blood.[16] Christ fulfills what the law of Moses symbolized. Just as
the symbols are fulfilled in Christ and the Church, so also the commandments
are fulfilled by love of God and love of neighbor: "On these two commandments depend all the law and the prophets" (Matt. 22:40).

In Book 19, Faustus is willing to grant that Jesus said what Matthew 5:17
reports him to have said. Faustus argues, however, that Jesus said it to placate
his enemies at the time, and Jesus did not actually mean the Jewish law or

---

16. See Fredriksen, *Augustine and the Jews*, 250.

the Jewish prophets. Faustus identifies three kinds of law: the Jewish law, the natural law of the gentiles, and the law of the truth (the law of Christians). He also states that not only the Jews but also the gentiles and the Christians have prophets. According to Faustus, the commandments that Jesus goes on to mention, such as "You shall not kill" (Matt. 5:21), are found long ago among the gentiles. It is these gentile laws that will be fulfilled by the law of truth. The law of the Jews, by contrast, is rejected by Jesus in a series of statements where he tells his audience, "You have heard that it was said" (Matt. 5:38), and then goes on to teach the opposite. Faustus emphasizes once more that he and Catholics should agree on this point, because both Manicheans and Catholics reject circumcision, the food laws, animal sacrifice, and so forth. If Christ had come to fulfill and not to destroy the Jewish law, then both Manicheans and Catholics would need to become Jews so as to observe these commandments. If Catholics imagine that Christ does not destroy the Jewish law, then by their own rejection of the Jewish law they are destroying the Jewish law and simultaneously disobeying Christ.

Augustine, in reply, begins by once more quoting 1 Corinthians 10:6, "All these were symbols of us," and in confirmation of Christ's mission of fulfillment he adds 2 Corinthians 1:19–20, "Jesus Christ . . . was not Yes and No; but in him it is always Yes. For all the promises of God find their Yes in him." He then dismisses Faustus's notion that there are three kinds of law (and prophets) to which Jesus might be referring. John 1:17 and 5:46 are clear that Jesus has in view the law of Moses. Paul says of the law of Moses, "The law is holy, and the commandment is holy and just and good" (Rom. 7:12). The law of Moses humbled its recipients by showing them how easily they failed, thereby making them ready for faith in Christ. The law served as a "custodian" (Gal. 3:25) preparing for the freedom that faith in Christ gives through the grace of the Holy Spirit. Christ fulfills the righteousness of the law, and by faith, transformed by the grace of the Holy Spirit, we share in his fulfillment. Even in grace we fail to fulfill it perfectly, and so we rely on Christ to intercede for us and mediate God's forgiveness to us (see 1 John 2:1–2). In this way, Christ fulfills the prophecies and the divine promises. The fact that the prophecies and promises have been fulfilled is the reason Christians no longer obey the commandments that symbolized this fulfillment. Christians are not circumcised in the flesh, for example, because Christ's resurrection fulfilled the spiritual birth symbolized by circumcision. Yet this does not mean that Christians are now bereft of sacraments. On the contrary, since the resurrection of the dead has happened to Christ but not to us, Christ has given us the sacrament of baptism to symbolize our participation in Christ's death and resurrection.

Augustine develops further this theology of sacramental signs. Every religion, he argues, requires visible signs in order to unite people. Giving the example of Simon Magus, Augustine points out that these visible signs are misused by those who latch on to their outward aspect and fail to see that their purpose is holiness, charity, and faith, but even so the signs should not be rejected. God gave his chosen people visible signs that symbolized the coming of Christ, and many of his chosen people performed these sacraments in faith, hoping for God's salvation rather than trusting in the outward form. When Christ came, he fulfilled the sacraments that symbolized him. He instituted more powerful (and fewer) sacraments that unite his people in him and, when performed in faith, lead us to the resurrection life that he now possesses. Just as those living before Christ obeyed their sacramental signs often at great personal cost because of their faith in what was to come, so also, living after Christ, we too should not hesitate to endure all hardships for baptism and the Eucharist, in faith that we will receive the resurrection and eternal life won by Christ. What we believe in by faith has already been accomplished in Christ.

The sacraments of the Old Testament and of the New testify to the same faith—namely, faith in Christ, who redeems his people and leads them to everlasting life with God.[17] The change in sacraments does not indicate a change in the realities of faith, as if there were no unity between Old and New Testaments. Rather, the old sacraments signify the Christ who is to come, and the new sacraments signify the Christ who has come. The God who ordains the sacraments, and the purpose for which he ordains them, remains the same, despite the necessary change in the bodily actions and words of the sacramental signs. Again, the change in sacraments was necessary to ensure that Christians did not signify, by obeying the sacraments of the Mosaic law, that Christ was still to come. Christ has indeed come and fulfilled the sacraments that symbolized his coming.

Why, then, did St. Paul circumcise Timothy (see Acts 16:1–3)? If Christ fulfilled the old sacraments that symbolized his coming, then how is it that we find Paul, after Christ has died and risen, still performing the old sacraments as if Christ had not in fact come? Augustine explains that the old sacraments, since they were truly from God, could not simply be rejected as if they were things that had no value. Rather, it had to be shown that they had been fulfilled, not merely negated. Their divine ordination meant that the apostles had to treat them with respect, especially given the unity of faith between the Old and New Testaments. A change in sacramental signs had to be undertaken slowly or else it could have been misunderstood as a rejection of the Old Testament

17. For contrasting views of Augustine's sacramental theology, see Phillip Cary, *Outward Signs: The Powerlessness of External Things in Augustine's Thought* (Oxford: Oxford University Press, 2008), 236–43, and J. Patout Burns, "Providence as Divine Grace in St. Augustine," in *Augustinus Afer: Saint Augustin: Africanité et universalité*, ed. Pierre-Yves Fux, Jean-Michel Roessli, and Otto Wermelinger (Fribourg: Éditions universitaires, 2003), 211–18. Burns emphasizes the centrality for Augustine of the "bodily and social mediation of salvation" (212). On the significance of Augustine's anti-Manichean polemic for his evaluation of external things, see Henry Chadwick, *Augustine: A Very Short Introduction* (Oxford: Oxford University Press, 2001), 89–90. See also John C. Cavadini's helpful correction of Cary's position in "The Darkest Enigma: Reconsidering the Self in Augustine's Thought," *Augustinian Studies* 38 (2007): 119–32.

and the God of the Old Testament—the very thing the Manicheans had done. Those who had been raised under the Old Testament's sacramental signs were not forced to give them up, but at the same time those gentiles who came to faith were not forced to adopt the Old Testament sacraments.[18]

Augustine recognizes, of course, that there nonetheless arose a serious controversy among the first Christians about whether the gentiles needed to obey the Old Testament sacraments. This was the theme of the council of Jerusalem described in Acts 15, and it also appears in Paul's letters (for example, Gal. 2).[19] It was difficult for those who had been born prior to Jesus's death and resurrection, and who had thus grown up under the Old Testament sacraments, to accept that the prophetic sacraments had served their purpose now that Christ had in fact come. The apostles walked a fine line between seeming to reject the value of these divinely ordained sacraments and failing to acknowledge that their prophetic role had now ended. Augustine argues that the apostles, led in this regard by Paul, made the right pastoral decision in permitting those who had grown up under the law to keep the sacraments of the law, while insisting that new believers recognize Christ's fulfillment of the Mosaic sacraments. The apostles' insistence that the Mosaic law and its sacraments had been fulfilled by Christ, so that observance of these sacraments now had to cease lest Christian sacramental practice falsely testify that Christ has not yet come, resulted in breakaway groups such as the Symmachians (Nazareans) that continued to require all believers in Christ to obey the Mosaic law. These groups were known to both Augustine and Faustus.

Augustine also distinguishes between commandments that have to do with conduct and laws that are in some way symbolic. Christians continue to obey the commandments that have to do with conduct, such as "You shall make for yourselves no idols" (Lev. 26:1). Christians worship the God who gave these commandments, and so Christians obey them through the grace of the Holy Spirit given by Christ. As regards the symbolic laws, Christians obey them not in themselves but in their fulfillment in Christ. The commandments are fulfilled by a person who has faith working through love (see Gal. 5:6). The symbolic laws (the sacraments) are fulfilled by the coming of what they symbolized. Regarding the latter, Augustine notes that "they were not destroyed but fulfilled, because Christ showed that they were neither invalid nor deceptive when he made known what their significance promised."[20]

18. For discussion see Fredriksen, *Augustine and the Jews*, 256–57.

19. For Augustine's debate with Jerome in this regard, see R. S. Cole-Turner, "Anti-Heretical Issues and the Debate over Galatians 2:11–14 in the Letters of St. Augustine and St. Jerome," *Augustinian Studies* 11 (1980): 155–66; Peter J. Gorday, "Jews and Gentiles, Galatians 2:11–14, and Reading Israel in Romans," in *Engaging Augustine on Romans: Self, Context, and Theology in Interpretation*, ed. Daniel Patte and Eugene TeSelle (Harrisburg, PA: Trinity Press International, 2002), 199–236, at 204–18.

20. Augustine, *Answer to Faustus, a Manichean* 19.19, p. 250.

Returning to Faustus's claim that Christ fulfilled the law of the gentiles and destroyed the law of Moses, Augustine emphasizes that Christ fulfilled Moses's law and strengthened it by attending to the inner dispositions from which flow our actions. Some commandments, however, were indeed shown by Christ to be suited for the people of Israel but not for Christians. Augustine argues that God gave some commandments that fit the particular time but not all times. For example, Exodus 21:24, "eye for eye, tooth for tooth," helped to form the people of Israel in their time and place but was abolished by Jesus, in a certain sense at least. Yet even in this case, Jesus abolished it only because his coming fulfilled the time, so that a new time has begun. Fulfillment, not abolition, is the core reality. With respect to Faustus's notion that Christ fulfilled the law of the gentiles by adding (for example) restraints on anger and lust (see Matt. 5:22, 28), Augustine points out that if the gentiles did not know to restrain their anger and lust, none of them could have been righteous, whereas in fact through faith some of them were righteous, among them Enoch, who "walked with God" (Gen. 5:24). Regarding Christ's commandment that people not swear at all (see Matt. 5:34), Augustine observes that both Paul and the Manicheans swear oaths. Christ here is warning against perjury and against the danger, caused by a habit of swearing oaths, of unintentionally falling into perjury. Not swearing at all frees us from the danger of perjury, but in certain circumstances oaths are permitted. Thus Christ does not negate, but instead strengthens, the Mosaic law regarding oaths (see Lev. 19:12).

Faustus had pressed the point that Christ rejected the Mosaic law that required the Jews to love their neighbors but did not require them to love outsiders (for example, Lev. 19:18). Augustine responds that Paul too teaches that some persons are hateful to God and deserve to die (see Rom. 1:30–32). The key here is to distinguish the way in which charitable persons love their enemies from the way in which charitable persons hate their enemies. The enemies of charitable persons should be loved as human beings, but their sin should be hated. We should love a person's human nature but hate the sinful distortion of human nature in that person. It is a mark of true love for the sinner to want the sinner to be freed from sin. Similarly, the Mosaic law about "an eye for an eye" served to restrain uncontrolled vengeance. Jesus did not reject vengeance altogether: someone who has suffered an injury still deserves repayment. It is not wrong for a Christian to ask for the payment of a debt. Even so, Jesus makes clear that the fine line between desiring repayment in a just manner and desiring repayment in an uncontrolled, angry, and bitter manner is not easy to walk, and so it is safest, spiritually speaking, not to demand repayment at all. In this sense, rather than abolishing the Mosaic law, Christ's teaching ensures that what the Mosaic law sought—the avoidance of uncontrolled vengeance—will be more easily attained. Augustine's interpretation here fits with his interpretation of Christ's commandment against swearing oaths. In the same way, he argues that Christ's rejection of divorce fits with the intention of Deuteronomy 24:1, which was to restrain people from dismissing their wives. Moreover, by making us charitable through the grace of the Holy Spirit, Christ not only teaches about the law but enables us to fulfill it, so that we can love God and neighbor and attain to the kingdom of heaven.

Augustine also adduces texts from the Old Testament (especially the Wisdom literature) that teach, as Christ does, against anger and lust and in favor of love of enemy and mercy. Similarly, when Christ teaches against divorce, he appeals in his argument to Genesis 2:24. Not only does Christ not negate the law of Moses; he agrees with Moses, against the Manicheans, in appreciating the good of marriage.

Augustine again observes that the goal of being made holy and living in everlasting union with God is present in both Testaments. Although this goal and the path by which we attain it are often hidden in the Old Testament and are clearly revealed only in the New, the holy people of the Old Testament lived by faith and thus were already united to the goal. By faith, guided by the many symbols of the Old Testament, they already believed in the one who would come, filled with the Holy Spirit, to take away sin and to unite us with God in resurrection and eternal life. The coming of Christ thus fulfills God's promises and, by the outpouring of grace, enables us to fulfill God's law of love.

Books 22 and 30–32

Book 22 is the longest of all the books in *Answer to Faustus, a Manichean*. Faustus argues that neither he, nor the Manicheans, are enemies of the Law and the Prophets. On the contrary, he is willing to believe that what was written in the Old Testament books about the patriarchs and prophets is false. If the Old Testament books are true, however, then it is clear that the patriarchs and prophets lived unrighteous lives.

The law of the gentiles, Faustus maintains, was good. This law, shared by the best men of all nations, can be found in such commandments as "You shall not commit adultery" (Exod. 20:14). But the Jewish writers took this law and intermingled it with all sorts of nonsense about circumcision, animal sacrifices, and so forth. To be holy, we need to obey the true law, but the intermingled nonsensical laws have nothing to do with holiness, as Catholics show by not obeying them. In rejecting the Jewish laws (and Judaism), Faustus does not thereby reject the law, properly understood. The prophets and patriarchs wrote and did abominable things. Perhaps the prophets, in writing about the patriarchs, lied about them, in which case the reputation of the patriarchs could be salvaged. Faustus bemoans the Old Testament's portrait of God. The true God would not have worried about the first man and woman eating from a particular tree, for example. Nor would he have been jealous, angry, and bloodthirsty against various peoples, including his own. He would not have destroyed thousands of men because a few among them had committed a small sin. He would not have threatened to obliterate the whole human race. Faustus can only hope that the prophet or prophets who wrote such things were lying. Certainly such authors were not holy.

Abraham's copulation with his wife's maidservant, with his wife's knowledge, strikes Faustus as disgusting, as does Abraham's lying to Abimelech and to Pharaoh. What kind of husband would cause, by his own lies, his wife to become a king's concubine? Abraham's nephew, Lot, is a drunk who has incestuous intercourse with his two daughters. Isaac too is a liar, and Jacob a philanderer with his two wives and their maidservants. Judah has intercourse with his daughter-in-law, who deceives him by posing as a prostitute. Moses is a murderer and robber, and takes many wives. David has countless wives and still commits adultery with Bathsheba because of his rapacious lust, after which he orders that Bathsheba's husband be killed. Solomon too has countless wives and concubines. Hosea even blames God for commanding him to marry a prostitute. Far from being holy, these men are criminals, and the God that they depict is hardly better—unless the whole Old Testament is a lie, which would be much better than supposing it to be true.

Augustine here is led to offer an extended defense and explanation of the behavior and writings of the Old Testament prophets and patriarchs, as well as the God whom they portray. After briefly distinguishing once more between the commandments—fulfilled by love of God and neighbor—and the promises/ symbols of the law, he begins with the portrait of God and creation in Genesis 1. First John 1:5 states that "God is light," and this divine light (wisdom) makes all created light, whether spiritual or bodily. God did not, therefore, previously dwell in the "darkness" that "was upon the face of the deep" (Gen. 1:2). Nor when God "saw that the light was good" (Gen. 1:4) did that surprise God. Nor are we to suppose that God's question "Where are you?" (Gen. 3:9) means that God did not know where Adam was.

Augustine then points out that if Faustus is committed to reading the Old Testament in a flat-footed manner, by supposing that the Old Testament teaches that God dwelt in darkness or that God was surprised to see that his work was good, then Faustus will also have to apply the same defective exegetical technique to the New Testament. Christ, after all, chose Judas among the twelve; does this mean that Christ lacked foresight? In his parable of the wise and foolish virgins, Christ speaks of shutting the door on the five foolish virgins; does this mean that Christ is eager to lock us out? When Christ teaches that we must lose our lives for his sake, does this mean that Christ is bloodthirsty? When Christ warns sternly about judgment and punishment, does this mean that Christ is an arbitrary and wrathful God? In a parable, for example, Christ says that those who lack a wedding garment will be thrown "into the outer darkness" (Matt. 22:13). Is Christ, then, arbitrary and wrathful? The same question pertains to the Father who hands over his innocent Son to death (Rom. 8:32) or to the God who permits his saints to endure terrible tribulations.

Having shown that Faustus's mode of exegesis would distort the New Testament (which Faustus accepts) in the same way that it distorts the Old Testament, Augustine observes that pagans could teach Faustus something about reading Scripture. Pagans, Augustine thinks, could understand that God is Creator of the world and that God rejoices in the world's goodness. Pagans could understand that God is not to be blamed if he gives a good law and people do not follow it, even if God foreknows that many will fail to follow it. Pagans have some sense of divine providence and of the symbolic role of animal sacrifices, even if pagans have abused sacrificial worship by offering it to demons. Pagans might be open to learning the truth of prophetic discourse. Pagans certainly can understand different modes of speech, and they will recognize that the term "jealous," for instance, can have a much wider range of meaning than Faustus allows. Pagans would be able to understand that God, in sparing neither the wicked nor the just, does so to punish the wicked and to purify and perfect the just.

Faustus's notion of a dark, ignorant, bloodthirsty, jealous, and arbitrarily wrathful Old Testament God thus gives way, on a fair reading, to the God who is light, who foreknows all things, who jealously guards his people against idolatry, who punishes justly, and who purifies those who are on the way to salvation. By contrast, the Manichean God, whom Augustine goes on to describe, truly is monstrous in his relation to the things that he begets from his own substance. After all, the Manicheans believe that God is trapped, as spirit, within animals and foods that are offered in sacrifice to idols. Manicheans believe that God weakly gives up his own members, begotten of his own substance, to the realm of darkness without their free consent, and that God's members are punished in this realm of darkness by being caught up into the darkness.

What about Faustus's charge that the patriarchs and prophets were vicious rather than virtuous? No matter how vicious they were, Augustine avers, they were not as vicious as the Manichean God. In his view, no further answer would be needed if he were responding only to the Manicheans, but the purpose of his response is also to instruct Christians. The principle on which Augustine builds his answer is that "not only the language but also the life of those persons was prophetic, and that the whole kingdom of the nation of the Hebrews was a great prophet because it was prophetic of someone great."[21] To this principle, Augustine adds the point that sin is a violation of God's eternal law.[22] The Holy Spirit heals fallen humans so that, through faith, we can know what God's eternal law is and obey his law by works of love.

---

21. Augustine, *Answer to Faustus, a Manichean* 22.24, p. 316.
22. See Richard J. Dougherty, "Natural Law," in *Augustine through the Ages*, ed. Allan D. Fitzgerald, OSA (Grand Rapids: Eerdmans, 1999), 582–84.

On these foundations, the first question that Augustine takes up is whether
Abraham violated the eternal law by having sexual intercourse with Hagar,
Sarah's maidservant. Here he argues that Abraham sought this sexual inter-
course solely for the purpose of having children, a purpose that accords with
God's law for sexual intercourse. Sarah too acted from the desire to have
children. Although God had promised that Abraham would have a child, he
had not told him how this would come about. Since Sarah was barren, it was
reasonable for Sarah to call upon her maidservant to serve as the mother of
Abraham's child; and Abraham was reasonable to obey Sarah's wishes. Since
Hagar was Sarah's maidservant, Augustine considers that Sarah could justly
command Hagar in this regard.

Regarding Abraham's supposedly deceiving Abimelech and Pharaoh, Augustine points out that Sarah truly was Abraham's half-sister. Abraham did
not lie; he simply did not tell the whole truth. He withheld part of the truth
for good reason—namely, fear that he would be killed by these kings so that
they could take Sarah by force. In stating only that Sarah was his sister, he
trusted that God would ensure that Sarah would not be abused, and his trust
was shown to be well-founded. Augustine also suggests that Sarah is a figure
of the Church, which, in a hidden way, is the chaste bride of Christ in the
midst of the earthly kingdoms of the world, symbolized by Abimelech and
Pharaoh. He also interprets Lot symbolically, not only with respect to Lot's
life in Sodom (which can symbolize the life of the saints among the wicked),
but also even as regards his drunken sexual intercourse with his daughters
(which can symbolize the illegitimate use of the Mosaic law made by those
Israelites whose understanding of the law was darkened).

Augustine does not thereby justify the vicious behavior of Lot in getting
drunk or of Lot's daughters in their incestuous actions. Rather, he argues that
their evil actions were permitted by God, and were recorded in Scripture, for
our prophetic instruction. As for Lot and his daughters, God justly judged
their evil actions. Yet Augustine observes that Lot's daughters undertook
this behavior for the sake of having children after the destruction of the men
of Sodom and Gomorrah, and not simply out of lust. Above all, he makes
clear that Scripture narrates these actions without approving them, although
Scripture narrates them for a reason.

Augustine considers that having many wives need not be a violation of God's
eternal law. It is custom, not the eternal law, that determines how many wives
are permissible at a given time and place. Since the fundamental purpose of
marriage within God's providential order is the propagation of the human
race,[23] the number of wives permissible to one man depends on the need for

23. On the goods of marriage, see Donald X. Burt, OSA, *Friendship and Society: An In-
troduction to Augustine's Practical Philosophy* (Grand Rapids: Eerdmans, 1999), 83–86; Carol
Harrison, *Augustine: Christian Truth and Fractured Humanity* (Oxford: Oxford University
Press, 2000), 158–69.

the begetting of children. So long as the man does not seek wives on account of lust, having more than one wife does not necessarily violate God's law. As for the role of the maidservants, Augustine interprets it in the same way as he did for Abraham and Sarah. Jacob was obedient to his wives in the matter of sexual intercourse, and the purpose was consistently the begetting of children for the good of the household. Augustine also draws symbolic meanings from the two wives, the two maidservants, and various events in their lives. For example, Leah symbolizes action, Rachel contemplation. Jacob's active life of moral virtue (Leah) is fulfilled by contemplative wisdom (Rachel). The active life of virtue is loved for its fruits, just as Leah is honored for her children. The contemplative life needs the time that we all too often give to the active life, just as Rachel is sometimes jealous of Leah.

Scripture does not defend the actions of Judah, who sinned by having sexual intercourse with his daughter-in-law and by selling his brother into slavery. Yet Scripture counts Judah among the twelve patriarchs of Israel, and Judah is honored because David and Christ descend from him. How could God have permitted this? Augustine replies that even Judas served as one of the twelve apostles. Since Judah is a sinner, furthermore, Jacob's prophecy regarding Judah (Gen. 49:10) clearly describes not Judah but one who will come from his line, thereby preparing the people for Christ. When David sinned most egregiously, the prophet Nathan rebuked him. David's sins are not honored, although David's good deeds are, especially his humble repentance. Repentant sinners who bear much spiritual fruit in God's eyes excel those who do not commit egregious sins but who nonetheless lack interior humility. Augustine observes that in accord with his humanity, Christ descended not only from good people, but from wicked people; in accord with his divinity, Christ was miraculously born of a virgin.

Faustus despises Moses, but Augustine ardently praises him. Chosen by God to lead Israel, Moses was humble, obedient, vigorous, vigilant, and patient with his often wayward people. Even so, Moses violated God's eternal law by killing the Egyptian. At that time, Moses's zeal for God was powerful but not yet rightly ordered; he had not yet been trained for obedience by God's revelation of himself on Mount Sinai. Similarly, Saul showed a powerful zeal for God in persecuting the Church, but when Christ converted him on the Damascus road, Paul's zeal became rightly ordered and effective. Again, Peter's defense of Jesus by cutting off the ear of the servant of the high priest was disordered, but Peter's zeal, when rightly ordered by Christ's resurrection, enabled him to shepherd the Church. Scripture praises not the vice but the zealous heart that, when disciplined, has the potential for great good.

What about Abraham's near-sacrifice of Isaac, Moses's despoiling of the Egyptians, and Moses's and Joshua's wars? Did Abraham, Moses, and Joshua sin in these actions, and did God violate his own eternal law by commanding them? Augustine explains that God is the lawgiver whose authority governs human lives and possessions. The Egyptians were oppressing the Israelites by forcing them to work for next to nothing. On their own authority, the Israelites could not have rightly stolen from the Egyptians. But God, who has authority over all things, commanded the redistribution, and Moses was just in implementing it. Regarding the taking of life, God likewise has authority over all lives. If God had deemed that Isaac should die at that time, his will in this regard would have been just, and given God's rightful authority Abraham would have been just in carrying out God's command. Wars undertaken by legitimate human authority can also be just, so long as their true goal is peace rather than vengeance or the desire to dominate others. It is not only the Old Testament that permits soldiering, but also the New (see Luke 3:14; Matt. 8:9; 22:21).[24] Just wars do not violate God's law, and so God can act directly to punish pride and achieve peace by commanding war. All lives are in the hand of God, and Moses and Joshua would have sinned had they disobeyed God's commands.

Yet Augustine does not end there, as if killing and war were unqualified goods. In the Old Testament, God shows that human kingdoms and military victories are under his power and judgment. God's sovereignty over temporal kingdoms, however, is a figure of what is revealed in the New Testament—namely, the true eternal kingdom of God. In the New Testament, Christ conquers by renouncing this life, and he leads his followers into a kingdom not of this world. The martyrs follow Christ by laying down their lives for this eternal kingdom, rather than by conquering earthly kingdoms. Believers worship God not in hope of a temporal kingdom—as might seem to be the case when the Old Testament's witness to the kingdom of Israel is not read as a figure—but in hope of an eternal kingdom. Assured of the resurrection of the body, believers give their lives for this eternal kingdom willingly, like sheep among wolves (see Matt. 10:16). In spreading the kingdom of God, we must imitate Christ's cross rather than Moses's and Joshua's wars. This does not negate the Old Testament's demonstration that earthly kingdoms are under the power and judgment of God, a lesson that Christian rulers must continue to take to heart. In God's providence, his commands differ for different times.

Augustine concludes that we should not, like Faustus, criticize what God has willed for others. The will of God is just. We are just when we love God and love everything else for God's sake, that is to say, when we love the will of God as we see it worked out and accomplished in others. We cannot know, however, precisely how God is working in others. If God permits someone to

24. For Augustine's response to Faustus on this point, see Allen Verhey, "Neither Devils nor Angels: Peace, Justice, and Defending the Innocent: A Response to Richard Hays," in *The Word Leaps the Gap: Essays on Scripture and Theology in Honor of Richard B. Hays*, ed. J. Ross Wagner, C. Kavin Rowe, and A. Katherine Grieb (Grand Rapids: Eerdmans, 2008), 599–625, at 604–9. See also David Lenihan, "The Just War Theory in the Work of Saint Augustine," *Augustinian Studies* 19 (1988): 37–70.

die at a young age, for example, we cannot know whether this was a punishment or a blessing. An early death could be a just punishment, or it could be a divine blessing that saves the person from trials that would have caused the person to fall spiritually. This ignorance should instruct us when we see how God differently commands his followers in the Old and New Testaments. We know that Christ's followers are called by God to die at the hands of sinners rather than to seek to defend the kingdom of God by military means, but this knowledge should not set us up to condemn the Israelites who were commanded by God to punish pride and establish peace through military conquests. Likewise, Paul's command that a sinner be excommunicated (1 Cor. 5:5) has Moses's capital punishment of Israel's rebels (Exod. 32; Num. 16) as its figure, but this prophetic meaning does not thereby signify that Moses sinned. On the contrary, Moses rightly obeyed God, just as Paul did. The outward action differed, but the inward disposition of love toward God and neighbor was the same. Neither Moses nor Paul offered the other cheek when he was attacked—Paul called his attacker a "whitewashed wall" (Acts 23:3)—but in both cases their inward disposition was in accord with Christ's command to love one's enemies.

Faustus singled out Hosea, who married a prostitute by God's command, and Solomon for special scorn. In response, Augustine points out that surely a prostitute can repent and become a chaste wife. Christ, after all, teaches that "the tax collectors and the harlots go into the kingdom of God before you" (Matt. 21:31). Solomon, for his part, receives the condemnation of Scripture, not only for his lust but also for his idolatry. Solomon is an exemplar of virtue in some ways, but a warning against vice in other ways.

Augustine devotes the remainder of Book 22 to showing how the lives of the men criticized by Faustus also have a prophetic role in Scripture. Even their evil deeds, he argues, can prefigure goods that God will bring about. Evildoers do not of course mean for this to be the case, nor does God approve their wicked actions. Nonetheless, God can use their evil deeds for his purposes.[25] An example of this is Caiaphas's speech, which he meant for Jesus's destruction but which unwittingly prophesied Jesus's saving work (John 11:50–51). In his figural interpretation of Judah's sexual intercourse with his daughter-in-law, Augustine makes much of the meaning of the names "Tamar" and "Judah" (including its Latin meaning), as well as the meaning of the name of the town to which Judah came, "Timnah." Sitting at the gate, Tamar symbolizes the Church, called from the nations and desiring the seed of Abraham; she receives in secret the marks of holiness, symbolized by the ring, necklace, and staff. The names "David," "Uriah," and "Hittite" come in for similar figural exposition. Solomon's foreign wives symbolize, perhaps, the churches in gentile nations.

---

25. For philosophical discussion, see G. R. Evans, *Augustine on Evil* (Cambridge: Cambridge University Press, 1982), 96–98.

Solomon's surpassing wisdom, followed by his terrible fall, symbolizes the mingling of good and bad people in the Church. The prophetic significance of Hosea's marriage to Gomer, a prostitute, is explained by the prophet himself in Hosea 1–2, and its fulfillment is made clear by Paul and Peter (see Rom. 9 and 1 Pet. 2). Moses's despoiling of the Egyptians symbolizes the fruitful use that the Church can make of some pagan philosophy. Moses's command that the idolaters who worshiped the golden calf be killed (Exod. 32) foreshadows the destruction of vices. What Moses did to the golden calf symbolizes the spiritual power of righteous zeal, the Word of God, and the water of baptism.

Augustine gives many more examples, but the key point is clear: everything in the Old Testament has a figural meaning. Every word and deed in the Old Testament can be fruitfully reread in light of Christ so as to discern prophetic meaning. This is because the Old Testament tells the story of God's formation of his people, and Christ fully reveals how and for what goal God forms his people. At the same time, Augustine defends the holiness of the patriarchs and prophets, as we have seen: the books of the Old Testament are not to be rejected on the grounds that their authors were not worthy of the New Testament. He finds that the Old Testament contains examples of humans in all spiritual conditions, so that we can imitate the good (especially in their repentance) and reject the bad. If we find something in the Old Testament that does not seem to have a figural meaning or seems superfluous, this is an invitation to seek more deeply the figural or mystical meaning. God gives us the Old Testament, like the New, for our salvation. Finally, Augustine observes that even if the patriarchs were as bad as Faustus says, they were not nearly as bad as the Manichean God, whose very substance is embedded in the bodies of sinners and who yielded his members, at some past point in time, to the forces of darkness. In arguing that the patriarchs were unworthy of imitation, Faustus fails to see that it is his own false God who is unworthy of imitation. Indeed, Faustus himself, merely by the goodness of his existence, is much better than the Manichean God he worships.

In Book 30, Faustus replies to how Catholics apply 1 Timothy 4:1–3 to the Manicheans.[26] First Timothy 4:1–3 states, "In later times some will depart from the faith by giving heed to deceitful spirits and doctrines of demons, through the pretensions of liars whose consciences are seared, who forbid marriage and enjoin abstinence from foods which God created to be received with thanksgiving by those who believe and know the truth." Faustus does not believe that Paul actually wrote this, but he is willing to suppose for the sake of argument that Paul did. If Paul did write it, then Paul must be saying that Moses and the prophets taught demonic teachings. After all, it is Moses and

26. For discussion see François Decret, "L'utilisation des épitres de Paul chez les Manichéens d'Afrique," in Le epistole Paoline nei Manichei, i Donatisti e il primo Agostino (Rome: Istituto Patristico Augustinianum, 1989), 29–83, at 44–51.

the prophets who claim that God deems some foods unclean, thereby enjoining abstinence "from foods which God created to be received with thanksgiving by those who believe." Such foods include the flesh of pigs, rabbits, shellfish, and so forth. The prophet Daniel records that he himself, as well as Hananiah, Azariah, and Mishael, abstained from meat and fasted in obedience to God's law, a further instance of the behavior that Paul rejects in 1 Timothy. Even if Paul said such a thing, therefore, Paul was speaking against the Old Testament (and in favor of the Manicheans). Faustus adds that Catholics encourage consecrated virginity and abstain from meat during Lent, and so Catholics too come under Paul's condemnation, if the passage was in fact written by Paul. Further, if Paul were the author of 1 Timothy 4:1–3, he would be condemning both himself and Christ, because Paul favored virginity and Christ encouraged those who "have made themselves eunuchs for the sake of the kingdom of heaven" (Matt. 19:12). Faustus also claims that the apostle John was a virgin.

Against Faustus's attempt to show that if Catholics accept 1 Timothy 4:1–3 they will also have to reject the Old Testament, Augustine remarks that Faustus has failed to recognize why Catholics quote this passage in opposition to Manichean teachings. Certainly Catholics sometimes abstain from meat, and Catholics also encourage virginity. To abstain from meat or to encourage virginity is not to fall into "the teachings of demons." Nor does the Mosaic law teach demonic doctrine through its food laws, because these laws were symbolic, as Augustine has previously explained. Rather, the Manicheans take the crucial extra step by arguing both that certain foods are evil by their nature, and that marital intercourse is evil by its nature. It is this exaggeration that constitutes "the teachings of demons," because these Manichean doctrines vilify the work of the Creator God. By denying that the true God created certain foods and by rejecting marriage because it propagates the human race and thus continues the cycle of embodiment, the Manicheans spread the view that God is not the Creator and that matter is evil by nature.

Another text often quoted against the Manicheans is Titus 1:15, "To the pure all things are pure, but to the corrupt and unbelieving nothing is pure; their very minds and consciences are corrupted." Book 31 takes this verse as its subject. As he did with 1 Timothy 4:1–3, Faustus argues that Titus 1:15 applies much better to Moses and the prophets than it does to the Manicheans. After all, Moses and the prophets reject the view that "all things are pure." They must therefore be "corrupted" in "their very minds and consciences." Such men could have known nothing of God. In the same vein, Catholics who purport to obey the New Testament also abstain from foods. If Titus 1:15 is correct, this abstinence shows that Catholics too are "corrupted." Having turned Titus 1:15 against Catholics, Faustus takes up another text often quoted against Manicheans, Acts 10:12–16, where Peter in a trance sees a sheet with "all kinds of animals and reptiles and birds of the air" let down from heaven, and where God declares all these foods clean. Faustus considers that this text commits Catholics to eating such disgusting foods as snakes and other vermin.

Augustine responds, as in the previous chapter, by noting that the issue has to do not with the Old Testament food laws or with other abstinence from foods, but rather with the Manichean claim that some things are evil by nature. Moses affirms that God, upon creating all things, pronounced them "very good" (Gen. 1:31). This is the very point that Manicheans deny, because they consider that matter comes from Satan rather than from God. The supposition that material things are evil by nature is what Paul has in view when he tells Titus that "to the corrupt and unbelieving nothing is pure."

In Book 32, Faustus defends his selective reading of the New Testament. As we have seen, he does not accept certain parts of the New Testament as authentic. Rather, when verses seem to conflict, he accepts only the verses that fit with Manichean doctrine and assumes that the other verses have been interpolated. He points out that Catholics read the Old Testament in this same way. Indeed, Catholics ignore almost the entirety of the Old Testament, whereas they obey the entirety of the New Testament. It would be much more logical, Faustus thinks, for Catholics to agree that both the Old Testament and the New Testament have interpolated material, especially since Jesus and his apostles did not write the New Testament but instead it was written much later. Faustus blames the later writers for pretending that their writings were authored by the apostles or by the earliest followers of the apostles.

On this basis, Faustus reiterates his earlier observations that Catholics reject most of the Old Testament laws and that Catholics prefer to ignore the unsavory doings of the patriarchs and prophets. He also brings up, as clearly unacceptable and absurd, the law that requires a surviving brother to marry the wife of his dead brother, if his brother died without having children, and to father children with her. If this law and the others like it are bad, then the Old Testament, as the source of many such laws, should be rejected. At the very least, Catholics should stop hypocritically blaming Manicheans for being selective in what to accept from the New Testament. He lists various laws from the Old Testament that, if they were accepted by Catholics, would decisively undermine Catholic faith, including laws that curse those who hang upon a tree (Deut. 21:23), that curse men who do not raise up offspring in Israel, that curse uncircumcised males (Gen. 17:14), and that condemn to death Sabbath violators (Num. 15:35).

Faustus is aware of the Catholic answer that the Old Testament foretells the coming of Christ and that the laws bind God's people only up to the time of Christ's coming, at which point Christ teaches what laws still apply. This answer should, however, explain to Catholics why the Manicheans accept the New Testament selectively. After all, the Manicheans affirm the New Testament's promise that Christ will send the Paraclete, and the Paraclete teaches the Manicheans what to accept from the New Testament. Just as Catholics think that Christ allows them to reject many (or most) Old Testament laws, so also Manicheans think that the Paraclete allows them to accept as authentic only those sayings in the New Testament that truly honor the Son of the Father. Among the New Testament sayings that do not honor the Son are those that connect him to the flesh or to Judaism—for example, that he was born of a woman, that he was circumcised, that he offered the prescribed temple sacrifices, that he was baptized, and that he was tempted by the devil in the wilderness. The Manicheans accept his crucifixion, mystically understood, and they also accept as authentic most of his teachings.

Augustine replies that by contrast to Faustus's view of the New Testament, Catholics do not consider the Old Testament to be corrupted.[27] He repeats that God's commandments were appropriate to the time and place, and truthfully symbolized Christ. The Old Testament predicted its own fulfillment, as in Jeremiah 31's prophecy of a new covenant. This fulfillment is repeatedly attested by Paul, whose authority the Manicheans accept. Paul teaches that Christians, including gentiles, are "Abraham's offspring" (Gal. 3:29); that the laws regarding food, festivals, and the Sabbath were "a shadow of what is to come" (Col. 2:17); and that "these things happened to them as symbols, but they were written down on account of us, upon whom the end of the ages has come" (1 Cor. 10:11). If Faustus had understood Paul's words, says Augustine, he would have understood that (for example) the law commanding the surviving brother to marry the wife of his dead brother, if his brother died childless, not only does not command a crime but also has a symbolic meaning with regard to Christ. The symbolic meaning has to do with preaching the gospel in order to raise up children for Christ, who has died, rather than for oneself. Faustus would also have observed that the Christian celebration of the Eucharist fulfills the Jewish celebration of the Pasch. The Jewish sacrament points to the one who is to come, while the Christian sacrament remembers the one who has come. Augustine also repeats his argument that while the first Christians distanced themselves only slowly from the Jewish sacraments, in order to show respect for the law of Moses, later Christians rightly did not observe the law of Moses, since Christ has fulfilled it. Due to the difference in times, sacraments that foreshadowed the coming of Christ are no longer fitting sacraments for those who know that Christ has come. The fulfillment is not a negation: "We praise, accept, and approve all the things that were written in those books of the Old Testament as having been written with the greatest truth and the greatest usefulness for eternal life."[28]

27. For discussion see Roland J. Teske, SJ, "Augustine's Appeal to Tradition," in *Tradition and the Rule of Faith in the Early Church: Essays in Honor of Joseph T. Lienhard, S.J.*, ed. Ronnie J. Rombs and Alexander Y. Hwang (Washington, DC: Catholic University of America Press, 2010), 153–72, at 154–59; Thomas F. Martin, OSA, "Augustine, Paul, and the *Ueritas Catholica*," in *Tradition and the Rule of Faith*, 173–92, at 176–80.

28. Augustine, *Answer to Faustus, a Manichean* 30.14, p. 417.

Augustine goes on to defend the New Testament against Faustus's charge that it contains internal contradictions and was not written by the apostles. He challenges the basis upon which the Manicheans identify the Paraclete with Mani. The Paraclete is the Holy Spirit, who was given to the apostolic community when Jesus was glorified. The authority of Mani thus cannot suffice for determining which of the teachings of the New Testament about Christ are true. Manichean doctrine has no real basis other than personal opinion for determining which New Testament teachings are acceptable. Indeed, only by accepting the truth of the Old Testament can Manicheans learn to recognize the truth of the New Testament witness to Christ, and give up Mani's inventions about Christ.[29]

Conclusion

The first set of books—4, 6, 9, and 10—grounds Augustine's reply to Faustus in Paul's typological teaching that "these things happened to them as symbols, but they were written down on account of us, upon whom the end of the ages has come" (1 Cor. 10:11) and that "these are only a shadow of what is to come; but the substance belongs to Christ" (Col. 2:17). In the second set of books—12–19—Augustine focuses on the fact that even though the Old Testament foreshadows the New, the advent of Christ does not negate the Old Testament. The Old Testament remains necessary for attesting to the truth of the realities. For example, we learn the meaning of the name "Christ" from the Old Testament, without which we cannot appreciate the Christ of the New. Having rejected the Old Testament, the Manicheans are unable to understand the New Testament's portrait of Christ. The Old Testament does not claim to contain its goal within itself, but instead promises that it will be fulfilled by God's Messiah. Augustine's view of the Old Testament as figurative, then, does not undermine the value of the Old Testament.

The third set of books—22 and 30–32—affirms the value of the Old Testament from a different angle. Augustine criticizes Faustus for a flat-footed reading of the Old Testament. If one insists on a rigidly anthropomorphic interpretation of God's wrath in the Old Testament, then one will be compelled to find in the New Testament a divine Father who thirsts for the blood of his innocent Son. Since the patriarchs and prophets encountered God and wrote about him, their testimony to God would be impaired if it could be shown that they were egregious, untrustworthy sinners. Augustine both defends the patriarchs and prophets, and shows that the sins of the patriarchs, such as David's adultery with Bathsheba, are condemned rather than commended.

---

29. See Augustine, *Answer to Faustus, a Manichean* 32.22, p. 423. See also Robert A. Markus, *Signs and Meanings: World and Text in Ancient Christianity* (Liverpool: Liverpool University Press, 1996), 32–33, 40.

Augustine also differentiates New Testament fasting and Old Testament abstinence from certain foods, from Manichean rejection of matter as evil by nature. Here again a more appreciative reading of the Old Testament would have enabled Faustus to understand the teachings of Christ and the Church. Once the prophetic character of the Old Testament laws has been recognized and the enduring value of the Old Testament affirmed, the truth about the Creator God becomes clear.

As Creator of all, this God is neither evil nor opposed by an eternal principle of evil. Rather, he uses scriptural and sacramental signs to lead his people typologically, both before and after the coming of Christ, to union with himself in love.

3

Homilies on the First Epistle of John

P reached largely during Easter week around the year 407, Augustine's
Homilies on the First Epistle of John provides the occasion for one of
his most extraordinary treatments of Christian love. It also abounds with
anti-Donatist remarks.[1] As a set of homilies on a biblical text, it examines how
Scripture and interpreters of Scripture function in building up the Church in
love. Augustine wants to persuade the Donatists that they have misunderstood
Christ's Body the Church, but he also wants to show how such arguments can
be undertaken without failing in love. In his prologue, he states that reading
1 John should ignite a fire of love within us, "so that we all may rejoice in one
charity. Where there is charity there is peace, and where there is humility there
is charity."[2] No enemy can truly harm us so long as we love God. Even so,
how are we to rejoice in charity, humility, and peace when there are divisions
among those who claim the name of Christ?

The *Homilies on the First Epistle of John* can be divided into two sections.
The first section, homilies 1–5, explores fellowship with God in light of our
imperfect charity and given the presence in the Church of wicked persons who,
having been baptized, claim the name Christian. In this section, Augustine
challenges the perfectionism of the Donatists while agreeing with them that

---

1. See Eoin G. Cassidy, "Augustine's Exegesis of the First Epistle to John," in *Scriptural In-terpretation in the Fathers: Letter and Spirit*, ed. Thomas Finan and Vincent Twomey (Dublin: Four Courts, 1993), 201–20, at 206–10; Boniface Ramsey, "Introduction" to Saint Augustine, *Homilies on the First Epistle of John*, trans. Boniface Ramsey (Hyde Park, NY: New City, 2008), 9–17, at 12.

2. Augustine, *Homilies on the First Epistle of John*, Prologue, pp. 19–20.

perfect charity is the goal of Christian life. The second section, homilies 6–10, criticizes the Donatists for dividing what Jesus came in the flesh to unite: his Church. This section also argues that love cannot be perceived simply on the basis of the external appearance of an action, and so coercion of the Donatists should not be assumed to be an act of hatred. Augustine emphasizes that we must love our enemies both because they are fellow human beings and so that they might become our brothers in eternal life. If we love love, we will love God and our brethren, and thus we will love the unity of the Church. Loving Christ cannot be separated from loving his members. Throughout both sections, Augustine observes that since Christ promised that the Church would be spread throughout the nations, the Donatist Church's North African boundaries show that it cannot be the Church of Christ.

Homily 1

The First Epistle of John begins with a claim to eyewitness authority: "That which was from the beginning, which we have heard, which we have seen with our eyes, which we have looked upon and touched with our hands, concerning the word of life" (1 John 1:1). Augustine notes the connection between this opening and that of the Gospel of John. Since we could not see the invisible God, he became visible for us. The incarnate Word healed our spiritual illness so that we might be able once again to see him.[3] Since in Greek the word for "witness" is "martyr," Augustine points out that John's witness configured him to Christ's Pasch: human witness to God is joined to God's (prior) witness to humans.[4] The marriage of the Word and human flesh took place in the Virgin Mary's womb, and the incarnate Word, Jesus Christ, is not two but one. This unity is maintained even when we recognize that the whole Christ includes his Body: "The Church is joined to that flesh, and Christ becomes the whole, head and body."[5]

We see the incarnate Word by faith, which we share with those who knew him in the flesh, since even his closest disciples could only perceive by faith the divinity of the one whose humanity they saw and touched.[6] Through faith, we gain the blessing that is the fellowship of charity, a fellowship with Christ and the Father. As John says, "That which we have seen and heard we proclaim

3. For discussion see Lewis Ayres, "Augustine, Christology, and God as Love: An Introduction to the Homilies on 1 John," in *Nothing Greater, Nothing Better: Theological Essays on the Love of God*, ed. Kevin J. Vanhoozer (Grand Rapids: Eerdmans, 2001), 67–93, at 70–71.

4. See Ayres, "Augustine, Christology, and God as Love," 72–75, 85.

5. Augustine, *Homilies on the First Epistle of John* 1.2, p. 22. See Ayres, "Augustine, Christology, and God as Love," 76–79; Tarsicius J. van Bavel, "The 'Christus Totus' Idea: A Forgotten Aspect of Augustine's Spirituality," in *Studies in Patristic Christology*, ed. Thomas Finan and Vincent Twomey (Dublin: Four Courts, 1998), 84–94.

6. Ayres, "Augustine, Christology, and God as Love," 79–80.

also to you, so that you may have fellowship with us; and our fellowship is with the Father and with his Son Jesus Christ" (1 John 1:3). Augustine comments that Christ became incarnate and endured so many humiliations in order to teach us that "God is light and in him is no darkness at all" (1 John 1:5).[7] God is utterly transcendent, uncreated wisdom. We need to share in this wisdom, this light, if we are to live. In Augustine's words, "There must be fellowship with God; there is no other hope for eternal life."[8] Yet God's light reveals our sin. The danger, then, is that we sinners might lose hope for attaining fellowship with God.

Augustine emphasizes that God nourishes us on our way to God. Our sins do indeed cut us off from fellowship with God. But as John teaches, "The blood of Jesus his Son cleanses us from all sin" (1 John 1:7). In baptism, we are truly cleansed. We may have been old and near death as regards our sins, but by confessing ourselves in need of Christ and by receiving baptism, we are reborn.[9] Even so, baptized believers do not become utterly sinless. John says that "if we say we have no sin, we deceive ourselves, and the truth is not in us" (1 John 1:8). Augustine likewise affirms that "so long as a person bears flesh, he cannot but have at least slight sins."[10] No matter how slight, these sins weigh us down. Only when we have sufficient humility to confess our sins can we be said to love, rather than still being impeded by pride.[11] To receive Jesus's cleansing, we must acknowledge our need for his mercy. John states, "If we confess our sins, he is faithful and just, and will forgive our sins and cleanse us from all unrighteousness" (1 John 1:9).

Can we then sin with impunity, assuming that if we confess our sins the Lord will cleanse them? The quest for this position of security is itself a sin, a form of pride. To imagine that we can stand before God on any basis except profound repentance is to lack holy fear before the Lord. But if we cannot have assurance in advance, how can we hope for forgiveness when we fall into sin after baptism? The answer is that if we confess our sin in humble repentance, Jesus will be our advocate. Our only security is to recognize that we are beggars and to trust ourselves entirely to his mercy.

A model for us in this regard is John himself. Although he was the beloved disciple, he confessed his own sins and recognized his own need for the Redeemer. His humility is exemplary, and it is this humility that makes him a

---

7. Ayres, "Augustine, Christology, and God as Love," 81–83.

8. Augustine, *Homilies on the First Epistle of John* 1.5, p. 25.

9. See J. Patout Burns, "Christ and the Holy Spirit in Augustine's Theology of Baptism," in *Augustine: From Rhetor to Theologian*, ed. Joanne McWilliam (Waterloo, Ontario: Wilfrid Laurier University Press, 1992), 161–71, at 163.

10. Augustine, *Homilies on the First Epistle of John* 1.6, pp. 26–27. See Peter Burnell, *The Augustinian Person* (Washington, DC: Catholic University of America Press, 2005), 72, 75–77; James Wetzel, *Augustine and the Limits of Virtue* (Cambridge: Cambridge University Press, 1992), 184–85.

11. Ayres, "Augustine, Christology, and God as Love," 83–84.

true witness.[12] Indeed, Augustine argues that the source of heresy (false witness) is the proud claim to be righteous—the claim made by the Donatists. Saints and bishops must not present themselves as mediators or advocates on behalf of the community, because all members of the community must rely entirely on the one mediator Jesus Christ. Only the holiness of Jesus Christ suffices to intercede with the Father. Certainly, bishops pray for the people, but as sinners they also ask for the people's prayers. Even Paul asks for the prayers of his communities.

Jesus intercedes not only for believers' sins, "but also for the sins of the whole world" (1 John 2:2). This shows that the Church for which Jesus intercedes is found in all the nations, not simply in part of the world. Yet the Donatist churches flourish only in North Africa and cut themselves off from Christians in the rest of the world.[13] The Donatists thereby reveal that their movement is not marked by charity. They do so in two ways: first, by their claim that their bishops are particularly holy, and second by their claim that the true Church now exists only in North Africa. Rather than loving only those who are holy, Christians are called to love sinners. The way of charity requires love for our enemies "in such a way that you wish them to be brothers."[14] Christ's new commandment of love requires us to forgive each other rather than hate each other because of past arguments and divisions. What use is it when people convert from the idolatry of paganism to the light of Christian faith yet still hate their brother? As John says, "He who says he is in the light and hates his brother is in the darkness still" (1 John 2:9). Charity is the path by which we can be sure to remain united to Christ and his Church. If we leave the Church because we have been offended by our brethren, we have failed in love. None of us are indispensable to Christ or to the Church; rather, Christ and the Church are indispensable to us.

How can we be sure where the Church is? John teaches that the one who hates his brother "does not know where he is going, because the darkness has blinded his eyes" (1 John 2:11). Blinded by pride, such a person will not be able to see Christ or the Church. Yet the Church, like the moon, is evident to one who can see. Augustine points out that the Church is where, as was promised to Abraham, all nations are blessed. It cannot be that the Church exists solely in North Africa. The Donatists were offended by their African brethren, and they therefore cut themselves off from the Church not only in North Africa

---

12. See Cassidy, "Augustine's Exegesis," 207.

13. See Jason Byassee, *Praise Seeking Understanding: Reading the Psalms with Augustine* (Grand Rapids: Eerdmans, 2007), 216, 220–21; Michael Cameron, "Augustine's Construction of Figurative Exegesis against the Donatists in the *Enarrationes in Psalmos*" (PhD diss., University of Chicago, 1996); Coleen Hoffman Gowans, *The Identity of the True Believer in the Sermons of Augustine of Hippo: A Dimension of His Christian Anthropology* (Lewiston, NY: Edwin Mellen, 1998), 195–96.

14. Augustine, *Homilies on the First Epistle of John* 1.9, p. 30.

but also in the rest of the world. In taking such offense at their brethren's lack of holiness, they showed that they lacked charity, which requires us to love even our enemies in hopes that our enemies might one day become fully our brethren.[15] Despite their refusal to tolerate the faults of Catholics, moreover, they later tolerated the followers of Maximian in order to preserve the unity of their movement.

Homily 2

Augustine begins with the story of the two disciples on the road to Emmaus. They were sad because they had hoped that Jesus was the Messiah. When the risen Jesus meets them, they do not recognize him. Without revealing his identity, Jesus showed that his sufferings had been foretold in Scripture, and finally he revealed himself to them in the breaking of the bread. In manifesting himself to the eleven disciples, Jesus made sure that they were able to touch him so that they would not think he was a ghost. Through the preaching of the disciples, thousands of Jews in Jerusalem believed in the gospel. Augustine draws particular attention to the fact that the risen Lord strengthened his disciples by the biblical testimony that the Christ would suffer and rise again so as to bring about the salvation of all the nations. It cannot be, therefore, that the Church is now only in North Africa. Indeed, the Donatists are not even in communion with the Church in Jerusalem, because they reject the validity of its sacraments (especially baptism). On the day of Pentecost, the Holy Spirit enabled the apostles to speak in many languages, but the Donatists imagine that the true Church is now confined to only two languages. In severing the unity of the Church, the Donatists have shown that they walk in darkness rather than in the light of charity.

Christians are reborn through the forgiveness of sins in Jesus Christ. We belong to Christ in love, and this unity should not be broken on account of partisanship either for Donatus or for Augustine. We are Christ's sons; we are in time, whereas Christ exists from all eternity, outside of time. We are "fathers" in Christ (1 John 2:14) by recognizing that Christ is before all time. We cannot love both the world and God (1 John 2:15). If like vessels we are filled with the love of the world, we cannot be filled with God's love. We must empty ourselves so as to be filled. Having been reborn in baptism, we must live in charity. Commenting on 1 John 2:17, "the world passes away, and the lust of it; but he who does the will of God abides for ever," Augustine asks, "Which do you want, to love temporal things and to pass away with time or not to love the world and to

---

15. For emphasis on orthodox faith's acceptance of a certain amount of imperfection and ambiguity in this life, see Carol Harrison, "*De profundis*: Augustine's Reading of Orthodoxy," in *Orthodox Readings of Augustine*, ed. George E. Demacopoulos and Aristotle Papanikolaou (Crestwood, NY: St. Vladimir's Seminary Press, 2008), 253–61.

live forever with God?"[16] We are caught up in the temporal stream that is flow-ing onward, whereas Jesus is like a tree by the stream; we must hold on to the wood of the cross in order to have eternal life. The Lord became temporal so that we might become eternal. Sin had imprisoned us in things that are passing away; the Lord visited us and redeemed us from this imprisonment. Certainly we are still mortal, but we are united to an anchor that will give us eternal life.

God made all things good, but the danger is that we will cleave to the beautiful created things and turn away from the infinitely more beautiful Creator. This distortion, rooted in concupiscence, "is not of the Father but is of the world" (1 John 2:16). Augustine makes clear that John here condemns not God's creation but the "world" in another sense—namely, the lust for the things of this world taken out of the context of God's creative love. We can-not place our happiness in worldly things; this would be like a bride loving her wedding ring more than she loves her bridegroom. God gave us created things as the pledge of his love, and God wishes to give us himself. Following 1 John 2:16, Augustine examines what constitutes "the lust of the flesh" (food, sexual intercourse),[17] "the lust of the eyes" (curiosity, theurgy, public shows, evil deeds), and "the pride of life" (worldly ambition for glory, power, or wealth). He connects these three kinds of sins with the three temptations by which the devil sought to overthrow Christ. Christ resisted these sins by affirming the necessity of depending on God and of serving God alone. Augustine urges us, too, to hold fast to God in charity and to resist the concupiscence of the world. The choice is between eternal death and eternal life. Those who love earthly things "will be earth," while those who love God will be adopted sons of God.[18] Believers will become like God by sharing in his love.

Homily 3

Augustine's third homily begins with John's addressing his audience, "Children, it is the last hour" (1 John 2:18). When we are baptized, we become children in Christ. Christ nourishes us through mother Church and her breasts, the two Testaments of Scripture. The nourishing milk that we receive is the "sacraments" or mysteries that have taken place in history for our eternal salvation. Whether prophetically or explicitly, all of these mysteries have to do with Jesus Christ. Nourished by the milk of the temporal mysteries of Christ's humanity, we are made ready to eat the bread of the eternal truth of Christ's divinity. We are led by visible things to the invisible Word of the Father. When we have been made pure

16. Augustine, *Homilies on the First Epistle of John* 2.10, p. 46.
17. See Mathijs Lamberigts, "A Critical Evaluation of Critiques of Augustine's View of Sexu-ality," in *Augustine and His Critics: Essays in Honour of Gerald Bonner*, ed. Robert Dodaro and George Lawless (London: Routledge, 2000), 176–97.
18. Augustine, *Homilies on the First Epistle of John* 2.14, p. 51.

of heart, we know Christ as the Word of God, equal to the Father. Now is the "last hour" because our salvation urgently depends upon knowing Christ as God.

The "last hour" is marked by the coming of "many antichrists" (1 John 2:18). The "antichrists" are those who, as John says, "went out from us, but they were not of us" (1 John 2:19). The name "antichrist" means "contrary to Christ," and those who leave the Church, whether in heresy or in schism, are contrary to Christ. To avoid being contrary to Christ, one must remain a member of his Body, and one must act in charity rather than in sin. Because Christ's Body will not be perfect until the eschaton, there are some who are in the Church but who are wicked. Lacking charity, they are in the Church but not of the Church. They receive baptism and the Eucharist, but when trials come, they show their true colors. The indwelling Holy Spirit enables Christians to "recognize the good and the bad."[19]

What about those who leave the Church but then return? Are they "antichrists"? Augustine points out that such persons demonstrate, by choosing to return, that they are not opposed to Christ. Since Christ is truth, liars are opposed to Christ. The liar, says John, is "he who denies that Jesus is the Christ" (1 John 2:22). Catholics and Donatists both confess that Jesus is the Christ, but the Church has manifestly been divided by Donatists separating from Catholics. As members of a worldwide Church, Catholics possess the inheritance promised in Scripture. Those who have left this inheritance "went out from us" (1 John 2:19). Although both Catholics and Donatists confess that Jesus is the Christ, then, it is their deeds that must be compared. Certainly many people in the Church do deeds that are opposed to Christ; they remain in the Church only because they haven't yet been tested.

Others are opposed to Christ because they refuse to worship Christ and instead worship only the Father. John warns in this regard, "No one who denies the Son has the Father. He who confesses the Son has the Father also" (1 John 2:23). Rather than being insulted when someone calls us an antichrist, we should ensure that we are indeed lovers of Christ. The reward of loving Christ is to dwell eternally with the Son and the Father. Augustine quotes John's exhortation, "Let what you heard from the beginning abide in you. If what you heard from the beginning abides in you, then you will abide in the Son and in the Father. And this is what he has promised us, eternal life" (1 John 2:24–25). We must work not for wealth or for an abundance of possessions but for eternal life; the alternative is eternal fire. Christians are made strong in the pursuit of eternal life by the sacrament of anointing, which confers the Holy Spirit and strengthens our charity. Augustine understands John to be speaking of this anointing when John says that "the anointing which you received from him abides in you, and you have no need that any one should teach you; as his anointing teaches you about everything" (1 John 2:27). But

---

19. Augustine, *Homilies on the First Epistle of John* 3.5, p. 56.

why then do preachers preach, and furthermore why should John write his letter, if the anointing teaches us all that we need to know? Augustine distinguishes the exterior word and the interior word: unless the person interiorly understands, no amount of exterior wisdom can have an impact. The interior Holy Spirit must make fruitful the exterior words of the preacher, no matter how wise these words are. Christ and the Holy Spirit are our interior teachers, on whom we depend. The preacher is like a farmer who pours water on the tree; the water has its use, but the farmer himself does not form the fruit.

Homily 4

Augustine begins his fourth homily by returning once more to the difference between the preacher's exterior words and the interior words of Christ and the Holy Spirit; it is God speaking to us from within that makes the exterior words of the preacher persuasive to us, and that begets our faith. Yet we cannot be passive: God "speaks within to those who make room for him."[20] To make room for God, we must refuse to make room for the devil, who tempts us. So long as God dwells in our hearts, the devil can only tempt us from without. God's interior anointing enables us to refuse to consent to these temptations. In this way we will be ready for Jesus's "coming" (1 John 2:28). We believe what the apostles witnessed. Jesus sent the apostles to preach the gospel to all nations. They preached what they had seen, whereas we believe in faith what we haven't seen. Those who do not believe will "shrink from him in shame at his coming" (1 John 2:28). To receive the promised inheritance of eternal life, we must keep faith not only in words but also in deeds.

Certainly, in this life we cannot yet be perfectly righteous. The angels are perfectly righteous, but we are not; our minds and hearts are not continually drawn to God. We receive righteousness from faith in Christ, and the first step is to confess our sins rather than to defend ourselves. Only when we have no concupiscence, no interior struggle, and a perfect desire for God will we have perfect righteousness. The present life, then, is the site of a spiritual battle. In this spiritual battle against sin, we must rely on God's strength, not our own. We cannot conquer the temptations of the devil on our own. Adam fell because he imagined that he could be his own power, self-sufficient rather than subject to God. Adam fell in paradise, whereas Job, by trusting in God, conquered in the ash heap. We can only conquer the devil through humility, in dependence on God. Thus John says that "every one who does right is born of him" (1 John 2:29)—that is, of Christ the Son of God.

Reflecting on 1 John 3:1, "See what love the Father has given us, that we should be called children of God," Augustine observes that many are called something

20. Augustine, *Homilies on the First Epistle of John* 4.1, p. 64.

but are not what they are called. Many are called Christians but are not so in deeds or in faith, hope, and charity. To live a holy life requires not doing a good number of things that others take for granted. Worldly persons will scorn those who aim at holiness, just as worldly persons scorned and persecuted Jesus. Having been reborn in baptism, "we are God's children now" (1 John 3:2), but we still await in hope our final perfection. John says that "it does not yet appear what we shall be, but we know that when he appears we shall be like him, for we shall see him as he is" (1 John 3:2). Augustine focuses on the word "is." Christ is the unchanging, eternal Son of God. Everyone will be resurrected, and everyone will see Christ the judge in his humanity. But only the blessed will see his divinity. The Christian life, then, is a journey toward a full vision of Christ. Augustine describes the vision as excelling "all the earthly beauties of gold, of silver, of glades and fields, the beauty of sea and sky, the beauty of sun and moon, the beauty of the stars, the beauty of the angels, all things, because it is from this that all things are beautiful."[21] When we see the eternal Creator of all things, we will be like him. This is the great promise that Christians have received.

The Christian life, says Augustine, can be boiled down to the holy desire to participate in this divine beauty. As the interior teacher, God expands our hearts so that our desire becomes larger and larger, "so that, when there comes what you should see, you may be filled."[22] The problem with fallen humans is that our desires are too small: we cleave to finite created things rather than desiring their infinite Creator. The purpose of our lives is to give God the time to stretch our desires, so that we come to long more and more for him. Augustine urges us to desire and pursue God. Consumed by love for God, we will no longer desire to cleave to this world. God wants to fill us with himself, and this will not be possible if in our hearts we have substituted the things of this world for God. We must be emptied out and purified so that we can be filled with God. Along these lines, John states that "every one who thus hopes in him purifies himself as he is pure" (1 John 3:3). God will make us pure, but only if we are willing. We must ask God for his help. God helps us through Christ, the sinless one who takes away our sins. In faith, we see and know Christ; our righteousness is now by faith, and we await its perfection in the vision of God, with the caveat that we will never be infinitely righteous so as to be equal to God. Because of Adam's fall (in imitation of the devil) we are sinners, but because of Christ's death we are made righteous.

Homily 5

When John teaches that "no one born of God commits sin" (1 John 3:9), this seems in tension with his earlier remark that "if we say we have no sin, we

---

21. Augustine, *Homilies on the First Epistle of John* 4.5, p. 69.
22. Augustine, *Homilies on the First Epistle of John* 4.6, p. 69.

deceive ourselves" (1 John 1:8). Surely John was born of God, and we too are reborn in baptism. But if John cannot say that he has no sin, and one born of God cannot sin, then it would seem that neither John nor we have been born of God. Augustine argues that John has in view a particular sin, acting against Christ's commandment of charity. It is this sin that destroys our rebirth in Christ Jesus. So long as we love, we are in Christ. Recall that the Lord asks Peter three times, "Do you love me?" (John 21:15–17). Peter had denied him three times; now Peter affirms his love three times. We have only this to give back to God—namely, the love that God gives us. Receiving the gift of charity from God, we give it back to him "in such a way that you not only don't hate your brother but are prepared to die for your brother."[23] Perfect charity involves the willingness to die for others. If we do not have charity, then even if we have been baptized we cannot say that we are in Christ. If we love, we are "children of God"; if we do not love, we are "children of the devil" (1 John 3:10). Charity is the sole dividing point, the pearl of great price. Augustine states that "if you love the brother whom you see, you will see God at the same time, because you will see charity itself, and God dwells within it."[24]

The opposite of love is envy. The devil tempted Adam and Eve out of envy at their goodness; Cain likewise murdered Abel out of envy. John observes that God accepted Abel's sacrifice but rejected Cain's, because Cain's "deeds were evil and his brother's righteous" (1 John 3:12). How we treat our brethren shows whether we love. As a lover of the world rather than of God, Cain hated Abel. If we have love in our hearts, then we are like plants in winter; we can be assured that we will blossom and bear the fruit of eternal life, no matter whether we lack honor here and now. If we have hatred in our hearts, then we are already like a murderer, even if we have as yet done nothing to our brother. In this condition, we will receive eternal punishment, not eternal life (see 1 John 3:15). Whereas the hate-filled person conceals an envious and murderous heart, the charitable person will even die for his brethren, as Jesus did and as he commanded Peter to do.

Augustine is aware, however, that many of us will hardly dare to claim that we love our brethren so much that we would die for them. Are we then cut off from Christ? In this regard, says Augustine, John provides solace. Immediately after stating that "we ought to lay down our lives for the brethren" (1 John 3:16), John warns that "if any one has the world's goods and sees his brother in need, yet closes his heart against him, how does God's love abide in him?" (1 John 3:17). Certainly, giving our superfluous goods to our brother is less demanding than giving up our life for our brother. Augustine urges us not to lose heart, then, if our charity is less than perfect. Charity need not be perfect all at once; it must

23. Augustine, *Homilies on the First Epistle of John* 5.4, p. 78.
24. Augustine, *Homilies on the First Epistle of John* 5.7, p. 82.

be nourished and perfected. The way to do this is through almsgiving.[25] Christ paid the price for all sins; at the very least, then, we should gladly pay a price to relieve the worldly needs of our brethren. In this way, even if our charity isn't yet perfect, we show that we love not "in word or speech but in deed and in truth" (1 John 3:18). We thereby nourish the seed of charity that has been planted in us by baptism, so that we will eventually be able to bring a great crop to harvest.[26]

Homily 6

Augustine repeats his injunction that those without perfect charity need not lose hope. Charity is possessed when we give alms. If we nurture this imperfect charity by meditating on the promise of eternal life, God will increase our charity to the point where we become willing to lay down our lives for others. Yet people without charity also give away their goods and even lay down their lives for others. It is possible to do such things for human praise or for unjust causes. How can we tell when charity motivates our actions? God knows our heart, and we must "reassure our hearts before him" (1 John 3:19) by consulting our conscience.[27] As John says, "Beloved, if our hearts do not condemn us, we have confidence before God" (1 John 3:21). External appearances cannot prove whether we have charity; only God and our own conscience can know our heart. Even if God and our conscience condemn us, all is not lost. If we confess our sin and beg God to help us, he will do so. If on the contrary we find genuine unselfish love within ourselves, we are keeping Christ's commandment to love. John assures us that in this condition, we will "receive from him [God] whatever we ask" (1 John 3:22).

But why then did Paul, who was certainly filled with charity, not receive from God what Paul asked for—namely, the removal of his thorn in the flesh? Augustine answers that Paul, in charity, desired union with God above all things. When God refused to remove the thorn in the flesh, God did not remove it because the thorn conduced to Paul's salvation, and so in this way God fulfilled Paul's primary desire. When we ask for something and God does not give it to us, therefore, this need not mean that we lack charity. Rather, it may mean that God, as the good physician, is healing us in the way that he knows best. Rather than testing God, we should simply love God and our brethren, and we should understand that God allows us to suffer in certain ways for our own good. Our love itself calls out to God, and God will do whatever is necessary

25. For discussion see Boniface Ramsey, OP, "Almsgiving in the Latin Church: The Late Fourth and Early Fifth Centuries," *Theological Studies* 43 (1982): 226–59.

26. See Dany Dideberg, *Saint Augustin et la première épître de saint Jean. Une théologie de l'agapè* (Paris: Beauchesne, 1975), 89–91.

27. See Dideberg, *Saint Augustin et la première épître de saint Jean*, 105–6. For Augustine's understanding of "heart" (*cor*), see John C. Cavadini, "The Darkest Enigma: Reconsidering the Self in Augustine's Thought," *Augustinian Studies* 38 (2007): 119–32, at 129–32; Gowans, *Identity of the True Believer*, especially chaps. 1 and 2.

to fulfill this love's desire by bringing us to eternal life. When we love God, his Spirit "abides in us" (1 John 3:24) and enables us to understand our hearts. In the Holy Spirit, our hearts will reveal "a love of peace and unity, a love of the Church spread throughout the earth."[28]

We do not know all our brethren in God's Church, but we nonetheless gaze with them upon the same beloved, God himself. The test of charity is to inquire whether our heart loves our brethren in God; if so, then the Holy Spirit truly dwells in us. Augustine notes that John cautions us not to "believe every spirit, but test the spirits to see whether they are of God" (1 John 4:1). Having been baptized does not guarantee that the Spirit dwells in us. Those who are cut off from the Church, whether by open heresy or schism or by hidden wickedness, may have the sacrament of baptism, but they do not have the Spirit's nourishing effects. John states that "many false prophets have gone out into the world" (1 John 4:1), and Augustine reasons that this is where heretics and schismatics are. For testing whether we have the Spirit of God and possess charity, John gives us a rule: "By this you know the Spirit of God: every spirit which confesses that Jesus Christ has come in the flesh is of God, and every spirit which does not confess Jesus is not of God" (1 John 4:2–3). But the Arians, Eunomians, Novatians, and so forth all confess that Jesus Christ has come in the flesh. Are we then to suppose that these false teachers possess the Spirit of God?

Augustine's answer is that we should look at deeds, not words. Christ came in the flesh in order to die out of love for us and to lead us to eternal life. He came in the flesh because of his charity. It follows that if we lack charity, we cannot truly confess that Christ came in the flesh.[29] Charity unites, while lack of charity divides. Those who divide the Church through schism bear the fruit not of charity but of lack of charity. They divide the Body of Christ, the very Body that Christ came in the flesh in order to unite. Some in the Church secretly cause divisions, while others openly separate themselves from the Church and produce division. In both cases, such persons "dissolve Jesus, and . . . deny that he has come in the flesh."[30] They bear witness to the fact that they lack Jesus's Spirit of charity. Those who rend the Church that he came to gather deny his coming, if not by words then by deeds.

Homily 7

Augustine begins by comparing life in this world to Israel's wandering in the desert. With God's commandments showing the way, Israel in due time arrived at its homeland. Similarly, God is preparing us now for eternal life, and if we follow his commands, we certainly will arrive there. The water that sustains

28. Augustine, *Homilies on the First Epistle of John* 6.10, p. 97.
29. See Dideberg, *Saint Augustin et la première épître de saint Jean*, 128–30.
30. Augustine, *Homilies on the First Epistle of John* 6.14, p. 103.

us in the desert is charity. We must drink charity in order to avoid dying in the desert. In eternal life we will be perfectly refreshed by charity. Charity requires that we forgive those who sin against us; lacking charity, we cannot forgive but remain mired in hatred. We deny Jesus's coming in the flesh when we refuse to forgive our brethren, because he came out of love in order to forgive sins.[31]

John teaches us that "you are of God, and have overcome them; for he who is in you is greater than he who is in the world" (1 John 4:4). In this way John undermines our pride. We have overcome, but only by the power of the Holy Spirit dwelling in us. Worldly persons expect us to avenge ourselves rather than to forgive in charity. This is what John means in saying, "They are of the world, therefore what they say is of the world, and the world listens to them" (1 John 4:5). In refusing revenge, we are imitating Jesus. Commenting on 1 John 4:6—"We are of God. Whoever knows God listens to us, and he who is not of God does not listen to us. By this we know the spirit of truth and the spirit of error"—Augustine notes that we had better listen if we wish to know God and to possess the spirit of truth. What is it that we must listen to? John continues: "Beloved, let us love one another; for love is of God, and he who loves is born of God and knows God. He who does not love does not know God; for God is love" (1 John 4:7–8). Those who possess the Spirit of truth, and who listen to God's apostle, show this by their deeds of love. Since God is love, only the lover can know God, and "to act against love is to act against God."[32] When we do not love our brethren, we show that we do not love God.

Augustine remarks that John here says both that "love is of God" and that "God is love." God, then, is "of God." The Son and the Holy Spirit both are God of God. Drawing on Romans 5:5, Augustine points out that the love of God that is poured into our hearts is, in particular, the Holy Spirit.[33] Baptized persons can be wicked and can be called Christians, but because they do not love, they do not have the indwelling Spirit. When we lacked love and needed healing, God showed us his love by sending "his only Son into the world, so that we might live through him" (1 John 4:9). In this way, God proves that he is love. Yet it might seem that God the Father merely did what Judas did: they both handed over the Son. Indeed, the Son handed over himself. Did the Father and the Son thereby commit a wicked act, or perhaps Judas performed a good act? The difference consists in intention: the Father and the Son acted out of supreme love, whereas Judas acted out of hate.[34] Likewise, a painful beating can be given out of love (as punishment), whereas pleasurable flattery can be given out of hate. The exterior appearance of the deed is not a sure

31. See Ayres, "Augustine, Christology, and God as Love," 85, 87.

32. Augustine, *Homilies on the First Epistle of John* 7.5, p. 107. See Ayres, "Augustine, Christology, and God as Love," 86.

33. See Bertrand de Margerie, SJ, *An Introduction to the History of Exegesis*, vol. 3, *Saint Augustine*, trans. Pierre de Fontnouvelle (Petersham, MA: Saint Bede's, 1991), 120–25.

34. See Ayres, "Augustine, Christology, and God as Love," 86, 88.

guide as to whether it is a charitable deed. Augustine comments, "Love, and do what you want. If you are silent, be silent with love; if you cry out, cry out with love; if you chastise, chastise with love; if you spare, spare with love."[35] So long as a person acts in charity, the act will not go astray.

We are not the source of our love. John teaches, "In this is love, not that we loved God but that he loved us and sent his Son to be the expiation for our sins" (1 John 4:10). Christ offered himself for the forgiveness of our sins. The only appropriate response to such a gift is to imitate it by loving and forgiving each other (see 1 John 4:11). God is the source of our love, but what do we mean when we say "God"? John observes, "No man has ever seen God" (1 John 4:12). Augustine urges us not to try to imagine God, because inevitably we will end up imagining a spatially vast entity. Rather we should recall that "God is love." Love has no shape, no appearance of its own. Love instead can be known by what it does: it leads to the Church, it gives to the poor, and so forth.[36] We do not see love itself, but we applaud its deeds. Love is a great treasure, and we can have it for free. We must recognize it for the delightful treasure that it is, rather than thinking of it indifferently. Love should prompt zeal: we should love ourselves and other persons by loving what God has made and by seeking to remove the sins and errors that we humans have made. Correction can be loving. We must be like a loving father who corrects his son, or like a dove that protects its nest without bitterness.

The image of the dove recalls the Holy Spirit who descended upon Jesus at his baptism. Just as acting against charity is to act against the Holy Spirit, so also acting in charity can require defending the unity of the Body of Christ. Augustine warns that "those who violate charity have created a schism"—the Donatist schism.[37] Donatist baptism is not invalid, because the sacraments are the Lord's, but the Donatists err in baptizing people outside the Lord's Body. The Donatist Church has broken away from the unity of the Catholic Church. Baptized Donatists must return to the one Church in order to be in Christ and be filled with the Holy Spirit.

Homily 8

To praise God's love with words is good, but to praise God's love with deeds is even better. We cannot always speak of charity, but we can always act charitably.

---

35. Augustine, *Homilies on the First Epistle of John* 7.8, p. 110. See Frederick H. Russell, "Persuading the Donatists: Augustine's Coercion by Words," in *The Limits of Ancient Christianity: Essays on Late Antique Thought and Culture in Honor of R. A. Markus*, ed. William E. Klingshirn and Mark Vessey (Ann Arbor: University of Michigan Press, 1999), 115–30, at 126; Cassidy, "Augustine's Exegesis," 214–16. See also John R. Bowlin, "Augustine on Justifying Coercion," *Annual of the Society of Christian Ethics* 17 (1997): 49–70.

36. See Ayres, "Augustine, Christology, and God as Love," 89–90.

37. Augustine, *Homilies on the First Epistle of John* 7.11, p. 113.

Charity must always be in our hearts; it is like the general of an army of virtues. The other virtues are commanded by charity. Yet if charity is like a general, it is one that does not wish for human praise. After all, we are able to act charitably only because the Holy Spirit dwells within us and acts through us. The praise belongs to God. Our bad actions come from ourselves, but our good actions have God as their source. Does this mean that, in confessing our sins, we demean ourselves? On the contrary. Like Paul, we confess our sins in order to glorify God who heals us. Pride sinks us lower, whereas humility raises us up through the power of God. In the course of daily life we must do a large variety of things, but in all of these actions we need charity.

John, however, seems to have emphasized love of our brethren while hardly mentioning love of God and leaving love of enemy entirely unmentioned. This focus on loving our brother contrasts with Jesus's emphasis on loving our enemies. In this context, Augustine notes that love "implies a certain benevolence toward those who are loved," and he wishes to explore what this means.[38] Benevolent love is different, for example, from loving food because we enjoy consuming it. Benevolent love seeks to bestow good upon the beloved. Do we love God and our enemies in this way, and does God love us in this way?

Almsgiving exemplifies benevolent love, yet the one who gives alms (for example, food, clothing, burial, peacemaking) wishes that there were no need for the alms and no lack endured by others. Almsgiving can increase our pride because it places us in a position of superiority vis-à-vis another person. When we love with benevolent love a person who does not need our benevolence, then we get a sense of the love that we owe to God. Pride is a form of avarice because it exceeds the measure in its greedy desire not only to be made to the image of God, but to be over God. Such pride is brought down by lowly things, such as the frogs and flies by which God subjected Pharaoh. Not all who are brought low, however, are filled with pride. Christ wills to suffer, and God permits some to suffer whom he loves. In the new creation, the holy martyrs will no longer be subject to the wild beasts as they were in the Coliseum. God's benevolent love includes his permission of suffering.

Augustine states that "a Christian must live in such a way as not to exalt himself over other people."[39] To love other people requires that we wish them to be our equal. A teacher, for example, must not want his student to always remain a student. Just as we can teach out of pride rather than out of charity, so also we can give other alms and do other good works out of pride. Pride has its martyrs just as charity does. Augustine again recommends questioning our conscience, so as to test whether we are acting out of charity or cupidity. In this light, we can return to the love of enemy. To love our brother is to

---

38. Augustine, *Homilies on the First Epistle of John* 8.5, p. 119. See Cassidy, "Augustine's Exegesis," 212–13.

39. Augustine, *Homilies on the First Epistle of John* 8.8, p. 122.

wish for his true good, eternal life; the same holds for love of enemy.[40] We should love our enemy (that is, one who does not have charity) that he may become our brother in eternal life. God too loves us sinners for what we will be, his adopted children. God also loves us because he creates us and gives us the goodness of human existence. We too must love our enemy because he is a human being made by God. We should love his goodness, not his lack of goodness. We should pray for him, have mercy on him, and ask God to do good for him. In this manner, we are loving our enemy in the same way that we love our brother, because we want the same thing for both of them—namely, the perfection of human existence in God. Just as a physician does not want his patient to remain ill and loves the patient rather than the illness, so also loving our enemies does not mean wishing that they remain enemies due to lack of charity. When we were his enemies, Christ loved us and, by his love, changed us. So long as we love, the attacks of our enemies upon our temporal goods can do us no permanent harm.

John promises that "if we love one another, God abides in us and his love is perfected in us" (1 John 4:12).[41] We are called therefore to love God who dwells within us, so that God may make us perfect in love. Indeed, John adds, "By this we know that we abide in him and he in us, because he has given us of his own Spirit" (1 John 14:13). To know whether we have received the Holy Spirit, we must inquire within our hearts and ask whether we are filled with charity. Even if we do not see charity there, we should not despair. The divine physician wants to heal us. As John says, "The Father has sent his Son as the Savior of the world" (1 John 4:14). In faith, we should put our hope in this Savior and desire eternal life. Again, faith in Christ requires confessing him not only in words but in deeds. Thus John teaches, "Whoever confesses that Jesus is the Son of God, God abides in him, and he in God. So we know and believe the love God has for us. God is love, and he who abides in love abides in God, and God abides in him" (1 John 4:15–16). When God dwells in us, of course, we do not contain him in a spatial way; we do not provide for him some perfection that he lacks. Rather, it is we who are changed. God loves us freely rather than because he is seeking something from us. He seeks us because we need to seek him. He wants to give us eternal life as his adopted sons in the Son.

Homily 9

Augustine instructs us to examine ourselves to see whether we are progressing in charity. When we have perfect charity, John says, we will "have confidence for the day of judgment" (1 John 4:17). If we are progressing in charity but

---

40. See Dideberg, *Saint Augustin et la première épître de saint Jean*, 67–73; Oliver O'Donovan, *The Problem of Self-Love in St. Augustine* (New Haven: Yale University Press, 1980), 123.

41. See Dideberg, *Saint Augustin et la première épître de saint Jean*, 167–68.

are not yet perfect, we will still fear the day of judgment. This fear of judgment stimulates our efforts to mortify our passions and do good works. We then begin to desire what we once feared, because of our hope for the eternal crown. In faith, hope, and charity, we pray with desire rather than with fear that God's kingdom come, and we groan at the Lord's delay. Augustine compares the person who struggles to endure death patiently because he would prefer to continue with earthly life, with the person who "lives patiently and dies in delight."[42] The latter person is characterized by perfect charity, because he confidently desires to meet God.

A person who possesses such confidence has become like God, who is love. John states that when we have attained perfect love, we are confident "because as he is so are we in this world" (1 John 4:17). Christ loved his enemies in this world, and so do those who are perfect in charity. Prior to perfection in charity, our conscience reminds us of our imperfection and stimulates fear. Augustine praises such fear, which he compares to a physician's scalpel: the fear of God provides a medicinal pain that removes the festering of cupidity and opens our hearts to the health of charity.

But if "perfect love casts out fear" (1 John 4:18), why does Psalm 19 praise the fear of the Lord as "enduring for ever" (Ps. 19:9)? Augustine differentiates chaste fear from fear of punishment. Fear of punishment does not yet love the Lord as he should be loved. God is infinite goodness, infinitely desirable. Fear of punishment desires to avoid pain rather than desiring to possess good. The latter motivates chaste fear. Chaste fear desires never to lose the presence of God. Perfect charity and chaste fear go together, since perfect charity desires always to possess the Lord. By contrast, fear of punishment can change our hearts so that we desire God for his goodness; love thus "casts out" fear of punishment. The person with chaste fear awaits with longing the arrival of God's kingdom.

John states, "We love, because he first loved us" (1 John 4:19).[43] Augustine comments that God, who is infinitely beautiful, loved us when our souls were ugly with sin. In loving ugly persons, God "didn't do so in order to leave them loathsome but in order to change them and, from being ugly, to make them beautiful."[44] The beauty of the soul consists in its love. In becoming human and dying on the cross, Jesus Christ took on our ugliness so as to reveal the beauty of his charity. When we love the beautiful Lord, we become like him. To boast in our own beauty, however, would destroy it. Rather we can be beautiful only by keeping our eyes upon the beautiful God. In loving God, we love the one who loves sinners so as to make them good. For this reason we cannot claim to love God if we hate our brother (see 1 John 4:20). If we love

---

42. Augustine, *Homilies on the First Epistle of John* 9.2, p. 134.
43. Dideberg, *Saint Augustin et la première épître de saint Jean*, 209, 219–21.
44. Augustine, *Homilies on the First Epistle of John* 9.9, p. 141.

God, Augustine reasons, we love love, since God is love. Augustine adds that we see God (who is love) by love.

If we hate our brother, we do not have love and we cannot see God. Hatred for our brother shows that we do not love love, but instead we choose to hate. Christ commands us to love others as he loved us, and we show our hatred for God by rejecting his command. Nor is loving God sufficient without zeal; we must continually seek to grow in love for God, rather than loving our earthly pilgrimage. The danger is always present that we will turn from cleaving to God to cleaving to a created thing. Charity averts this danger by recognizing God as the infinite good who promises us all things in him. We can only love God if we love to obey his commandment, which is to love our brother. In this light Augustine concludes, "Let us hold onto the unity of the Church, let us hold onto Christ, let us hold onto charity."[45]

Homily 10

John teaches, "Every one who believes that Jesus is the Christ is a child of God" (1 John 5:1). Augustine comments that the one who does not believe that Jesus is the Christ is the one who does not obey Jesus's commandment of love. Many claim to believe in Jesus, but "faith without works doesn't save," because "faith's work is love itself."[46] Without love, works are useless, because we are not yet walking in the way of Christ that leads to eternal life. Without Christ we are too weakened by sin to undertake the journey. Christ enables us to perform the works of love that unite us with him. Both the demons and Peter confess that Jesus is the Son of God, but only Peter says this with love. Peter desires union with Christ, whereas the demons desire Christ to depart. Only when we believe with love do we rightly believe. As John says, "Every one who loves the parent loves the child. By this we know that we love the children of God, when we love God and obey his commandments" (1 John 5:1–2).

In faith, then, Christians love the Father and the Son and also the children of God. In loving the Son, we love the sons (children); in loving the Head, we love the members. Likewise, in loving the sons, we love the Son. The unity of Head and Body is such that in the end "there shall be one Christ loving himself. For, when the members love each other, the body loves itself."[47] We become members of the Son by love. We cannot love our brother without loving Christ, because in rightly loving our brother, we love Christ's members, and in loving Christ's members, we love Christ. When we love Christ we love the Son and his Father. Just as if we love God the Father we must love God the Son (since

45. Augustine, *Homilies on the First Epistle of John* 9.11, p. 144.
46. Augustine, *Homilies on the First Epistle of John* 10.1, p. 145.
47. Augustine, *Homilies on the First Epistle of John* 10.3, p. 148.

they are one God), so also if we love Christ, we must love his members. We cannot separate loving Christ from loving God, or loving Christ from loving his Church.[48] The fire of love fuses the many into one.

Nonetheless, obeying Christ's commandment of love can seem impossible in practice. Augustine suggests that the problem has to do with our lack of effort. In pursuit of money or honor, we work zealously; in pursuit of God, we do little. The irony is that attaining God is easier than attaining great wealth or honor, and God infinitely exceeds the value of mere temporal wealth or honor, which we can possess only for the briefest of times. God is infinitely more powerful than the potential patron whom we strive so hard to impress. We attain God through love, which becomes possible for us by faith in Christ who takes away sin and who is the path to eternal life. Our works of love have as their goal that we rest in God's love. When we have finished our works, we will attain to our end, not in the sense of being ended or consumed but in the sense of being eternally perfected and fulfilled. So long as we place our end in God rather than clinging to the temporal goods of our earthly journey, nothing can harm or constrict us: "You love God, you love the brotherhood, you love God's law, you love God's Church; it shall be forever."[49]

When we love, we are secure. We are only in danger when the pleasures of the world threaten to dull our love for God and take away what is supremely lovable. Those who love will not harm themselves or others. But what if we have to correct or punish someone? From the perspective of the person being disciplined, our action can seem like hatred. Equally, however, flattering can seem like love while in fact being an act of hatred. The key is to love each person, including our enemies, like a brother. Our brothers are already our friends and fellow Catholics; our enemies may become our brothers. To love and be loved is already the pinnacle of earthly life; how much greater, then, will be eternal life.[50] Since the way to eternal life is to love Jesus Christ, we need to know where his Body is, where his members are. Christ's Body is the Church

48. See Joseph Ratzinger, "The Holy Spirit as Communio: Concerning the Relationship of Pneumatology and Spirituality in Augustine," trans. Peter Casarella, *Communio* 25 (1998): 324–37, at 332–33.

49. Augustine, *Homilies on the First Epistle of John* 10.6, p. 153. See William S. Babcock, "*Cupiditas* and *Caritas*: The Early Augustine on Love and Fulfillment," in *Augustine Today*, ed. Richard John Neuhaus (Grand Rapids: Eerdmans, 1993), 1–34; O'Donovan, *Problem of Self-Love*, 132. See also Hannah Arendt, *Love and Saint Augustine*, ed. Joanna Vecchiarelli Scott and Judith Chelius Stark (Chicago: University of Chicago Press, 1996), 18–35, 77–92, as well as the exposition and critique of Arendt's position offered by the following scholars: Eric Gregory, *Politics and the Order of Love: An Augustinian Ethic of Democratic Citizenship* (Chicago: University of Chicago Press, 2008), chaps. 4–6; Burnell, *Augustinian Person*, 111–19; Thomas Breidenthal, "Jesus Is My Neighbor: Arendt, Augustine, and the Politics of Incarnation," *Modern Theology* 14 (1998): 489–504; Rowan Williams, "Politics and the Soul: A Reading of the City of God," *Milltown Studies* 19 (1987): 55–72, at 68–69.

50. See Gregory, *Politics and the Order of Love*, 329.

that began in Jerusalem and spread to all nations. The Donatist Church, with its North African boundaries, cannot be the Body of Christ but must instead have separated itself from the Body.

Having separated themselves from the Body, the Donatists' efforts to honor the Head are like that of a person who kisses one's head while stamping on one's feet. Not only the members suffer, but also the whole person, head and body. Similarly, by persecuting Christ's members, Saul was persecuting Christ. The Head sits at the right hand of the Father, but his Body is present on earth, and so we must love the Head through his Body. The final words that Christ speaks while on earth, before ascending to heaven, commend his Church as being located in all nations: "You shall receive power when the Holy Spirit has come upon you; and you shall be my witnesses in Jerusalem and in all Judea and Samaria and to the end of the earth" (Acts 1:8). Similarly, his words to Saul from heaven reveal that in persecuting Christ's members, Saul is persecuting Christ: "Saul, Saul, why do you persecute me?" (Acts 9:4).

We must take to heart Christ's final words before his ascension. We should obey them as rigorously as we would the last words of a man whom we loved greatly; indeed, we should obey them far more rigorously, since we know that Christ is not dead and buried but risen and ascended. This is even more the case since Christ has repeated his words from heaven, in the conversion of Saul. The Donatists, by refusing to forgive the *traditores*, have divided the Church and caused Christ's members to suffer; Christ sees this and will judge it. The sufferings of the Donatists arise from their dividing the Church. The Donatists need not listen to Augustine, but they should listen to Christ when he tells them that his Church will be in all nations. It is this Church, spread throughout all nations, that forgives sins through baptism in Christ's name. No matter how deplorable the actions of the *traditores*, the fact remains that the Donatists' African movement cannot be the Church promised by Christ.[51]

Conclusion

Can the claim of Christians to know the path of love be a humble claim? Or does it inevitably turn into a form of pride vis-à-vis other human beings and communities? As we have seen, Augustine argues that the safeguard is love itself. He recognizes that Christians in name only will abuse this. But he insists that Christ Jesus's cross and resurrection give us a new ability to love: in Christ, God the Father pours his love into us through the Holy Spirit. The test case is the love of enemies, including (in Augustine's case) the Donatists. True love treats the enemy as a brother in Christ, since that is what Christ wants the enemy to become. The charitable person bemoans the enemy's lack

---

51. See Cassidy, "Augustine's Exegesis," 208.

of love and seeks the enemy's conversion into a friend. Given true love for Christ's Body, Christian leaders at times must seek their enemies' true good by inflicting coercive discipline, so as to stop the wounding of the Body of Christ.

Yet *Homilies on the First Epistle of John* does not stand or fall upon the success (or failure) of Augustine's application of this argument to the Donatists. Rather, Augustine rightly emphasizes that love of God and neighbor requires that we patiently endure life in this world with the goal of attaining the fullness of what we have begun in this world—namely, communion with God the Trinity. Our love of neighbor does not require that we attain, here and now, to the perfection of the Church. When the many finally fully participate in the One—the members through the Head—we will find God's plenitude to be infinitely greater than any finite created good. Fellowship with God, not a perfect earthly society, is the goal of Christ's Body.

4

On the Predestination of the Saints

Introduction

In response to criticisms advanced by leading monks of Gaul against his anti-Pelagian writings, Augustine in 428 composed two works (or one work comprising two books), *On the Predestination of the Saints* and *On the Gift of Perseverance*. His opponents advocated a view that Augustine himself had once held—namely, that predestination depended on God's foreknowledge of the person's free act of faith.[1] In *On the Predestination of the Saints*, however, Augustine argues that God's grace causes the free charitable actions by which we attain to eternal life.[2] The order of salvation depends on God's decision from eternity with respect to whether to give grace to particular persons. In emphasizing the radical priority of the grace of the Holy Spirit, Augustine focuses the debate away from the difficulties caused by the fact that God does not predestine all persons—although Augustine readily acknowledges these difficulties—and toward the praise of God for curing our pride by his gift of love and thereby enabling our intimate participation in the trinitarian life.

---

1. See Henry Chadwick, *The Church in Ancient Society: From Galilee to Gregory the Great* (Oxford: Oxford University Press, 2001), 471.

2. On Augustine's use of biblical texts in *On the Predestination of the Saints*, see Thomas F. Martin, OSA, "*Modus inveniendi Paulum*: Augustine, Hermeneutics, and His Reading of Romans," in *Engaging Augustine on Romans: Self, Context, and Theology in Interpretation*, ed. Daniel Patte and Eugene TeSelle (Harrisburg, PA: Trinity Press International, 2002), 63–90, at 80–84. The importance of these biblical texts is particularly evident when they are absent, as they are in G. R. Evans's survey of *On the Predestination of the Saints* in her *Augustine on Evil* (Cambridge: Cambridge University Press, 1982), 134–36.

Election and Grace

Paul is the apostle of grace, and so Augustine begins by connecting his purpose in *On the Predestination of the Saints* to Paul's missionary zeal.[3] Paul
tells the Philippians that he does not tire of writing to them about the same
things, so long as it serves their salvation (see Phil. 3:1). At the end of the
letter to the Galatians, whose central theme is grace, Paul nonetheless warns,
"Henceforth let no man trouble me" (Gal. 6:17). In order to proclaim grace,
he will write tirelessly; but disputations about grace must come to an end at
some point. Writing to Prosper and Hilary, Augustine confesses that he too is
feeling somewhat troubled, because his writing on grace does not seem to be
bearing fruit. Yet he is willing to write once more to Prosper and Hilary out
of love for them and for the subject.

In Augustine's view, at stake is whether we wish to stand before God as
pagans or as followers of Christ Jesus. Given the finitude of the pagan "gods"
and the pride of the philosophers, pagans can be said to adhere to Virgil's
phrase, "Each man has hope in himself." By contrast, Christians recognize
themselves as dependent entirely on God for existence and for salvation. This is
the teaching not only of Paul but of the whole of Scripture. Augustine quotes
Jeremiah 17:5, "Thus says the Lord, 'Cursed is the man who trusts in man.'"
Those who are mature in Christ, he suggests, will recognize the truth of this
statement. Those who are not yet mature, but who have true faith in Christ,
will learn its truth in the course of their journey of faith.

Why is it that only grace, and not our own strength, gives us a participation in the victory won by Christ? Augustine reminds us that this victory is
over sin. Since Adam and Eve's fall, the entire human race had been wounded
by sin, so as to be in need of a deliverer.[4] The human race could not deliver
itself. Sin disordered the human will. A healthy will would love God over self,
but a diseased will cannot do so—this is precisely the nature of the disease.
The diseased will, being diseased, cannot heal itself. The unjust will is mired
in its own injustice, and cannot justify itself. In order to perform a work that
is truly good, therefore, the will must be made good by God. The healing and
transformative work of God upon the will is grace. Grace elicits our good
works rather than our good works leading God to give us grace. Indeed, given
our dependence on God, we never cease to need God's grace at any stage of
our good work. It is by God's grace that we begin a good work and by God's
grace that we bring it to completion.

---

3. See Thomas F. Martin, OSA, "*Vox Pauli*: Augustine and the Claims to Speak for Paul,
an Exploration of Rhetoric at the Service of Exegesis," *Journal of Early Christian Studies* 8
(2000): 237–72; J. Patout Burns, "The Interpretation of Romans in the Pelagian Controversy,"
Augustinian Studies 10 (1979): 43–54.

4. For Augustine on the transmission of original sin, see John M. Rist, *Augustine: Ancient
Thought Baptized* (Cambridge: Cambridge University Press, 1994), 317–20.

On these points, Augustine says, the persons to whom he has been asked to write agree. Even so, on their view, faith is not itself the work of grace, but God rewards our first act of faith by strengthening it through grace. This view, Augustine notes, is not really separable from that held by Pelagius. Nor is it consistent with the New Testament. In this regard he quotes Romans 11:35–36, "'Or who has given a gift to him that he might be repaid?' For from him and through him and to him are all things." Paul here makes it clear that we are not the giver of gifts to God; rather, everything that we have is from God. It is true, says Augustine, that the act of faith is meritorious. It is a good act, and God certainly does reward it. But in rewarding a good work of ours, God rewards his gifting that moved us to freely do the good work.[5] All things are radically from God, not only in the order of creation, but also in the order of new creation. Even Pelagius, Augustine adds, admitted (under pressure) that merit never has priority to grace.

Faith, then, is God's gift to us; God causes it in us.[6] In this regard Augustine quotes Philippians 1:29, "For it has been granted to you that for the sake of Christ you should not only believe in him but also suffer for his sake." God grants to us our faith. Paul serves as a good example of this, since he received his faith through God's grace on the road to Damascus; as he writes about his apostolic mission, "Not that we are sufficient of ourselves to claim anything as coming from us; our sufficiency is from God" (2 Cor. 3:5). Similarly Paul says, "For by the grace given to me I bid every one among you not to think of himself more highly than he ought to think, but to think with sober judgment, each according to the measure of faith which God has assigned him" (Rom. 12:3). We must follow Paul in refusing to claim anything, including our act of faith, as originating from ourselves rather than from God. Otherwise, if grace is given only after we have initiated the act of faith, grace becomes a reward for our good action and thereby ceases to be grace. Indeed, if we can originate the act of faith without God, then why would we need God to sustain and perfect the act of faith? These latter actions require no more power than does the first act of faith. We must not imagine that we are responsible for a part of faith, and God for another part, or that we have the primary role and God the secondary.

Augustine conceives of his own view not only as an effort to share in Paul's teaching, but also as an effort to be faithful to the witness of the great African bishops who have come before him. His own view, in other words, is not his

---

5. For free will in this context, see James Wetzel, *Augustine and the Limits of Virtue* (Cambridge: Cambridge University Press, 1992), 216–22.

6. See Robert Louis Wilken, *The Spirit of Early Christian Thought: Seeking the Face of God* (New Haven: Yale University Press, 2003), 287–88. On the ecclesial character of faith in Christ, see Basil Studer, OSB, "The Bible as Read in the Church," in *History of Theology*, vol. 1, *The Patristic Period*, ed. Angelo Di Berardino and Basil Studer, trans. Matthew J. O'Connell (Collegeville, MN: Liturgical Press, 1997), 353–73, at 354–55.

own invention but is deeply biblical and ecclesial, so that he is not attempting to claim first place for himself. Thus he cites "that pious and humble doctor . . . the most blessed Cyprian, who said, 'We must take glory in nothing, since nothing is our own.'"[7] Cyprian, Augustine notes, defends this claim by citing 1 Corinthians 4:7, "What have you that you did not receive? If then you received it, why do you boast as if it were not a gift?"

Yet Augustine admits that prior to 396, he himself stood in opposition to Cyprian. To show this, he quotes a lengthy passage from his *Retractions*, in which he reviews his *Exposition of Certain Propositions from the Epistle to the Romans* and shows that he held that the act of faith comes from us, whereas other good works come from God. On this view, God foreknows from eternity those who will have faith; and in light of this foreknowledge God gives the grace that enables those who have faith to do good works. Augustine makes clear that, like his opponents, he was led to this position by concerns about the teaching about divine election (predestination) in Romans 9, where Paul emphasizes that God's election of one person but not another "depends not upon man's will or exertion, but upon God's mercy" (Rom. 9:16).[8] In his *Exposition of Certain Propositions from the Epistle to the Romans*, Augustine interpreted this to mean that God's mercy follows upon our faith. Augustine in this way distinguished the act of faith from "man's will or exertion." He sought to affirm both our freedom in the act of faith and the nonarbitrary character of God's election or predestination of some humans but not others.

In the passage from his *Retractions* that he quotes in *On the Predestination of the Saints*, Augustine points out that there is no reason for supposing that our act of faith, like our other good acts, is not also caused by God's gracious mercy. This was the conclusion that he reached in 396, in *Ad Simplicianum*.[9]

---

7. Augustine, *On the Predestination of the Saints* 3.7, in St. Augustine, *Four Anti-Pelagian Writings*, trans. John A. Mourant and William J. Collinge (Washington, DC: Catholic University of America Press, 1992), 223. For Augustine's interpretation of Cyprian, see Rist, *Augustine*, 298; Mathijs Lamberigts, "Augustine on Predestination: Some *Quaestiones Disputatae* Revisited," *Augustiniana* 54 (2004): 279–305, at 302. See also Éric Rebillard, "A New Style of Argument in Christian Polemic: Augustine and the Use of Patristic Citations," *Journal of Early Christian Studies* 8 (2000): 559–78.

8. See Augustine's interpretation of Romans 8:29 in his *Propositions from the Epistle to the Romans* 55.4, in *Augustine on Romans*, ed. and trans. Paula Fredriksen Landes (Chico, CA: Scholars Press, 1982), 29. For his change of mind, see Augustine, *To Simplician—on Various Questions*, Book 1, question 2 (on Rom. 9:10–29), in Augustine, *Earlier Writings*, ed. and trans. J. H. S. Burleigh (Louisville: Westminster John Knox, 2006), 385–406.

9. For the basic continuity of Augustine's theology of grace, see Carol Harrison, *Rethinking Augustine's Early Theology: An Argument for Continuity* (Oxford: Oxford University Press, 2006), especially 265–87. Harrison shows that Augustine's shift is not as radical as supposed, for example, by James Wetzel, *Augustine: A Guide for the Perplexed* (London: Continuum, 2010), 6–8. See also James Wetzel, "Pelagius Anticipated: Grace and Election in Augustine's *Ad Simplicianum*," in *Augustine: From Rhetor to Theologian*, ed. Joanne McWilliam (Waterloo, Ontario: Wilfrid Laurier University Press, 1992), 121–32.

Again quoting from his *Retractions*, he notes that in *Ad Simplicianum* he examined Romans 9:10–29 and came to realize that Cyprian's dictum—"We must take glory in nothing, since nothing is our own"—is right. Since we receive everything from God, there is no space for an action that is solely or primarily our own. God does not respond to our good action and reward it by grace; rather, God's grace causes our free good action, because God's gifting stands at the very heart of everything. To suppose otherwise is the path of pride, the very opposite of Christ's humility.

Augustine carefully examines the context of 1 Corinthians 4:7. Paul, says Augustine, had found that there were divisions in the Corinthian congregation. Members of the congregation prided themselves on being followers of a particular apostle, and indeed imagined themselves to be wiser than others. They lacked understanding of the radical nature of their debt. Paul responds to them by emphasizing that "God chose what is low and despised in the world, even things that are not, to bring to nothing things that are, so that no human being might boast in the presence of God" (1 Cor. 1:28–29). No boasting in human strength is permitted, because we cannot make ourselves holy in God's sight. It is not us but God who "is the source of [our] life in Christ Jesus, whom God made our wisdom, our righteousness and sanctification and redemption; therefore; as it is written, 'Let him who boasts, boast of the Lord'" (1 Cor. 1:30–31). Augustine quotes this passage and then pairs it with another strong affirmation of the priority of God's grace: "What then is Apollos? What is Paul? Servants through whom you believed, as the Lord assigned to each. I planted, Apollos watered, but God gave the growth. So neither he who plants nor he who waters is anything, but only God who gives the growth" (1 Cor. 3:5–7). The point is that no human can take credit for faith; God's grace brings it about according to his plan. God's goodness causes ours, rather than our goodness eliciting his. The conclusion is: "So let no one boast of men" (1 Cor. 3:21).[10]

Augustine is aware that his opponents might reply that Paul has in view only gifts of our nature, so that while we are radically dependent on God for existence, we are not radically dependent on God for our freely chosen faith. Paul, says Augustine, is not talking about the gifts that all humans share by nature. Instead, Paul is responding to those who imagine themselves to be distinguished from others by spiritual superiority. Puffed up with pride, people boast even about their faith. Paul's point is that we cannot boast in such things because we receive them entirely from God rather than from our own resources. Augustine states, "That person whose pride the Apostle was trying to restrain was not puffing himself up in comparison to the beasts, nor in comparison to another man because of any gift of nature that might exist

10. Mathijs Lamberigts contrasts "psychological" and "metaphysical" levels of Augustine's teaching on predestination: see Lamberigts, "Augustine on Predestination," 304–5.

even in the worst of men. Rather, he was puffed up because he attributed some good thing which pertained to the morally good life to himself and not to God."[11] Insofar as we claim to be the source of our faith, we have contradicted Paul's warning about receiving everything from God.

Does this mean that our free will is uninvolved in the act of faith? Does God simply force us to believe? Augustine recognizes that some freely choose to believe and that others, equally freely, choose not to believe. In the act of faith our free will is prepared and moved by God's grace, but grace does not negate our freedom; rather, grace enables us freely to embrace a good that we otherwise could not have embraced.[12] The fact that God chooses some but not others expresses divine mercy and judgment, respectively. Emphasizing God's election, Augustine quotes Romans 11:5, where Paul states that God's people are "chosen by grace." Paul adds that "if it is by grace, it is no longer on the basis of works; otherwise grace would no longer be grace" (Rom. 11:6). Salvation comes from God; as Augustine says, "there preceded nothing which they might first give so that it might be given to them in recompense. God saved them for nothing."[13]

Yet is the act of faith a work? It might be that no works precede grace, but that faith (and thus God's foreknowledge of our faith) precedes grace. Augustine answers that Jesus himself calls faith a work of God that we must do. In John 6:29, Jesus says, "This is the work of God, that you believe in him whom he has sent." What then of Paul's distinction between faith and works (cf. Gal. 2:16)? Augustine explains that Paul's point is that faith is primary; only when we are united to Christ by faith can we do his works of love. Furthermore, Paul explicitly rules out the notion that faith precedes God's grace when he writes that "by grace you have been saved through faith; and this is not your own doing, it is the gift of God—not because of works, lest any man should boast" (Eph. 2:8–9). But are there not examples of good people who lack faith and whose goodness merits that God give them faith? Augustine answers that good people who do not know Christ explicitly nonetheless

11. Augustine, *On the Predestination of the Saints* 5.10, p. 230. For Augustine's interpretation of Romans 2:13–16 in this regard, see Simon J. Gathercole, "A Conversion of Augustine: From Natural Law to Restored Nature in Romans 2:13–16," in *Engaging Augustine on Romans*, 147–72.

12. See Paul R. Kolbet, *Augustine and the Cure of Souls: Revising a Classical Ideal* (Notre Dame, IN: University of Notre Dame Press, 2010), 137–38. For the view that irresistible grace leaves no real room for human freedom, see Josef Lössl, "Augustine on Predestination: Consequences for the Reception," *Augustiniana* 52 (2002): 241–72; Lamberigts, "Augustine on Predestination," 305; Gene Fendt, "Between a Pelagian Rock and a Hard Predestinarianism: The Currents of Controversy in *City of God* 11 and 12," *Journal of Religion* 81 (2001): 211–27.

13. Augustine, *On the Predestination of the Saints* 6.11, p. 232. For an appreciative account of Augustine's theology of predestination (while dissenting from his theology of reprobation), see James Wetzel, "Snares of Truth: Augustine on Free Will and Predestination," in *Augustine and His Critics: Essays in Honour of Gerald Bonner*, ed. Robert Dodaro and George Lawless (London: Routledge, 2000), 124–41.

pray and must possess faith of some kind. God builds this faith up so that it becomes explicit faith in Christ. The point is that God's favor is the source of our faith, as well as of its development and perfection.[14] This radical priority of grace makes possible rather than excludes our free cooperation, as can be seen in the psalmist's saying, "Unless the Lord builds the house, those who build it labor in vain" (Ps. 127:1). Faith is the foundation of the house, and the Lord must build this foundation in order for us to do so too.

Augustine notes that Jesus makes clear that only God can give us the participation in God that is eternal life. This participation has its source entirely in God's gracious action. We are not its source. Thus Jesus says, "All that the Father gives me will come to me" (John 6:37); "No one can come to me unless the Father who sent me draws him" (John 6:44); and "Every one who has heard and learned from the Father comes to me" (John 6:45). Not only, then, does our coming to the Father and the Son depend entirely upon grace (by which the Father draws us), but also all whom the Father has chosen will come.[15] If we hear and learn from the Father, then we will come; God's grace is such that there is no option for someone who hears and learns to refuse ultimately to come. This is because God moves us by his grace, a movement that causes our will to freely embrace his goodness. When someone truly confesses faith in Christ, we can know that interiorly the Father has drawn that person. Again, why cannot a hard-hearted person resist being drawn? Augustine answers that the grace of conversion consists precisely in taking away, by the divine action, the hardness of our hearts so that we love God. As God promised through the prophet Ezekiel, God takes away our hearts of stone and gives us hearts of flesh.

The nettlesome question now arises: If all whom the Father gives to the Son will come to the Son, then why should anyone perish? Why does not the Father teach and draw everyone? In replying, Augustine turns to Romans 9. Like Paul, he appeals to God's mercy and judgment; since all have sinned, when God draws anyone away from perdition it is sheer mercy, and when God permits someone to remain alienated from him, it is just judgment. Citing Exodus 33:19 and Malachi 1:2–3, Paul states that God "hardens the heart of whomever he wills" (Rom. 9:18), and Augustine interprets this to mean that God executes just judgment upon such persons. In this context, Paul himself raises and answers the central problem: "You will say to me then, 'Why does he

14. See Basil Studer, OSB, *The Grace of Christ and the Grace of God in Augustine of Hippo: Christocentrism or Theocentrism?*, trans. Matthew J. O'Connell (Collegeville, MN: Liturgical Press, 1997), 53.

15. Donato Ogliari challenges Augustine in this regard: "If predestination belongs to God's inscrutable and eternal decree, just what is the precise weight of Christ's redeeming role? Would not his mediation simply mean that it is 'piloted' by God's predestination *ab aeternitate*?" See Ogliari, "The Role of Christ and of the Church in the Light of Augustine's Theory of Predestination," *Ephemerides Theologicae Lovanienses* 79 (2003): 347–64, at 354.

still find fault? For who can resist his will?' But who are you, a man, to answer back to God? Will what is molded say to its molder, 'Why have you made me thus?' Has the potter no right over the clay, to make out of the same lump one vessel for beauty and another for menial use?" (Rom. 9:19–21).

To this answer, Augustine adds that the Father does, in a certain sense, teach everyone. He observes that in the same discourse in the Gospel of John, Jesus cites Isaiah 54:13 (John 6:45: "they shall all be taught by God"). This prophecy is fulfilled, says Augustine, in the sense that God teaches everyone who is taught. No one learns from anyone other than God; no one comes in another way. But this does not remove the force of the truth that God does not draw all persons. Augustine refuses to gainsay or ameliorate Paul's remark that "God, desiring to show his wrath and to make known his power, has endured with much patience the vessels of wrath made for destruction, in order to make known the riches of his glory for the vessels of mercy, which he has prepared beforehand for glory, even us whom he has called" (Rom. 9:22–24). Indeed, this remark appears as a rhetorical question in Paul but as a statement in Augustine. Yet does not Paul's thought move in a different direction elsewhere, so that Paul could be invoked in favor of the view that God in fact does draw all persons? For example, Paul writes to Timothy that God "desires all men to be saved and to come to the knowledge of the truth" (1 Tim. 2:4).[16] How is this passage consistent with John 6 or Romans 9?

This is a difficult problem, and Augustine seeks to answer it by appealing again to his view that God does indeed teach everyone in the sense that those who are taught are taught by God. Thus God desires all "to come to the knowledge of the truth," but does not draw all, because he in fact teaches the truth to all those whom he desires to be saved, and he permits others to perish. Augustine quotes 1 Corinthians 1:18, "For the word of the cross is folly to those who are perishing, but to us who are being saved it is the power of God." If none were in fact perishing, then Paul would speak entirely differently. The key principle for Augustine, in light of the words of Jesus in the Gospel of John, is summed up in Paul's use of the story of Jacob and Esau: God elects the former but not the latter, so that election clearly "depends not upon man's will or exertion, but upon God's mercy" (Rom. 9:16). Just as in the time of Elijah, God permits many to perish by idolatry, but he saves some by grace. Grace would not be grace if God's election depended in any way upon our works (cf. Rom. 11:5–6).

Augustine is aware of the circular argument that results from his position. God does not teach all because those who are perishing do not wish to learn. He teaches all who are open to learning. Yet God is the one who, by his grace, converts sinners so that we become open to learning. All humans

16. For Augustine on 1 Timothy 2:4, see Lamberigts, "Augustine on Predestination," 285–88; Ogliari, "Role of Christ," 351.

depend upon God for conversion, and so the question remains as pressing as ever: No matter that those who do not convert are to blame for their own free rejection of God's Word, nonetheless why does God not convert everyone?[17] If God allows some to perish, it might also seem that the Church need not pray for her persecutors. In fact, the Church prays for everyone living, because God may yet turn the hearts of those who now oppose him. Paul too prays for those among his fellow Jews who did not accept Christ: "Brethren, my heart's desire and prayer to God for them is that they may be saved" (Rom. 10:1). By his grace, God may give faith to anyone now living who lacks faith. Augustine takes the opportunity here to point out again that grace precedes faith and that faith is a gift. We cannot know and love the Triune God unless God heals us and draws us to him. And to suppose that all already have faith is gainsaid by Jesus, who knows "from the first" (John 6:64) who believes and who does not believe.

For Augustine, the key issue at stake in predestinarian arguments is the radical gift-character of salvation as an intimate participation in God.[18] God wills to draw us to himself, and what God wills is done. God's eternal plan cannot be frustrated. In other words, God truly has the power to accomplish his eternal purpose in creating us. Certainly God permits some to rebel against him permanently; his punishment of these is just. Since all have rebelled, his salvation is indeed a great grace; we do not deserve it. From this perspective, the question of why God saves one rather than another diverts our attention from the central truth of God's grace. With regard to the difficult question, Augustine concludes by emphasizing Paul's (and his own) awareness that this is an insoluble mystery but not one that should divert us from the revelation of God's love: "As to why God delivers this person rather than that one, 'How incomprehensible are his judgments, and how unsearchable his ways' [Rom. 11:33]. For it is better for us here to listen or to say, 'O man, who are you that replies against God?' [Rom. 9:20] than to dare to explain, as if we knew, what God has chosen to keep a secret."[19] The one thing that we can know about this secret is that its reason, whatever it might be, accords with God's infinite justice and love.

In an earlier work, *On the Time of the Christian Religion*, Augustine had defended Christianity against Porphyry's criticisms by arguing that Christ came at a fitting time and that people received salvation if they lived worthily even in times and places where there was no explicit knowledge of Christ.

17. See Peter Burnell, *The Augustinian Person* (Washington, DC: Catholic University of America Press, 2005), 83–88. Rist describes Augustine's position as "his extraordinary and ultimately unintelligible limitation of the love of God" (*Augustine*, 288).

18. See Studer, *Grace of Christ*, 132–35.

19. Augustine, *On the Predestination of the Saints* 8.16, p. 238. See Paul Rigby, "The Role of God's 'Inscrutable Judgments' in Augustine's Doctrine of Predestination," *Augustinian Studies* 33 (2002): 213–22.

Augustine's position in this regard was well known, and it might seem to suggest that faith in some way precedes grace. He therefore quotes a lengthy portion of this earlier work and in particular his statement therein that "the salvation offered by this religion [Christianity] was never lacking to him who was worthy of it, and whoever lacked it was unworthy of it."[20] This worthiness, he now emphasizes, is the work of grace. To buttress this point he cites Paul's statement to the Ephesians that "by grace you have been saved through faith; and this is not your own doing, it is the gift of God—not because of works, lest any man should boast. For we are his workmanship, created in Christ Jesus for good works, which God prepared beforehand, that we should walk in them" (Eph. 2:8–10). When Paul writes that God prepared these good works for us "beforehand" and that God created us "in Christ Jesus for good works," Augustine notes that God has an eternal plan of gifting, a plan that God knows and executes from eternity. This plan, says Augustine, "is the preparation for grace, while grace is the gift itself."[21] In other words, God eternally knows the gift that he wills to give us, but he gives this gift (grace) in time, in our historical lives. The effect of our eternal predestination is the grace that transforms us in history.

Faith, Grace, and Foreknowledge

If predestination is God's plan for the gifting that he accomplishes in history, does predestination also include his plan for sinners? Augustine answers that God foreknows our sins, but he does not make them happen. Predestination is simply God's plan for the transformative gifts that he actively gives. As an example of this plan, Augustine points to God's promise to Abraham that "I have made you the father of a multitude of nations" (Gen. 17:5). This promise shows God's preparation for grace, his plan of gifting. God promises that he will do something, not that we will do something. As Paul says, "That is why it [the promise] depends on faith, in order that the promise may rest on grace and be guaranteed to all his descendants" (Rom. 4:16). The promise does not rest on our good works. The promise rests instead on God's predestination, and it will be accomplished in us by his grace so that we do good works. Augustine comments, "For even though men do good works which pertain to the honoring of God, it is he who brings it about that they do what he has

20. Augustine, *On the Predestination of the Saints* 10.19, p. 241.
21. Augustine, *On the Predestination of the Saints* 10.19, p. 241. Augustine makes clear that predestination has to do only with the gift of grace, and that reprobation (as opposed to punishment) follows from divine permission. The view that Augustine advocates "double predestination" is nonetheless held by Jaroslav Pelikan in his *The Christian Tradition: A History of the Development of Doctrine*, vol. 1, *The Emergence of the Catholic Tradition (100–600)* (Chicago: University of Chicago Press, 1971), 297–98 (see 278–331 for a full account of the controversy over grace).

ordered; it is not they who bring it about that he does what he has promised. Otherwise, the accomplishment of God's promises would not be in the power of God, but in that of men."[22] Abraham believed not in human works, but rather in the power of God. Thus "he gave glory to God, fully convinced that God was able to do what he had promised" (Rom. 4:20–21). God's promises pertain to predestination because they describe what God is going to do for our salvation, whereas God foreknows much that he does not do (i.e., our sins).

It might seem, nonetheless, that Augustine has unfairly cut off a possible reading of Genesis 17 and Romans 4—namely, that God foreknows the faith of the nations and thereby can make his promise to Abraham. This is the view of Augustine's opponents, who argue that faith comes from us and constitutes the foundation for the good works that God's grace accomplishes through us. Could it be, then, that God foreknows the faith of the nations and on this basis predestines their good works? Augustine denies that Paul's argument can be squared with such a view of faith and grace. The problem is that if humans were the source of faith, then God would have to depend on humans in order to be able to accomplish his promise. By contrast, Abraham believed that "God was able to do what he had promised" (Rom. 4:21). Indeed, Augustine expresses surprise that anyone would think it better to suppose that salvation depends on our faith rather than on God's grace causing our free act of faith. Those who trust in their own power to have faith should attend to Paul's warning to the Corinthians, "Therefore let any one who thinks that he stands take heed lest he fall" (1 Cor. 10:12).

In defense of the claim that the human act of faith takes place prior to grace, however, Augustine's opponents cite Romans 10:9: "If you confess with your lips that Jesus is Lord and believe in your heart that God raised him from the dead, you will be saved." The human act of faith gives rise to the divine act of salvation. In reply, Augustine argues that both faith and salvation are God's to give. To illumine Romans 10:9, he points to Romans 8:13, which makes more clear the role of the Holy Spirit: "If by the Spirit you put to death the deeds of the body you will live." We can only live by the power of God, and likewise for us to die unto sin requires the action of the Holy Spirit. In addition, Augustine considers it significant that in 1 Corinthians 12 Paul lists faith among the things apportioned by the Holy Spirit. It is God who, by his Holy Spirit, will give us a "heart of flesh" (Ezek. 36:26) and cleanse us from idols so that we can worship him in faith and love. In this way, God's grace is truly grace—that is, a free gift that causes our good actions rather than a reward merited by our good actions.

Augustine further observes that those who hold that faith precedes grace get themselves into a tangle regarding infants who die before they are old enough to make an act of faith. For such infants, does baptism make a difference?

22. Augustine, *On the Predestination of the Saints* 10.19, p. 242.

Augustine's opponents think so. They propose that baptized infants are saved because God foreknows their future faith and good works, while unbaptized infants are damned because God foreknows their future evil works. As Augustine remarks, on this view God damns infants for sins that were actually never committed. But it is absurd to imagine that we are damned for what we would have done had we lived long enough to do it. In fact God only condemns (or rewards) a person "according to what he has done in the body" (2 Cor. 5:10). When unbaptized infants die, they are punished only for original sin, not for some putative sins that they would have committed in the future. Even the Pelagians recognize that one cannot be rewarded or condemned for something that has literally never been done. It is true that God allows some people to fall into sin at the end of long lives, rather than taking them to himself while they are young; but this is mystery enough rather than adding to it all the undone deeds of those who died young.

The Wisdom of Solomon too stands against the view put forward by Augustine's opponents. Explaining that God's providence accords with the fact that sometimes just persons die young, the Wisdom of Solomon states, "There was one who pleased God and was loved by him, and while living among sinners he was taken up. He was caught up lest evil change his understanding or guile deceive his soul" (Wis. 4:10–11). Augustine grants that the canonical status of the Wisdom of Solomon has been contested, by Jerome among others. Yet as eminent a bishop as Cyprian appeals to this passage in the Wisdom of Solomon in order to show that an early death need not be a disaster. The passage rightly shows that those who die young are not subject to condemnation for deeds that they would have done if they had lived. That Augustine's opponents find themselves advocating this absurdity shows the foolishness of their attack upon the priority of grace, by which God causes our participation in himself by knowledge and love.

The advocates of the priority of faith take this position in order to ensure that predestination is based on divine foreknowledge, if not of our works (which would be Pelagianism) then at least of our faith. This position avoids the trouble that comes from granting the radical priority of grace while denying that God saves all rational creatures. But as Augustine has shown, the position raises numerous difficulties of its own. The predestination of Christ is another such difficulty. The issue is this: Why has one instance of human nature been granted to be so unfathomably greater than all other instances of human nature? Surely the hypostatic union itself is a grace; and if grace is a reward of faith, then what has this particular human nature, united at the instant of its conception to the divine nature, done to receive such a reward? If predestination must be based on more than solely God's will, it would seem only fair that all instances of human nature, and not merely one, should be taken up into hypostatic union. Otherwise Christ's human nature would be alone predestined, and by nothing more than God's gracious causality, to enjoy hypostatic union.

Once we admit the radical priority of grace in the case of Christ's hypostatic union, we should be willing to admit the radical priority of grace in the case of our new creation in Christ. Augustine emphasizes in this regard that "the grace that makes any man a Christian from the time he begins to believe is the same grace by which one man from his beginning became Christ."[23] The Holy Spirit who overshadows Mary at the incarnation of Jesus is the same Spirit who makes us a new creation by forgiving our sin and giving us faith, hope, and love. From eternity, God has predestined the Head and the members in the Head (cf. Eph. 1:3–6). Just as his predestination to be the incarnate Son is not based on merit, neither is our predestination to be his members. When our faith leads us to receive baptism, this means not that faith precedes grace, but rather that the grace of faith leads us to full participation in Christ's body.

God calls all people to salvation, but as in Jesus's parable of the wedding banquet (see Luke 14:16–23), some refuse the call. The call of predestination is not the universal call, but rather is a particular call that causes salvation. In making this distinction, Augustine appeals to Paul's observation that "we preach Christ crucified, a stumbling block to Jews and folly to Gentiles, but to those who are called, both Jews and Greeks, Christ the power of God and the wisdom of God" (1 Cor. 1:23–24). By preaching to the multitude, Paul calls them all to faith; but only some are called in the special sense. It is about the latter persons that Paul says, "We know that in everything God works for good with those who love him, who are called according to his purpose. For those whom he foreknew he also predestined to be conformed to the image of his Son. . . . And those whom he predestined he also called" (Rom. 8:28–30). Paul similarly has the latter persons in view when he describes God's election of Jacob as proceeding "not because of works but because of his [God's] call" (Rom. 9:11). Augustine emphasizes that God's call does not depend here upon faith any more than it depends upon works. God's call bestows faith and unites to God those whom he predestines from eternity to be united to him.

Augustine thinks that this is also what Paul means when he says, with regard to Israel, that "the gifts and the call of God are irrevocable" (Rom. 11:29). Nothing happens without God's permission, and God ensures that even our bad deeds serve his goal of uniting his predestined people to himself. When Pilate, Herod, and some among the Jewish people conspired against Jesus, even this action—as the apostles confessed—accorded with what God "had predestined to take place" (Acts 4:28). God permitted some among Israel according to the flesh to be "hardened" (Rom. 11:7) so that the gentiles might come in; but others among Israel according to the flesh constituted "a remnant, chosen by grace" (Rom. 11:5), onto which the gentiles have been grafted. None of the

---

23. Augustine, *On the Predestination of the Saints* 15.31, p. 254. See Studer, *Grace of Christ*, 60–62.

elect of Israel perished, because, as Jesus says, "this is the will of him who sent me, that I should lose nothing of all that he has given me" (John 6:39).

The particular "call" of election, then, consists in God's eternal choosing of the person not because he or she believes but in order that he or she may believe. In this respect Jesus makes God's priority quite clear: "You did not choose me, but I chose you" (John 15:16). That God chose the apostles, and indeed all the elect, from eternity is apparent from Paul's statement that God "chose us in him [Christ] before the foundation of the world" (Eph. 1:4). The point that Augustine is making has to do both with the radical priority of predestination and with the fact that not all are predestined, called, justified, and glorified.

Yet the Pelagians, Augustine recognizes, argue that Ephesians 1 is on their side. On their view, God predestines persons to be his members, but he would hardly choose the impure. God predestines only the pure, and he recognizes these pure persons by means of his foreknowledge of what they will do.[24] Augustine notes, however, that Paul's language in Ephesians 1 runs counter to the Pelagian interpretation. In Ephesians 1:4, Paul says "that we should be" rather than "because we were going to be." The plain sense of this verse therefore shows that God's election causes human holiness rather than following upon God's foreknowledge of it. Lest there be any doubt, Paul adds that God's election is made "according to the purpose of his will, to the praise of his glorious grace which he freely bestowed on us in the Beloved" (Eph. 1:5–6). Election comes about because of God's good will, not because of his foreknowledge of our good will.[25]

Paul goes on to amplify even further this sense of God's free gifting: "In him we have redemption through his blood, the forgiveness of our trespasses, according to the riches of his grace which he lavished upon us" (Eph. 1:7–8). Our will becomes good only because God's good will, "the riches of his grace," causes it to become so in Christ, in accord with God's eternal plan of predestination. Paul concludes that in Christ, "according to the purpose of him who accomplishes all things according to the counsel of his will, we who first hoped in Christ have been destined and appointed to live for the praise of his glory" (Eph. 1:11–12). The good will of God accomplishes his purpose in us.

Augustine argues, then, that it is God who is powerful, not us. If we are to be transformed and to gain an intimate participation in the divine life, it is

---

24. For a defense of Pelagius and critique of Augustine, see Gerald Bonner, *Freedom and Necessity: St. Augustine's Teaching on Divine Power and Human Freedom* (Washington, DC: Catholic University of America Press, 2007), 125–32.

25. For Augustine on God's "foreknowledge" (*praescientia*), see James Wetzel, "Predestination, Pelagianism, and Foreknowledge," in *The Cambridge Companion to Augustine*, ed. Eleonore Stump and Norman Kretzmann (Cambridge: Cambridge University Press, 2001), 49–58; Barry A. David, "The Meaning and Usage of 'Divine Foreknowledge' in Augustine's *De libero arbitrio* (*lib. arb.*) 3.2.14–4.41," *Augustinian Studies* 32 (2001): 117–55.

only God who can give it to us. God gives it to us not because of our goodness but because of his. We become good because his grace makes us so. For this reason there is no room for human pride, and Christ's humility shows itself to be not only the cause but also the path of our salvation. We must obey Paul's exhortation to "work out your own salvation with fear and trembling," always in the knowledge that "God is at work in you, both to will and to work for his good pleasure" (Phil. 2:12–13). If we are to be holy, pride must be utterly uprooted and we must learn to understand ourselves as creatures whose existence, wisdom, and goodness come entirely from God. Citing 1 Corinthians 3:21 and 1:31, Augustine states, "This is why we cry out, 'Let no man glory in man,' and accordingly not in himself, but 'He that glories, let him glory in the Lord,' in order that we may 'be unto the praise of his glory.'"[26] In humility, we should praise the God who is accomplishing his eternal purpose of salvation, despite human sinfulness, for "the gifts and the call of God are irrevocable" (Rom. 11:29).

In predestining us, God foreknows the gracious work by which he will make us holy. But even though he foreknows that he will lead the elect to good works (rather than electing them because he foreknows their good works), is it possible that nonetheless he foreknows and rewards the *faith* of the predestined? Augustine's opponents have pressed this distinction between faith and works, and Augustine raises the issue again in order to address it in light of Ephesians 1. He emphasizes that Paul says that God "accomplishes all things according to the counsel of his will" and that we have been "destined and appointed" by God (Eph. 1:11–12). God "accomplishes all things," including our faith. We do not begin to believe in Christ through our own resources. Rather, we are moved to believe by the grace of the Holy Spirit. This accords with Jesus's statement, "You did not choose me, but I chose you" (John 15:16), and accords also with Paul's insistence that election takes place "not because of works but because of his call" (Rom. 9:11)—and thus not because of the faith of the person. We do not choose Jesus in faith before he chooses us by grace.

Indeed, Paul gives thanks to God because he has heard of the faith and love of the Ephesians (see Eph. 1:15–16). There would be no point in giving thanks to God if their faith had arisen from their own resources. In the same way, in his first letter to the Thessalonians, Paul praises God "that when you received the word of God which you heard from us, you accepted it not as the word of men but as what it really is, the word of God, which is at work in you believers" (1 Thess. 2:13). In thanking God for the faith of the Thessalonians, Paul shows that it is God who gave them faith. It is God who, by his grace, enables the Thessalonians to hear the gospel as the word of God. Augustine also interprets Colossians 4, 1 Corinthians 16, and 2 Corinthians 2 in this manner. When Paul prays that God will "open to us a door for the

---

26. Augustine, *On the Predestination of the Saints* 18.37, p. 263.

word" (Col. 4:3), rejoices that in Ephesus "a wide door for effective work has opened to me" (1 Cor. 16:9), and reports that in Troas "a door was opened for me in the Lord" (2 Cor. 2:12), Augustine considers that the "door" in these cases refers not merely to exterior preaching but to interior response. This interior response is a gift, and not all receive it. Jesus suggests as much by telling his disciples, with regard to the interpretation of his parables: "To you it has been given to know the secrets of the kingdom of heaven, but to them it has not been given" (Matt. 13:11). Similarly Paul says that his preaching of the gospel divides his hearers, so that "we are the aroma of Christ to God among those who are being saved and among those who are perishing, to one a fragrance from death to death, to the other a fragrance from life to life" (2 Cor. 2:15–16).

That God works in human hearts so as to give us faith appears explicitly in the story of Lydia, who heard Paul preaching in Philippi. The book of Acts states, "The Lord opened her heart to give heed to what was said by Paul" (Acts 16:14). The same point, says Augustine, appears in the books of Kings and Chronicles. To understand this it is necessary to recognize that God "in a marvellous and ineffable way works also in us that we will."[27] God's moving the human will does not negate its freedom; on the contrary, he moves us by inclining our hearts to freely desire him. Thus Solomon rightly prays, "The Lord our God be with us, as he was with our fathers; may he not leave us or forsake us; that he may incline our hearts to him, to walk in all his ways, and to keep his commandments, his statutes, and his ordinances" (1 Kings 8:57–58). Even if Solomon is speaking of the earthly kingdom of Israel, the same prayer pertains to those who seek the heavenly kingdom. We pray that God will "incline our hearts" so that we will know God in faith and love him in truth.

For his part, God promises to "put my spirit within you, and cause you to walk in my statutes and be careful to observe my ordinances" (Ezek. 36:27). This is the promise of grace. It is by grace, in accord with God's predestination, that we believe the gospel. As a final biblical example, Augustine recalls what the book of Acts says about the preaching of the gospel in Antioch of Pisidia: "And when the Gentiles heard this, they were glad and glorified the word of God; and as many as were ordained to eternal life believed" (Acts 13:48). Their ordination to eternal life is the primary cause of their free response of faith.

Conclusion

In his brief conclusion to On the Predestination of the Saints, Augustine sums up what motivated him to write it. Persuaded that the *increase* of faith and all other good works come from God, some leading Christians in Gaul nonetheless

27. Augustine, *On the Predestination of the Saints* 20.42, p. 268.

argued that the very first movement of faith comes from the human person rather than being God's gift. In response, therefore, Augustine argues that all is God's gift, including the act of faith. He makes this case on the basis of Scripture. Since God's grace and power to save are at the very heart of the gospel, it would be quite difficult to refute the biblical arguments that Augustine presents. We receive a share in "every spiritual blessing in the heavenly places" (Eph. 1:3) because God, from eternity and solely because of his own goodness and love, willed that it be so: God "chose us in him [Christ] before the foundation of the world, that we should be holy and blameless before him. He destined us in love to be his sons through Jesus Christ, according to the purpose of his will, to the praise of his glorious grace which he freely bestowed on us in the Beloved" (Eph. 1:4–6).

There remains, however, the mystery of why, if everything depends on God's infinite love, God does not transform and save all. Although this mystery cannot be plumbed, we must not suggest that God's superabundant love is lacking or deficient with respect to any rational creature.[28]

28. See Matthew Levering, *Predestination: Biblical and Theological Paths* (Oxford: Oxford University Press, 2011).

5

Confessions

In his *Retractions*, Augustine states that his reason for writing his *Confessions* (composed during the years 397–401) was to move the mind—his own and others'—toward God in love. This participatory dynamism must be paramount in any survey of the *Confessions*. In what follows, I seek to show how this dynamism works by surveying the thirteen books of the *Confessions* in four sections: 1, 2–6, 7–10, and 11–13. The goal is to obtain a sense of both the content of the *Confessions* and of how the *Confessions* succeeds in moving our minds to God.

A brief sketch of the work will be helpful before we proceed. Book 1 treats Augustine's infancy and boyhood. God's eternal presence provides the ground for Augustine's coming to be and his changing, finite existence. Even in his infancy, however, Augustine was alienated from the God who gave and sustained his existence. This alienation came both from Augustine's own sinful inclinations and from the sinfulness of the adults around him. Augustine's love was disordered, and he loved creatures rather than God. Books 2–6 show Augustine's love for finite things and his open rebellion against ontological and moral participation in God. His love for finite things extended to his worship (as a Manichee) of a spatial god. If Books 1–6 treat Augustine's immersion in spatiotemporal goods and his failure to appreciate their participation in God, Books 7–10 show how Augustine moved out of this culture and toward the love of God. The first step came through the books of the neo-Platonists, which freed Augustine from his spatial imaginings about God and evil. Comparing their insights with the Gospel of John's proclamation of the Word of God and our participation in the Word, he found that Scripture not only revealed this truth more clearly but also showed the path for ascent to the Word—namely, through the Word's descent. By imitating the Word's humility, our pride is healed and replaced by love. Because the Word has taken on our humanity and overcome our sin, we can share in the divinity of the Word. In light of the power of memory for the purposes of repentance and praise, Augustine concludes by calling to mind the finite things that he is still tempted to misuse and by praising Christ the mediator for enabling him to participate in God's life by faith, hope, and charity.

The first ten books of the *Confessions* thus move from ontological participation in God but moral separation from God as an infant and boy, to cleaving to finite things but longing for something more as a young adult, to the love of God through Christ as a mature adult. Books 11–13, then, insert this journey of love within Christian theology of creation and new creation. Augustine explores how time is real in the present moment, how time is measured by present consciousness, and how time (as created) participates in God's eternal present. Interpreting Genesis 1, he examines how God, from his free goodness, creates unformed things and gives them form. In love, Augustine seeks union with God the Trinity and observes God's beautiful works in order to contemplate God. Through spiritual interpretation, he presents the participation of creation in the new creation of all things in the Church, Christ's Body.

By means of the last three books of the *Confessions*, Augustine shows not merely that his own life has changed from self-seeking love of sexual pleasure and worldly career to self-giving love of God and eternal life. He also shows that Christian revelation, unlike his previous worldviews, affirms the goodness of God and of all created things and reveals both a transcendent origin and a transcendent end—centered on participation in eternal goodness, generosity, wisdom, love, and life. Augustine begins as a proud false interpreter and ends, by God's grace, as a humbled true interpreter,[1] whose understanding of his own life is only possible from within the story of the Triune God's love for us in creation, Christ, and the Church.[2]

1. See Brian Stock, *Augustine the Reader: Meditation, Self-Knowledge, and the Ethics of Interpretation* (Cambridge, MA: Harvard University Press, 1996).

2. For discussions of the structure of the *Confessions*, see Frederick J. Crosson, "Structure and Meaning in St. Augustine's *Confessions*," in *The Augustinian Tradition*, ed. Gareth B. Matthews (Berkeley: University of California Press, 1999), 27–38; Kenneth B. Steinhauser, "The Literary Unity of the *Confessions*," in *Augustine: From Rhetor to Theologian*, ed. Joanne McWilliam (Waterloo, Ontario: Wilfrid Laurier University Press, 1992), 15–30; Thomas F. Martin, OSA, "Augustine's *Confessions* as Pedagogy: Exercises in Transformation," in *Augustine and Liberal Education*, ed. Kim Paffenroth and Kevin L. Hughes (Lanham, MD: Lexington Books, 2008), 25–51; Robert McMahon, "Book Thirteen: The Creation of the Church as the Paradigm for the *Confessions*," in *A Reader's Companion to Augustine's* Confessions, ed. Kim Paffenroth and Robert P. Kennedy (Louisville: Westminster John Knox, 2003), 207–23; McMahon, *Augustine's Prayerful Ascent: An Essay on the Literary Form of the* Confessions (Athens: University of Georgia Press, 1989).

Book 1

The *Confessions* begins with quotations from the psalms in praise of God's power and wisdom. After these quotations, Augustine's first words are: "Man, a little piece of your creation, desires to praise you."[3] Yet humans have difficulty praising God: we are sinners doomed to death, and our pride blocks us from relationship with God. Even so, says Augustine, "to praise you is the desire of man, a little piece of your creation. You stir man to take pleasure in praising you, because you have made us for yourself, and our heart is restless until it rests in you."[4] Many of the key elements of the *Confessions* are here: As creatures, we yearn to share in God's life. God has created us for this end, and by grace God moves us toward it. We are restless until we attain rest in God. This restlessness shows us that we cannot do without sharing in God's life, but it also suggests that we have trouble finding God.

How can creatures find God? Augustine answers that we can seek him in prayer, and he will answer our prayer. More than this, God comes to find us in the humanity of Jesus and through the preachers of the gospel, and interiorly the Holy Spirit gives us faith. What does it mean to beg God to come to us? Since God is infinite spirit, we cannot contain him. Yet unless God were sustaining us in being, how could we be? We exist in God. If so, what do we mean by begging him to come to us more fully?

In these first few paragraphs, Augustine is exploring how to understand the relationship of creatures to the transcendent God. He asks God, "Do heaven and earth contain you because you have filled them? or do you fill them and overflow them because they do not contain you? Where do you put the overflow of yourself after heaven and earth are filled?"[5] Clearly this physical, spatial image does not work for God's being. Augustine proceeds to a list of attributes, which quickly turns into a list of paradoxes including "deeply hidden yet most intimately present" and "always active, always in repose, gathering to yourself but not in need."[6] He recognizes that these words fall infinitely short of God's reality. Furthermore, the list of attributes does not fulfill his existential need. As Augustine says, "Who will enable me to find rest in you? Who will grant me that you come to my heart and intoxicate it, so that I forget my evils and embrace my one and only good, yourself? What are you to me?"[7] We are restless, but God can seem abstract to both our minds and our hearts. Why does everlasting happiness or misery depend on loving a God whom we have such trouble finding? Augustine begs for a relationship with God that is personal,

3. Augustine, *Confessions* 1.1.1, trans. Henry Chadwick (Oxford: Oxford University Press, 1991), 3.

4. Augustine, *Confessions* 1.1.1, p. 3.

5. Augustine, *Confessions* 1.3.3, p. 4.

6. Augustine, *Confessions* 1.4.4, pp. 4–5.

7. Augustine, *Confessions* 1.5.5, p. 5.

that is intimate and clear: "In your mercies, Lord God, tell me what you are to me. 'Say to my soul, I am your salvation' (Ps. 34[35]:3). Speak to me so that I may hear. See the ears of my heart are before you, Lord. Open them and 'say to my soul, I am your salvation.'"[8]

Augustine begs God to cleanse his soul, so that he can have full communion with God. Augustine also begs God to have mercy on his ignorance: "What, Lord, do I wish to say except that I do not know whence I came to be in this mortal life or, as I may call it, this living death?"[9] We suddenly exist, and we are threatened with nonexistence, but we do not know the meaning of either our existence or our death. Yet we know that there must be some meaning, because we came into existence within a natural order that does not depend on human decision making, an order that has its own intelligible patterns and laws. Augustine describes his awakening, as an infant and small child, to this order in which he had come to share by birth. He remarks, "Where can a living being such as an infant come from if not from you, God? Or can anyone become the cause of his own making?"[10]

The radical receptivity of the infant leads Augustine to praise God as the infinite fullness of being and life, the immutable source of all changing things, "the one from whom every kind of being is derived."[11] Generations of creatures are born into the world and pass away, but God does not pass away with them. Instead, all generations have existence by participating in the unchanging God. Augustine knows that he cannot grasp what it means to be timeless and to be the unchanging source of all changing and temporal things. Remembering his infancy and early childhood, Augustine also reflects on the origin of sin, the beauty and harmony of the human form, and the acquisition of language due to intelligence and memory (as well as the misery of an educational system that relied on corporal punishment). His first conceptions of God were of a "large being with the power, even when not present to our senses, of hearing us and helping us."[12]

God did not help Augustine when he prayed that he would be spared corporal punishment at school; nor did God see to it that Augustine be baptized as a boy, even though during a serious childhood illness Augustine begged his mother to arrange for his baptism. Where was God too when Augustine cared more for the fictional character Dido, and for poetic stories about depraved gods, than for truth?[13] Furthermore, like many boys, Augustine practiced

8. Augustine, *Confessions* 1.5.5, p. 5.

9. Augustine, *Confessions* 1.6.7, p. 6.

10. Augustine, *Confessions* 1.6.10, p. 8.

11. Augustine, *Confessions* 1.7.12, p. 10. See Mary T. Clark, RSCJ, "Augustine on Immutability and Mutability," *American Catholic Philosophical Quarterly* 74 (2000): 7–27.

12. Augustine, *Confessions* 1.9.14, p. 11.

13. See Camille Bennett, "The Conversion of Vergil: The Aeneid in Augustine's *Confessions*," *Revue des Études Augustiniennes* 34 (1988): 47–69.

regular lying, stealing, and cheating, although he was furious with other boys for doing these things to him. Yet not only did God not cause these sins (whether Augustine's or those of others), but God also continued to bestow gifts on Augustine. Specifically, Augustine participated in God by existing, living, thinking, instinctively preserving his life, hating being deceived, hating ignorance, loving friendship, and loving to communicate. In all these ways Augustine was praiseworthy, and all these ways were God's gifts rather than Augustine's choices. By contrast, in his choices Augustine sought fulfillment in spatiotemporal realities rather than in their source: "My sin consisted in this, that I sought pleasure, sublimity and truth not in God but in his creatures, in myself and other created beings."[14] Augustine is aware that he was acting in a normal way for fallen humans. The point is that God does not abandon us, even when we abandon him through our choices.

Books 2–6

Augustine begins Book 2 by observing that in adolescence he fell into what, indebted to neo-Platonist language, he calls "a state of disintegration" and "multiplicity."[15] In other words, he was living without regard to God and with solely spatiotemporal goods in view. His adolescent erotic lust could have awakened him to God, since what he wanted "was simply to love and be loved"[16] and since his delight in beauty might have led him toward divine beauty. Instead, however, his attention was entirely attracted by this world without attending to the way in which this world shares in God. As a result, he lost contact with the principle of unity and order within himself and in this world, and his fragmentation enslaved him to things that are passing away. His own sexual lust and his parents' worldly ambition for him dominated his life. He rejoiced in using natural goods against their fruitful purpose, both with young women in fornicating and with young men in stealing pears and throwing them away. Turning away from God, he turned away from the ends for which God created these goods. By describing his love for rebellion itself, Augustine depicts the pride that seeks to make itself rather than God the center of all things.[17] As Augustine remarks, "So the soul fornicates (Ps.

---

14. Augustine, *Confessions* 1.20.31, pp. 22–23.

15. Augustine, *Confessions* 2.1.1, p. 24. See the analysis of John C. Cavadini, "Book Two: Augustine's Book of Shadows," in *A Reader's Companion to Augustine's* Confessions, 25–34. The authors in Paffenroth and Kennedy's volume benefit from the exhaustive commentary provided in James J. O'Donnell's edition of the *Confessions*, which includes the full Latin text plus an introduction and two volumes of commentary. See Augustine, *Confessions*, with commentary by James J. O'Donnell, 3 vols. (Oxford: Oxford University Press, 1992).

16. Augustine, *Confessions* 2.2.2, p. 24.

17. For discussion see James Wetzel, "Snares of Truth: Augustine on Free Will and Predestination," in *Augustine and His Critics: Essays in Honour of Gerald Bonner*, ed. Robert Dodaro and

72[73]:27) when it is turned away from you and seeks outside you the pure and clear intentions which are not to be found except by returning to you."[18]

In this context Augustine shows that in vices, we pathetically strive to be God on our own terms rather than receiving God's gifts in love. Thus cruelty aims to cause fear, but God alone is truly to be feared; curiosity desires knowledge, but God alone knows all; idleness seeks rest, but God alone gives perfect rest; envy wishes for excellence, but God alone is perfect; and so forth. The vices make the self into the center of all things, when in fact God is the center: only participation in God holds us in being and offers us hope for attaining the goods we seek. Because the vices are self-centered, they distort our efforts at friendship. Stealing the pears would not have been fun without his companions in the act. Vice turns even friendship, which is intended to unite us in love with God and neighbor, into an occasion for self-seeking.

It might seem that turning away from God would produce a hunger for a renewed participation in God, but Augustine finds that this is not the case. Rather than turning back to God, we vainly seek fulfillment in more spatio-temporal goods. In this light Augustine looks back upon his move to Carthage, where as a student he entered into a long-lasting sexual relationship with a local woman with no intention of marriage. He thus found another bad friendship, this time with a woman, to match the gang of male friends with whom he stole the pears. The simulacrum of friendship that he enjoyed with these friends, male and female, is compared by Augustine with his passion at that time for the theater. Lacking real compassion and charity for others, he would take pleasure in weeping and rejoicing with the fictional characters on the stage. His love was not real. The same unreality affected his intellectual activities: since he understood learning solely as a mode of satisfying ambition for temporal goods, rather than as the search for truth, his success as a student of rhetoric inflamed his ego rather than pointing him to the source of all truth.[19]

At this very time, however, Augustine's reading gave him a thirst for God. Cicero's *Hortensius* "altered my prayers, Lord, to be towards you yourself. It gave me different values and priorities. Suddenly every vain hope became empty to me, and I longed for the immortality of wisdom with an incredible ardour in my heart. I began to rise up to return to you."[20] Inspired by Cicero, Augustine suddenly wished to share in God's life through wisdom. The only

---

George Lawless (London: Routledge, 2000), 124–41, at 132–33; William E. Mann, "Inner-Life Ethics," in *The Augustinian Tradition*, 140–65, at 158–60.

18. Augustine, *Confessions* 2.6.14, p. 32.

19. For the rhetoric of the Second Sophistic in which Augustine was educated, and for Cicero's enduring influence on Augustine, see Calvin L. Troup, *Temporality, Eternity, and Wisdom: The Rhetoric of Augustine's* Confessions (Columbia: University of South Carolina Press, 1999), 13–32.

20. Augustine, *Confessions* 3.4.7, p. 39. For a much fuller account of Book 3 than I provide here, see Todd Breyfogle, "Book Three: 'No Changing Nor Shadow,'" in *A Reader's Companion to Augustine's* Confessions, 35–52. A reconstruction of Cicero's *Hortensius* is found in Kenneth B. Steinhauser, "Augustine Laughed: *De beata vita*," in *Tradition and the Rule of Faith in the Early*

thing that he found missing in the book was the name of Christ. Yet on reading the Bible, Augustine found it a poorly written collection of tales, far from the refined quest for wisdom proposed by Cicero. His newfound quest to share in God's life therefore took him not to Catholic faith but to the Manichean version of Christianity. Manichean theology attributed quantity and extension to spiritual realities, and thereby reduced them to the spatiotemporal level.

Augustine's pride in his intellectual refinement led him away from the Bible and into the foolishness of worshiping a spatial deity, a vast and luminous being at war with evil. He also did not understand that due to diverse circumstances, diverse legal codes can share in the one unchanging justice of God. He agreed with Manichean theology in rejecting the holiness of the persons of the Old Testament. His rejection of the Bible led him to a false theology according to which even "a fig weeps when it is picked, and . . . the fig tree its mother sheds milky tears."[21] On this view, divine spirit is contained in all matter and yearns to escape; the chewing of food by spiritually advanced Manichees was thought to enable the matter to be digested and the divine spirit to escape through burping and retching. This concept of divine spirit conceives of God as yet another spatial reality. Not surprisingly, Augustine continued living for temporal ambition and physical pleasure, and he also trusted in astrology, the power of the stars to determine human fate.

During this time Augustine had another opportunity, similar to reading *Hortensius*, to discover the truth about reality. A dear friend of his died, but only after receiving baptism and rejecting the Manichean doctrine to which Augustine had converted him. Augustine fell into a severe depression, during which he felt that death would swallow up everything.[22] In his grief he found that he could not call upon the God of the Manichees for help: "When I thought of you [God], my mental image was not of anything solid and firm. . . . If I attempted to find rest there for my soul, it slipped through a void and again came falling back upon me."[23] He had no relationship to God and instead was left solely to his own resources, which failed him. Looking back on this experience, Augustine draws the moral: human friendship can endure only in God. Friendship can be enduring only when our relationship to our human friends is caught up in our relationship to God.[24] Given the rushing current of

---

Church: Essays in Honor of Joseph T. Lienhard, S.J., ed. Ronnie J. Rombs and Alexander Y. Hwang (Washington, DC: Catholic University of America Press, 2010), 211–31, at 214–18.

21. Augustine, *Confessions* 3.10.18, p. 49.

22. See Genevieve Lloyd, "Augustine and the 'Problem' of Time," in *The Augustinian Tradition*, 39–60, at 41–43.

23. Augustine, *Confessions* 4.7.14, p. 60. James Wetzel rightly points out that this grief is the framing episode of Book 4. See Wetzel, "Book Four: The Trappings of Woe and Confession of Grief," in *A Reader's Companion to Augustine's* Confessions, 53–69.

24. See Joseph T. Lienhard, SJ, "Friendship in Paulinus of Nola and Augustine," in *Collectanea Augustiniana: Mélanges T. J. van Bavel*, ed. B. Bruning, M. Lamberigts, and J. van Houtem (Leuven: Leuven University Press, 1990), 279–96.

time and the quick approach of death, Augustine comments, "For whenever the human soul turns itself, other than to you, it is fixed in sorrows, even if it is fixed upon beautiful things external to you and external to itself, which would nevertheless be nothing if they did not have their being from you."[25] Transient things are a cause for giving praise to God, but we must not "become stuck in them and glued to them with love," because "in these things there is no point of rest: they lack permanence."[26]

By these words Augustine urges himself to continue to seek God's face through the things that God creates, rather than vainly trying to love these things on their own. The very existence of growth and decay should point us to the unchanging Word who orders the universe and makes its parts a whole. Augustine urges that wherever truth is, God will be discovered; when we love this Creator God, his love will secure our lives and show us our true goal. As Augustine puts it, "The good which you love is from him. But it is only as it is related to him that it is good and sweet. Otherwise it will justly become bitter; for all that comes from him is unjustly loved if he has been abandoned."[27] Teetering on the edge of eternity, in need of God in order to have any enduring goal, we find God's presence by awakening to the way in which finite things point to God. Yet God's presence is not merely something hidden: God comes to us in Christ Jesus, marries our mortal flesh in the incarnation, and endures and overcomes our death. By his ascension, Christ calls us to join him at the right hand of God. To ascend we must put away our pride and follow the path of humility, praising and loving God above the self. Augustine remarks, "Surely after the descent of life, you cannot fail to wish to ascend and live? But where will you ascend when you are 'set on high and have put your mouth in heaven'? (Ps. 72:9). Come down so that you can ascend, and make your ascent to God."[28]

This understanding of human life as participating in God through Christ and the Holy Spirit, who inspires our love, was not apparent to Augustine at the time of his friend's death and of his resulting move to Carthage,[29] a time during which he was making philosophical inquiries into the beauty of things. He particularly desired that his work be praised by an orator in Rome whom he had heard praised by people he respected. His worldly ambition was

25. Augustine, *Confessions* 4.10.15, p. 61.

26. Augustine, *Confessions* 4.10.15, p. 62. For Augustine's use of the image of glue, see Joseph T. Lienhard, SJ, "'The Glue Itself Is Charity': Ps 62:9 in Augustine's Thought," in *Augustine: Presbyter Factus Sum*, ed. Joseph T. Lienhard, SJ, Earl C. Muller, SJ, and Roland J. Teske, SJ (New York: Peter Lang, 1993), 375–84.

27. Augustine, *Confessions* 4.12.18, pp. 63–64.

28. Augustine, *Confessions* 4.12.19, p. 64.

29. For background to Augustine's career as a student and young teacher, which I have skimmed over here, see Neil McLynn, "Disciplines of Discipleship in Late Antique Education: Augustine and Gregory Nazianzen," in *Augustine and the Disciplines: From Cassiacum to* Confessions, ed. Karla Pollmann and Mark Vessey (Oxford: Oxford University Press, 2005), 25–48.

matched by his understanding of spiritual realities as vast entities, divided from a living substance that was evil. Following Manichean doctrine, he imagined that his soul was part of the divine substance. His reading of Aristotle led him to suppose that everything, including God, was a substance possessed of accidents. Augustine describes himself at this time as possessed of excellent intellectual gifts but having "my back to the light and my face toward the things which are illuminated."[30]

The answer to how to gain knowledge of the hidden God is to praise him in the Church: when we praise him, we discover the entire creation praising him, in its very being. Augustine recounts that he finally began to be freed from Manicheanism when he saw through the Manichees' false natural philosophy. For this step forward, as well as for his move from Carthage to Rome in search of more orderly students, Augustine credits God's hidden providence.[31] Arriving in Rome, he fell into a serious illness without desiring baptism; he credits his recovery to his mother's prayers. In Rome he associated both with Manichees and with skeptics called Academics.[32] He continued to imagine God as a vast material entity of dazzling light, opposed to a somewhat smaller evil entity. He soon left Rome, whose students were dishonest, and took up a position in Milan, where he attended the sermons of Ambrose, who freed Augustine from some of his earlier concerns about the Bible. While remaining an Academic skeptic, Augustine became a Catholic catechumen and abandoned Manicheanism. As a key element of his spiritual healing, Augustine points to his conviction, even during his spiritual wanderings, that God exists and that God providentially cares for us. Ambrose's sermons persuaded Augustine to accept that God providentially inspired the Bible and its authority.[33] Another key element in his spiritual healing was that his temporal ambitions were thwarted at this time. God was moving Augustine toward humility, the path of human participation in God. He had to learn that only God is glorious, worthy of all praise.

God also gave Augustine two friends, Alypius and Nebridius, with whom Augustine journeyed on the path toward friendship with the living God. Their discussions hinged on whether they should give themselves over entirely to seeking God. Death, Augustine reasoned, could not be annihilation, because God's creative power and care for his creatures is so evident in the universe.

---

30. Augustine, *Confessions* 4.16.30, p. 70. The image is from Plato's allegory of the cave.

31. For the importance of this theme, see Frederick J. Crosson, "Book Five: The Disclosure of Hidden Providence," in *A Reader's Companion to Augustine's* Confessions, 71–87. See also, on Augustine's benefactor at this time, Catherine Conybeare, *The Irrational Augustine* (Oxford: Oxford University Press, 2006), 16–20.

32. On the Academics, see John M. Rist, *Augustine: Ancient Thought Baptized* (Cambridge: Cambridge University Press, 1994), chap. 3.

33. For Augustine's portrait of Ambrose, see Debra Romanick Baldwin, "Models of Teaching and Models of Learning in the *Confessions*," in *Augustine and Liberal Education*, ed. Kim Paffenroth and Kevin L. Hughes (Lanham, MD: Lexington Books, 2008), 15–24, at 20–23.

If so, then happiness must be found with God after death, and so this life should be a preparation for death by coming to know God. But Augustine also reasoned that marriage and career were of value too, and he did not believe he could be celibate. At this time Monica arranged a marriage for him, and he sent away the woman with whom he had a son.[34] While waiting for marriage he obtained another sexual consort. At the same time, he grew in fear of judgment after death.

Here we reach the end of Book 6 and arrive at the beginning of Augustine's process of conversion in earnest. In Books 2–6, Augustine moves from adolescence to being more than thirty years old. In his adolescence, sexual lust and ambition entirely clouded his awareness and he sought temporal goods alone. In the years that followed (through Book 6), three central events happened to him that undermined his focus on temporal goods: reading *Hortensius* and falling in love with the life of wisdom, losing his close friend to baptism and death, and hearing Ambrose's sermons about the Old Testament history and prophecy. As we have seen, however, after each of these events a counter-event occurred that pushed Augustine back toward his focus on temporal goods: his dislike of the Bible and his consequent acceptance of the Manichean spatial portrait of God; the success of his career, which brought him new friends and took him from Thagaste to Carthage to Rome to Milan; and his fear of being celibate, which almost caused him to give himself fully over to his worldly career while still in an uncertain state about faith.

Books 7–10

Augustine begins Book 7 with his ongoing struggle to conceive of God in anything but a bodily way, and Book 10 ends with his praise of Jesus Christ the mediator. At the beginning of Book 7 he is still engaging in fornication, while at the end of Book 10 he is rejoicing over the forgiveness of sins accomplished by the Word incarnate. What happened during this period to bring about such change?

Although Augustine recognized that God must be incorruptible and unchanging, nonetheless whenever he thought of God, he pictured a vast spatial entity, because he "thought that anything from which space was abstracted was non-existent, indeed absolutely nothing, not even a vacuum."[35] Since God is present everywhere, it seems that God must be spatial, just as sunlight permeates air, or like an infinite sea permeating a finite sponge. Related to this problem is that of the nature of evil. Augustine tried to understand the Catholic teaching about evil—namely, that the free choice of the created will causes evil. But why would a good God have created him with such a dangerous

34. For discussion see Eric Plumer, "Book Six: Major Characters and Memorable Incidents," in *A Reader's Companion to Augustine's* Confessions, 89–105, at 104–5.

35. Augustine, *Confessions* 7.1.1, p. 111.

and destructive power? Why too would a rational creature whom God created purely good freely turn away from goodness? Why would a good will, rejoicing in God's goodness, turn bad? And if God permeates everything and is omnipotent, how did evil get in? In the midst of these questions,[36] however, Augustine was coming closer to God by more firmly embracing the faith of the Catholic Church, even if he did not yet have sufficient understanding of that faith to enter the Church.

Among his steps forward was his rejection of astrology, due partly to the different experiences of infants born at exactly the same time. Another, more important step forward was Augustine's now firm faith that "in Christ your Son our Lord, and by your scriptures commended by the authority of your Catholic Church, you have provided a way of salvation whereby humanity can come to the future life after death."[37] A third step came through neo-Platonic writings of Plotinus and Porphyry.[38] Here Augustine found arguments that dovetailed, in his view, with the confession of the divine Word. The neo-Platonist books gave Augustine his doctrine of participation: "The books say that before all times and above all times your only-begotten Son immutably abides eternal with you, and that souls 'receive his fullness' (John 1:16) to be blessed, and that they are renewed to be wise by participation in wisdom abiding in them."[39] But the books did not include the humility of the Word, his incarnation or Pasch, nor did they include Christ's instruction that we should imitate his humility. Proud of their knowledge, the neo-Platonists praised the gods and thus fell into foolishness.

Yet the neo-Platonist books led Augustine to discover his spiritual soul and its participation in the transcendent light of eternal truth and love.[40] On this

36. See Charles Mathewes, "The Liberation of Questioning in Augustine's *Confessions*," *Journal of the American Academy of Religion* 70 (2002): 539–60.

37. Augustine, *Confessions* 7.7.11, p. 119. See Goulven Madec, *La Patrie et la voie. Le Christ dans la vie et la pensée de saint Augustin* (Paris: Desclée, 1989).

38. On Plotinus's theology, see John Peter Kenney, *Mystical Monotheism: A Study in Ancient Platonic Theology* (Providence: Brown University Press, 1991), 91–156. For the debate regarding which neo-Platonist thinkers Augustine had read at this time, see Robert J. O'Connell, SJ, "Porphyrianism in the Early Augustine: Olivier DuRoy's Contribution," in *From Augustine to Eriugena: Essays on Neoplatonism and Christianity in Honor of John O'Meara*, ed. F. X. Martin, OSA, and J. A. Richmond (Washington, DC: Catholic University of America Press, 1991), 126–42; Frederick Van Fleteren, "Augustine's Ascent of the Soul in Book VII of *The Confessions*," *Augustinian Studies* 5 (1974): 29–72; Pier Franco Beatrice, "*Quosdam Platonicorum Libros*: The Platonic Readings of Augustine in Milan," *Vigiliae Christianae* 43 (1989): 248–81.

39. Augustine, *Confessions* 7.9.14, p. 122. See David V. Meconi, SJ, "The Incarnation and the Role of Participation in St. Augustine's *Confessions*," *Augustinian Studies* 29 (1998): 61–75; Meconi, "St. Augustine's Early Theory of Participation," *Augustinian Studies* 27 (1996): 81–98; Matthias Smalbrugge, "La notion de la participation chez Augustin. Quelques observations sur le rapport christianisme-platonisme," in *Collectanea Augustiniana*, 333–47.

40. For the difference between Augustine's Christian view of the soul and the neo-Platonic view, see John C. Cavadini, "The Darkest Enigma: Reconsidering the Self in Augustine's Thought," *Augustinian Studies* 38 (2007): 119–32, at 126–29. See also Rist, *Augustine*, 95–97.

basis, he rose from his soul to see the Creator: "When I first came to know you [God], you raised me up to make me see that what I saw is Being, and that I who saw am not yet Being. And you gave a shock to the weakness of my sight by the strong radiance of your rays, and I trembled with love and awe."[41] Augustine puts this insight into biblical terms by quoting Exodus 3:14, where God names himself "I am who am."[42] Finite participation in infinite Being allows for an analogy in which the dissimilarity is ever greater. Finite beings cannot be said "absolutely to be or absolutely not to be. They are because they come from you. But they are not because they are not what you are."[43] Since they are not infinite being and goodness, they are liable to corruption and privation; yet their being, insofar as it is, is real and good.[44] Augustine thereby discovered that evil is not a substance (which has to be good) but a corruption of or privation in a substance. All things praise God through their existence. Inquiring again into evil on the basis of his neo-Platonic reading, illumined by the teaching of Catholic faith, "I did not find a substance but a perversity of will twisted away from the highest substance, you O God, towards inferior things, rejecting its own inner life (Ecclus. 10:10) and swelling with external matter."[45] An evil will, instead of moving from created things to their Creator, occupies itself solely with created things.

This discovery, however, did not change Augustine's lifestyle. Instead he continued in his life of fornication, where he treated his partner as someone to be used for sexual pleasure rather than as someone created by God with an eternal destiny. Indeed he treated himself in this same way by living in lust for temporal goods rather than rightly ordering those temporal goods in relation to God. Intellectually, he was able to rise from contemplating bodies, to the soul, to the light of eternal truth: "So in the flash of a trembling glance it attained to that which is. At that moment I saw your 'invisible nature understood

41. Augustine, *Confessions* 7.10.16, p. 123. See Thomas Finan, "A Mystic in Milan: 'Reverberasti' Revisited," in *From Augustine to Eriugena*, 77–91. For recent efforts to understand *"esse"* (and *"idipsum"*) in Augustine's naming of God, see Ayres, *Augustine and the Trinity*, 201–8; Jean-Luc Marion, *"Idipsum*: The Name of God according to Augustine," trans. Christophe Chalomet, in *Orthodox Readings of Augustine*, ed. George E. Demacopoulos and Aristotle Papanikolaou (Crestwood, NY: St. Vladimir's Seminary Press, 2008), 167–89; and (more successfully) David Bentley Hart, "The Hidden and the Manifest: Metaphysics after Nicaea," in *Orthodox Readings of Augustine*, 191–226. Hart devotes three lengthy footnotes to critiquing David Bradshaw's contribution to *Orthodox Readings of Augustine*: Bradshaw, "Augustine the Metaphysician," 227–51 (the last eight pages of which are a response to Hart).
42. See Emilie Zum Brunn, "The Augustinian Exegesis of '*Ego sum qui sum*' and the 'Metaphysics of Exodus,'" in Zum Brunn, *St. Augustine: Being and Nothingness* (New York: Paragon, 1988), 97–118.
43. Augustine, *Confessions* 7.11.17, p. 124.
44. See F. B. A. Asiedu, "Augustine's Christian-Platonist Account of Goodness: A Reconsideration," *Heythrop Journal* 43 (2002): 328–43.
45. Augustine, *Confessions* 7.16.22, p. 126. See Rowan Williams, "Insubstantial Evil," in *Augustine and His Critics*, 105–23, at 106–16, 121.

through the things which are made' (Rom. 1:20)."[46] But he could not figure out how to enjoy God's presence. At the time he thought of Christ simply as a great man, a great teacher who enjoyed a "more perfect participation in wisdom."[47] He therefore failed to realize that the path to enjoying God consists in humility, charity, and praise.

In hindsight, Augustine observes that those who are being healed learn "no longer to place confidence in themselves, but rather to become weak. They see at their feet divinity become weak by his sharing in our 'coat of skin' (Gen. 3:21). In their weariness they fall prostrate before this divine weakness which rises and lifts them up."[48] To be in a relationship with the living God, to whom we entrust our lives in death, requires not intellectual power but humility in allowing God to draw us into relationship with him. Augustine says that his reading of the neo-Platonists, and his discovery of the God who is infinite Being (and his corresponding resolution of the nature of evil), led him to think of himself as wise; but without the real relationship to the God who redeems us from sin and draws us to himself, such supposed wisdom could only be deadly.

Augustine needed to see God's glory "not merely as an end to be perceived but as a realm to live in."[49] He needed charity, God's gift of real relationship with God. At this stage Augustine returned to the Bible and especially to the letters of St. Paul. Rereading Scripture in light of the best insights of the neo-Platonists regarding God and his Word, he discovered the revelation of God's grace (we have nothing that we have not received) and our need for healing in order to gain a living relationship with God. This healing we receive in the victory of Christ Jesus, who freely pays our penalty for sin and reconciles us to God. We receive salvation entirely from God; it is not something we can accomplish from our own resources. This is the key insight missing in the neo-Platonist books. As Augustine says, "It is one thing from a wooded summit to catch a glimpse of the homeland of peace and not to find the way to it, but vainly to attempt the journey along an impracticable route. . . . It is another thing to hold on to the way that leads there, defended by the protection of the heavenly emperor."[50]

Augustine was looking for stable life in God, not simply for the knowledge that God is. Yet he still did not know whether he was called to married life or to a celibate vocation; nor had he been baptized into Christ in the Church. Looking back on this time, he wonders why, since God is eternal and his

46. Augustine, *Confessions* 7.17.23, p. 127.
47. Augustine, *Confessions* 7.19.25, p. 129.
48. Augustine, *Confessions* 7.18.24, p. 128. See José Oroz Reta, "The Role of Divine Attraction in Conversion according to St. Augustine," in *From Augustine to Eriugena*, 155–67.
49. Augustine, *Confessions* 7.20.26, p. 130.
50. Augustine, *Confessions* 7.21.27, pp. 131–32. On Christ the way and the homeland, see Basil Studer, OSB, *The Grace of Christ and the Grace of God in Augustine of Hippo: Christocentrism or Theocentrism?*, trans. Matthew J. O'Connell (Collegeville, MN: Liturgical Press, 1997), 44–60.

creatures rejoice in him, "part of the creation oscillates between regress and progress, between hostilities and reconciliations?"[51] This was the situation in which Augustine found himself, oscillating between regress and progress. He needed God's help to return to God, and he also needed the help of human friends and exemplars. Augustine still held out against baptism and against giving up his sexual habit.

In this condition he was helped by various friends, above all Nebridius and Alypius, and by Simplicianus's story of the conversion of Marius Victorinus (a leading neo-Platonist) and Ponticianus's story of St. Anthony of Egypt and the spread of monastic vocations.[52] This latter story put Augustine into an agony: he wanted to give his life to Christ, and yet he did not fully want to do so. He feared what would happen to him if he gave up his present life. In his agony, he wept tears of repentance and on opening his copy of St. Paul's epistles, the first words he saw were Romans 13:13–14, where Paul calls upon believers to "put on the Lord Jesus Christ, and make no provision for the flesh, to gratify its desires."[53] This passage solved his last doubt, and he felt himself to be finally freed from the twin obsessions of his life—namely, sexual lust and ambition for his temporal career.[54] Along with Alypius, who became a Catholic at the same time, he could now devote himself to a life of love whose goal was union with God.

Augustine prepared himself for this life by reading the psalms, the model of how to participate in God through prayer and praise. He found his own plight in the psalms about God's enemies, of which he had been one. He rejoiced in the psalms of God's mercy.[55] In the days following his baptism, he "found an

51. Augustine, *Confessions* 8.3.8, p. 138. See Peter Burnell, *The Augustinian Person* (Washington, DC: Catholic University of America Press, 2005), 75–76; James Wetzel, *Augustine and the Limits of Virtue* (Cambridge: Cambridge University Press, 1992), 126–38, 175–86; Eugene TeSelle, "Exploring the Inner Conflict: Augustine's Sermons on Romans 7 and 8," in *Engaging Augustine on Romans: Self, Context, and Theology in Interpretation*, ed. Daniel Patte and Eugene TeSelle (Harrisburg, PA: Trinity Press International, 2002), 111–43, at 121–24; John K. Riches, "Readings of Augustine on Paul: Their Impact on Critical Studies of Paul," in *Engaging Augustine on Romans*, 173–98, at 181–88.

52. See Lewis Ayres, "Into the Poem of the Universe: *Exempla*, Conversion, and Church in Augustine's *Confessions*," *Zeitschrift für Antikes Christentum* 13 (2009): 263–81. For the salutary influence of Marius Victorinus, see Mary T. Clark, "Augustine the Christian Thinker," in *From Augustine to Eriugena*, 56–65.

53. See Henry Chadwick, "History and Symbolism in the Garden at Milan," in *From Augustine to Eriugena*, 42–55. See also Stephen A. Cooper, "Scripture at Cassiciacum: 1 Corinthians 13:13 in the Soliloquies," *Augustinian Studies* 27 (1996): 21–47.

54. On Augustine's attitude toward his temporal ambition, see Robert Dodaro, OSA, "Augustine's Secular City," in *Augustine and His Critics*, 231–59. See also Anna M. Wilson, "Reason and Revelation in the Conversion Accounts of the Cappadocians and Augustine," in *Collectanea Augustiniana*, 259–78, at 266–69.

55. See Jason Byassee, *Praise Seeking Understanding: Reading the Psalms with Augustine* (Grand Rapids: Eerdmans, 2007), 115–16.

insatiable and amazing delight in considering the profundity of your purpose for the salvation of the human race."[56] The Church's role in God's saving purpose was apparent to Augustine, not only in the liturgical hymns and psalms that lifted up his heart to God, but also in how the Catholics of Milan had united in the past year to thwart the empress Juliana's attempt to force Ambrose to give up basilicas for use in Arian worship. Likewise Augustine observed how God worked healings through the relics of the martyrs Protasius and Gervasius.

Augustine also describes the union of love in the faith that developed between him and his son, Adeodatus, and he praises the faith, hope, and love that marked his mother Monica's life, including her relations with a difficult mother-in-law and husband (whom she led eventually to baptism). The fruit of Christian communion showed itself in a conversation between Augustine and Monica in which they contemplated eternal life and even tasted it together for a moment: "And while we talked and panted after it, we touched it in some small degree by a moment of total concentration of the heart."[57] It seemed to mother and son that if the noisy expressions of creatures were removed, so that all creation stood aside for the Creator, they would encounter the Word himself speaking directly, as he seemed to do "when at that moment we extended our reach and in a flash of mental energy attained the eternal wisdom which abides beyond all things."[58] During this conversation both of them desired to be forever within this eternal wisdom, in everlasting joy, and Monica expressed her readiness to die now that her prayers for her son had been answered. She soon thereafter contracted a fever, and after nine days of illness, died in the presence of Augustine, his brother Navigius, and others.

Augustine examines his response to her death. Should Christians grieve the death of their loved ones, when they know that their loved ones are with God? At Monica's death Adeodatus immediately burst into tears, but Augustine showed no sign of grief, even though he was feeling "torn to pieces, since my life and hers had become a single thing."[59] After her burial (preceded by the celebration of the Eucharist),[60] he wept in private for his separation from her, and in writing about her he pours forth his prayers that God might have mercy on her and protect her. He was separated from her, but he was also united to her in Christ and he used that unity to call on all his readers for their prayers: "May they [his readers] remember with devout affection my parents in this transient light, my kith and kin under you, our Father, in our mother

---

56. Augustine, *Confessions* 9.6.14, p. 164.

57. Augustine, *Confessions* 9.10.24, p. 171. For Monica's important role in Augustine's Cassiciacum dialogues, see Conybeare, *Irrational Augustine*, chaps. 3–4.

58. Augustine, *Confessions* 9.10.25, p. 172. See John Peter Kenney, *The Mysticism of Saint Augustine: Rereading the Confessions* (London: Routledge, 2005), 78–86.

59. Augustine, *Confessions* 9.12.31, p. 175.

60. See John C. Cavadini, "Eucharistic Exegesis in Augustine's *Confessions*," *Augustinian Studies* 41 (2010): 87–108, at 88–95.

the Catholic Church, and my fellow citizens in the eternal Jerusalem."[61] This community of love endures beyond death, because the love of God bonds it together.

Monica's death concludes the narrative of events in Augustine's life. Book 10 serves as a retrospect. As Augustine says, "Late have I loved you [God], beauty so old and so new: late have I loved you. And see, you were within and I was in the external world and sought you there, and in my unlovely state I plunged into those lovely created things which you made. You were with me, and I was not with you."[62] He erred by putting his love in spatiotemporal things rather than in the God who made them. Had he understood earlier that they participate in God, their beauty would have led him sooner to the divine beauty.

In writing about the events of his life, Augustine has been engaged in an act of memory.[63] He knows, however, that nothing in his mind is or can be hidden from God. The goal of memory, then, is that we can find God, so that just as we are known to him, he will not be hidden to us. We find God when we repent of our sins and praise God for our blessings; these acts are God's gifts in us, and God makes himself present to us in them. Even more is this the case when we repent and praise God not only for our own good (for his glory as manifested in our healing) but also for the good of others. Augustine prays that by hearing how God powerfully transformed him, others will be inspired to depend on the power of God, to praise God in thanksgiving, and to pray for neighbors who have gone astray. As Augustine remarks, "You [God] have commanded me to serve them if I wish to live with you and in dependence on you."[64]

In loving God, what do we love? Love of God is an experience of spiritual goods that can best be described in terms of the (spiritual) senses: "a light, voice, odour, food, embrace of my inner man, where my soul is floodlit by light which space cannot contain, where there is sound that time cannot seize, where there is a perfume which no breeze disperses, where there is a taste for food no amount of eating can lessen, and where there is a bond of union that no satiety can part."[65] Since we cannot see God, how do we identify what we love in loving God? Beginning with the beauty of creatures who testify that they did not make themselves, we rise to the immaterial soul by which we

---

61. Augustine, *Confessions* 9.13.37, p. 178.

62. Augustine, *Confessions* 10.27.38, p. 201.

63. On "Augustine's identification of *memoria* with self" in *Confessions* 10, see Robert A. Markus, *Conversion and Disenchantment in Augustine's Spiritual Career* (Villanova, PA: Villanova University Press, 1989), 5; cf. 8–10. See also Pamela Bright's reflections on the place of Book 10 in the overall work: Bright, "Book Ten: The Self Seeking the God Who Creates and Heals," in *A Reader's Companion to Augustine's* Confessions, 155–66, as well as Stock, *Augustine the Reader*, 209–32.

64. Augustine, *Confessions* 10.4.6, p. 182.

65. Augustine, *Confessions* 10.6.8, p. 183. See Carol Harrison, *Beauty and Revelation in the Thought of Saint Augustine* (Oxford: Clarendon, 1992), 148–51.

know beauty; and from thence we attain to memory's storehouse of images and truth, including the first principles by which we know other things. This exploration of memory leads Augustine to observe that God dwells in his memory; he remembers discovering God's truth and the happiness that he found there. When he remembers God, he knows God and loves him with joy. Yet God did not always dwell in Augustine's memory: God, who is eternal truth, transcends Augustine's mind.

Augustine prays that God will mercifully give him continence, so as to overcome his fragmentation in sin. God can accomplish this in Augustine: "O charity, my God, set me on fire. You command continence; grant what you command, and command what you will."[66] He knows from his sexual dreams, rooted in his memory, that he is still weak. The pleasures of the table too make clear to him that he could still easily give himself up to temporal pleasures for their own sake rather than enjoying these pleasures in their right ordering to God. Here he examines in detail the other kinds of sense pleasures, as well as the vice of curiosity, which can entrap us if treasured without reference to the Creator.[67] Most important, perhaps, is his treatment of pride. He confesses to the ongoing temptation "to wish to be feared or loved by people for no reason other than the joy derived from such power, which is no joy at all."[68] What if, recognizing that God has given one a gift, one rejoices more in being praised by others than in the gift or in the Giver? As Augustine says to God, "Truth, in you I now see that, if I am praised, I should be touched not on my own account, but for the benefit of my neighbour. Whether that is my actual state of mind I do not know."[69] And what if one takes pride in rejecting pride? When we are pleased with ourselves, how can we be sure we are giving glory to God?

For Augustine, God is the light that enables us to know truth. Augustine's confessions have aimed at exposing his sins to this light of truth. Yet such confessions would be of no value, he concludes, without the mediator Jesus Christ. The neo-Platonic rites of purification (theurgy) cannot remove the sins of those who practice these rites, and not simply because of the pride of the practitioners. In order for sinful humans to share in God's life, as we were created to do, we need a mediator who is "mortal like humanity, righteous like God"—namely, the Word incarnate.[70] Augustine places his faith and hope in

66. Augustine, *Confessions* 10.29.40, p. 202.

67. See Cavadini, "Eucharistic Exegesis," 98–100; Kenney, *Mysticism of Saint Augustine*, 95–97; Harrison, *Beauty and Revelation*, 169–73.

68. Augustine, *Confessions* 10.36.59, p. 213.

69. Augustine, *Confessions* 10.37.62, p. 216.

70. Augustine, *Confessions* 10.43.68, p. 219. See Gérard Remy, *Le Christ médiateur dans l'oeuvre de Saint Augustin*, 2 vols. (Lille: University of Lille, 1979); Brian E. Daley, SJ, "A Humble Mediator: The Distinctive Elements of St. Augustine's Christology," *Word and Spirit* 9 (1987): 100–117; Carol Harrison, *Augustine: Christian Truth and Fractured Humanity* (Oxford: Oxford University Press, 2000), 36–38; David Tracy, "Augustine's Christomorphic Theocentrism," in

Jesus Christ, who bore our sins by his priestly cross. Having received life from Christ, we are called to imitate him by giving our lives in service to our neighbors. Life in Christ, a life of charity and praise in the eucharistic community,[71] is a true participation in the wisdom and love of the Trinity.

Books 11–13

The final three books trace Augustine's life to its origin and expose its end or goal.[72] Augustine wishes not merely to confess his sins and to praise the working of God's grace in his life, but also to praise God by contemplating God's works "from the beginning in which you made heaven and earth until the perpetual reign with you in your heavenly city."[73] Freed from his Manichean errors and nourished by Scripture, he wishes to contemplate the Triune Creator and Redeemer.[74]

By their mode of existence, finite things proclaim that they did not make themselves but instead were created. They are beautiful and good, but not in the infinite way that God is. But how did God create? Since he created from nothing, he did not create like a craftsman. There was no place or time before he created. He needed no instrument with which to create. When he spoke his creative word, it did not produce a vocal sound. Rather he spoke his eternal Word, who is our beginning and our end. Yet if creatures come to be through God's eternal Word, how is it that creatures themselves are not also eternal? The answer, says Augustine, consists in recognizing that God truly creates that which is not God. Without changing, the eternal God can create changing, temporal realities. In his eternal present, God radically transcends time.

Here Augustine inquires into what time is, and especially into what constitutes the present moment. Augustine notes that "if we can think of some bit of time which cannot be divided into even the smallest instantaneous moments, that alone is what we can call 'present'. And this time flies so quickly from future into past that it is an interval with no duration."[75] He goes on to

---

Orthodox Readings of Augustine, ed. George E. Demacopoulos and Aristotle Papanikolaou (Crestwood, NY: St. Vladimir's Seminary Press, 2008), 263–89, at 276–77.

71. See Cavadini, "Eucharistic Exegesis," 96.

72. For discussion see Robert P. Kennedy, "Book Eleven: The *Confessions* as Eschatological Narrative," in *A Reader's Companion to Augustine's* Confessions, 167–83, at 168–71.

73. Augustine, *Confessions* 11.2.3, p. 222.

74. See Cavadini, "Eucharistic Exegesis," 101–4; Kenney, *Mysticism of Saint Augustine*, 103–9.

75. Augustine, *Confessions* 11.15.20, p. 232. See Christopher J. Thompson, "The Theological Dimension of Time in *Confessiones* XI," in *Augustine: Presbyter Factus Sum*, 187–93; M. B. Pranger, "Time and the Integrity of Poetry: Ambrose and Augustine," in *Poetry and Exegesis in Premodern Latin Christianity: The Encounter between Classical and Christian Strategies of Interpretation*, ed. Willemien Otten and Karla Pollmann (Leiden: Brill, 2007), 49–62, at 57–61; Lloyd, "Augustine and the 'Problem' of Time," 45–58.

observe that neither the past nor the future now exists, although one can say that "there are three times, a present of things past, a present of things present, a present of things to come."[76] He argues that when we measure time, we are measuring present consciousness; whereas the divine mind, which is sheer present, has no temporality. Time is a finite, created participation in the eternal divine self-presence.[77]

Augustine also inquires into the beginning of things in time, when God had not yet given form to "unformed matter"—when there were no things, but when there also was not absolute nothingness.[78] In making heaven and earth (Gen. 1:1), God made an immaterial, intellectual realm that participates in God's eternity (without being coeternal) and a formless, material realm that had no change and therefore no time. Augustine praises heaven as the "House of God."[79] Yet he grants that other interpretations of Genesis 1:1 are possible. Moses wrote truth, but because he was describing an inexhaustibly rich reality, his words allow for various interpretations.[80] In Genesis 1:1–2, Augustine discerns the presence of the Trinity: God the Father creating in the Son (the "beginning") through the Spirit. By means of the triad of being, knowing, and willing, Augustine contemplates the Trinity, although he recognizes that the Trinity is infinitely beyond any creaturely analogy.

Augustine rejoices in the gratuity of God's creative act, the fruit of God's goodness rather than of any need on God's part. God created us so that we could share in his goodness. Not even the highest heaven merited existence; everything is God's gift. God was not required even to give form to the formless matter he created. He redeemed us too out of sheer goodness and mercy, and conformed us to the form of Christ. Like the creation, the Church contains a heaven and an earth—spiritual and carnal members—and the "earth" is in darkness before it receives the form of doctrine from the Holy Spirit.[81] The

---

76. Augustine, *Confessions* 11.20.26, p. 235.

77. For the implications of this, and the bridging of eternity and time by Christ Jesus, see John C. Cavadini, "Time and Ascent in *Confessions* XI," in *Augustine: Presbyter Factus Sum*, 171–85.

78. Augustine, *Confessions* 12.3.3, p. 247. See Rowan Williams, "'Good for Nothing'? Augustine on Creation," *Augustinian Studies* 25 (1994): 9–24, at 16–20.

79. Augustine, *Confessions* 12.15.19, p. 255; cf. 12.17.24, p. 258.

80. See Bertrand de Margerie, SJ, *An Introduction to the History of Exegesis*, vol. 3, *Saint Augustine*, trans. Pierre de Fontnouvelle (Petersham, MA: Saint Bede's, 1991), 77–79; Carol Harrison, "'Not Words but Things': Harmonious Diversity in the Four Gospels," in *Augustine: Biblical Exegete*, ed. Frederick Van Fleteren and Joseph C. Schnaubelt, OSA (New York: Peter Lang, 2001), 157–73, at 166–67; Thomas Finan, "St Augustine on the 'mira profunditas' of Scripture: Texts and Contexts," in *Scriptural Interpretation in the Fathers: Letter and Spirit*, ed. Thomas Finan and Vincent Twomey (Dublin: Four Courts, 1993), 163–99, at 176–82, 193–97. For the *Confessions* as a work of biblical exegesis (and for its principles of exegesis), see Thomas F. Martin, OSA, "Book Twelve: Exegesis and *Confessio*," in *A Reader's Companion to Augustine's* Confessions, 185–206.

81. See Isabelle Bochet, *"Le firmament de l'écriture": L'herméneutique augustinienne* (Paris: Institut d'Études Augustiniennes, 2004), 235–37.

insufficiency of the rational creature is shown by the state of fallen angels and of humans. We cannot provide ourselves with peace but must receive this peace as the gift of the Holy Spirit. The Holy Spirit inflames us with charity, by which we rise to God like fire ascending. As Augustine says, "Without you [God] it is evil for me, not only in external things but within my being, and all my abundance which is other than my God is mere indigence."[82] Augustine prays for the coming of the day when he will see God as he is, when faith and hope will be fulfilled in the heavenly Jerusalem. Faith and hope strengthen him but do not content him: "My God, where are you? I see you are there, but I sigh for you a little."[83]

We are sustained in our pilgrimage by Scripture, the authoritative "firmament" (Gen. 1:7) that God has established for destroying our pride, moving us to repentance and praise, and guiding our action and contemplation.[84] Above this firmament are the holy angels, who know God directly. Only God knows himself in an absolute, comprehensive sense. The "dry land" (Gen. 1:9) signifies the Church, fruitful in charity, while the "seas" are the evildoers restrained by the punishments attendant upon their sins. The "lights in the firmament" (Gen. 1:14) signify the members of the Church who receive gifts for strengthening the sight of the people of God. God makes us "lights in the firmament" by teaching us through the Church what is virtue and what is vice, and by moving our hearts to virtue. Through his saints, evangelizing the whole world, God gives light to all the earth.[85]

Augustine praises God through the creation: "All things are beautiful because you made them, but you who made everything are inexpressibly more beautiful."[86] He continues his spiritual interpretation of Genesis 1 by interpreting God's command to "let birds fly above the earth" (Gen. 1:20) as signifying the ongoing spiritual perfection of believers. Sharing in the sacraments is not enough without this desire for perfection. To be spiritually alive requires avoiding being "absorbed by the transitory world and conformed to it."[87] God creates beasts "according to their kinds" (Gen. 1:24); Augustine draws the tropological inference that by imitating our holy friends in the Church, we can control our passions.[88] Regarding the reformation of our rational soul,

---

82. Augustine, *Confessions* 13.8.9, p. 278.

83. Augustine, *Confessions* 13.14.15, p. 281. In 13.11, Augustine presents the triad existing-knowing-willing as an analogy for the Trinity: for discussion see Lewis Ayres, *Augustine and the Trinity* (Cambridge: Cambridge University Press, 2010), 134–38.

84. For discussion see Robert W. Bernard, "The Rhetoric of God in the Figurative Exegesis of Augustine," in *Biblical Hermeneutics in Historical Perspective: Studies in Honor of Karlfried Froehlich on His Sixtieth Birthday*, ed. Mark S. Burrows and Paul Rorem (Grand Rapids: Eerdmans, 1991), 88–99, at 89–92.

85. See Troup, *Temporality, Eternity, and Wisdom*, 127, 136.

86. Augustine, *Confessions* 13.20.28, p. 289.

87. Augustine, *Confessions* 13.21.30, p. 291.

88. See Cavadini, "Eucharistic Exegesis," 106–8.

Augustine notes that God did not create us according to our kind, but "in our [God's] image, after our likeness" (Gen. 1:26). The holy soul participates in the wisdom and will of the Trinity. As Augustine remarks, quoting St. Paul, "So man 'is renewed in the knowledge of God after the image of him who created him' (Col. 3:10)."[89] The division between male and female, for its part, images the rational soul (Augustine notes that women have "an equal capacity of rational intelligence").[90]

Caught up into the life of the Trinity, we exercise "dominion" (Gen. 1:26) by exercising spiritual judgment. This dominion is exercised by all who possess charity, without differentiation of male or female, or of bishop or layman. It is a dominion rooted in receptivity to God's will, and so our spiritual judgment receives, rather than interrogates, the words of Scripture. Similarly, we do not judge the angels. In the present life we cannot determine "which persons are spiritual and which carnal," since we do not know the plan that God has for each person.[91] What then do we judge, and how do we judge? We judge and approve what is right and disapprove what is wrong by sharing in the Church's liturgy, through the sacraments and through preaching. We also judge by approving what is right and disapproving what is wrong "in the works and behaviour of the faithful in their charitable giving."[92]

Read figuratively, the command "be fruitful and multiply" (Gen. 1:28) suggests to Augustine the many truthful meanings that can be found in one text. God encourages us to contemplate his works in their inexhaustible richness, which requires that we formulate many different concepts, guided by God's inspiration. As interpreters of Scripture, the saints bear fruit and multiply in this way. The "food" (Gen. 1:29) that God gives his holy people is the spiritual nourishment that we find in the good actions of others. Augustine counts seven times where God sees that what he has made is good, followed by an eighth time when God sees that it is "very good" (Gen. 1:31). He interprets this to mean that "particular things are good and all of them together very good," since the whole gives God glory even more than the parts.[93]

The whole that God sees is the Church that he has predestined to come to be in Christ and the Spirit. God does not see temporally, and so the eight times do not differ in God, but instead differ because "when a man sees something which is good, God in him sees that it is good. That is, God is loved in that which he has made, and he is not loved except through the Spirit which he has

---

89. Augustine, *Confessions* 13.22.32, p. 292.

90. Augustine, *Confessions* 13.32.47, p. 302. See Constance E. McLeese, "Augustinian Exegesis and Sexist Canon from the New Testament," in *Augustine and the Bible*, ed. and trans. Pamela Bright (Notre Dame, IN: University of Notre Dame Press, 1999), 282–300.

91. Augustine, *Confessions* 13.23.33, p. 293.

92. Augustine, *Confessions* 13.23.34, p. 294.

93. Augustine, *Confessions* 13.34.49, p. 303.

given."[94] The Holy Spirit healed the former Manichee Augustine, and enabled him to see that God's creation is good and that God authorizes Scripture and establishes the Church, which is ordered hierarchically and brings forth works of mercy. The Church, with its saints, sacraments, miracles, Scriptures, and ministers, is indeed very good. Yet the earthly form of the Church will pass away, so as to enter fully into the Sabbath that God has "sanctified . . . to abide everlastingly."[95]

In our earthly lives God works in us; in eternal life God will rest in us, and we in God—although God is "always working and always at rest."[96] Because God never ceases to do good, we exist and share in his life. He is peace, and we are called to share in his peace. But how can we know this peace who is the Triune God? Only, Augustine answers, through the receptivity of passionate prayer (see Matt. 7:7–8).

Conclusion

The *Confessions* argues that each and every moment of one's life, and one's life as a whole, has its true meaning in relation to the eternal living God. Augustine seeks to expand and enrich our understanding of what it means to be a historical creature, always in a state of change and always on the verge of the everlasting change that consists in handing over our being, in death, to the God whom we cannot know empirically. To understand our origin and to attain our end, we must come to realize that we have been disordered by a profound rebellion. This rebellion manifests itself in disordered desire: we seek happiness not in eternal things but in ambition, sexual pleasure, and so forth. Most important, our rebellion manifests itself in false worship. Augustine finds himself believing in astrology and worshiping a finite God who is engaged in an everlasting war with the evil forces that produced all material things.

Turning away from this rebellion requires the ability to conceive of a truly transcendent God, in whom all finite things participate. While neo-Platonic philosophy proves helpful in accomplishing this, and in resolving Augustine's imaginings about evil, nonetheless even this best philosophy does not show Augustine how to truly enter into communion with God. Only the humility of Christ reveals the path to God: he descends so that we can ascend, and our ascent comes about through imitating his humility and charity. Yet we cannot follow Christ's humility and charity by our own strength, because our desire is too disordered by sin. In order to be turned from the path of death to the path of eternal life, we require to be healed and transformed by the grace of the Holy Spirit. This requires of us an ongoing imitation of Christ's

---

94. Augustine, *Confessions* 13.31, p. 301.
95. Augustine, *Confessions* 13.36.51, p. 304.
96. Augustine, *Confessions* 13.37.52, p. 304.

self-sacrifice, where we constantly remember God's gifts to us in creation and redemption, and where we continually confess our disorder in repentant dependence upon God.

In short, as Augustine shows in his reading of Genesis, we must come to recognize our absolute dependence upon our Creator and Redeemer. We learn to live by repentance, praise, and prayer. This life is an ecclesial life, nourished by Christ's teachings and sacraments. In this life, the threat of everlasting dissolution and disintegration is replaced by the promise, in Christ, of eternal life in communion with the Father, Son, and Holy Spirit and with each other in love.

6

City of God

In a letter to his friend Firmus in which he comments on the structure of the *City of God* (composed during the years 413–26), Augustine explains that the work can either be divided into two parts or into five.[1] Divided into two parts, the work consists in ten books against the pagan gods, followed by twelve books on the origin, progress, and end of the City of God. Divided into five parts, the work consists in five books against pagan worship as beneficial for this life; five books against pagan worship (including that of the Platonists) as beneficial for the life to come; four books on the origin of the City of God; four books on its progress; and four books on its end.[2] As we will see, this

---

1. For the original audience of *City of God*, see Neil B. McLynn, "Augustine's Roman Empire," in *History, Apocalypse, and the Secular Imagination: New Essays on Augustine's* City of God, ed. Mark Vessey, Karla Pollmann, and Allan D. Fitzgerald, OSA (Bowling Green, OH: Philosophy Documentation Center, 1999), 29–44; Peter Brown, *Augustine of Hippo*, 2nd ed. (Berkeley: University of California Press, 2000), 297–305. Brown's biography presents Augustine as becoming increasingly dour as he aged, but in an epilogue added to the 2000 edition, Brown renounces this position in light of the discovery of new sermons and letters: see especially 445–47 as well as Carol Harrison, *Rethinking Augustine's Early Theology: An Argument for Continuity* (Oxford: Oxford University Press, 2006).

2. See the extract from Augustine's letter to Firmus published in Augustine, *City of God*, trans. Henry Bettenson (New York: Penguin, 1984), xxxvi. This letter was first published by C. Lambot, OSB, "Lettre inedite de S. Augustin relative au 'De civitate dei,'" *Revue Bénédictine* 51 (1939): 109–21. Gerald O'Daly follows this five-part structure in his *Augustine's* City of God: *A Reader's Guide* (Oxford: Oxford University Press, 1999), chaps. 6–10; in chap. 5 he traces the development of the work during the years of its composition. For the image of the two cities, see O'Daly, *Augustine's* City of God, chap. 4; Carol Harrison, *Augustine: Christian Truth and Fractured Humanity* (Oxford: Oxford University Press, 2000), 196–97, 206; Johannes Van Oort, *Jerusalem and Babylon: A Study into Augustine's City of God and the Sources of His Doctrine*

fivefold arrangement displays Augustine's achievement in reconfiguring history
and its ends. Beginning with the pagan worldview in which strictly immanent
gods and ends set the terms for what we can expect from historical existence,
Augustine painstakingly transforms it into a biblical understanding of history according to which our lives can only be rightly appreciated in terms of
ecclesial participation in the eternal God through Christ and the Holy Spirit.[3]

Books 1–5

In the *City of God*'s opening paragraph, Augustine states that his work will
defend the City of God and its founder—the Church and Christ Jesus—against
those who trust in pagan gods.[4] He describes the City of God as existing both
in time and in eternity, and he notes that the earthly journey of the City of
God is a difficult one because it is hard to convince "the proud of the power
and excellence of humility, an excellence which makes it soar above all the
summits of this world, which sway in their temporal instability, overtopping
them all with an eminence not arrogated by human pride, but granted by divine
grace."[5] Although it appears that the important historical agents and events
have to do with laying claim to temporal goods, in fact everything temporal
is passing away. What does not pass away is relationship with the God who is
infinite love, a relationship that requires following Christ's humility.

Augustine must explain why accepting Christianity did not prevent Rome
from being sacked by Alaric.[6] He points out that pagan history shows that

of the Two Cities (Leiden: Brill, 1991). For a standard reading of City of God, see Basil Studer,
OSB, The Grace of Christ and the Grace of God in Augustine of Hippo: Christocentrism or
Theocentrism?, trans. Matthew J. O'Connell (Collegeville, MN: Liturgical Press, 1997), 116–24.

    3. For an emphasis on the role of providence in history, similar to what I term "participa-
tory" history, see the brief study by Vernon J. Bourke, "The City of God and History," in his
Wisdom from St. Augustine (Houston: University of St. Thomas Press, 1984), 188–205. See
also the demonstration by Ernest L. Fortin, AA, that Augustine's understanding of "history"
is far from that of modern historical consciousness: Fortin, "Augustine's City of God and the
Modern Historical Consciousness," Review of Politics 41 (1979): 323–43. On the teleological
goodness of history and temporality in City of God (by contrast to their ambiguous status in
Confessions), see Ronnie J. Rombs, "Unum Deum . . . Mundi Conditorem: Implications of the
Rule of Faith in Augustine's Understanding of Time and Eternity," in Tradition and the Rule of
Faith in the Early Church: Essays in Honor of Joseph T. Lienhard, S.J., ed. Ronnie J. Rombs and
Alexander Y. Hwang (Washington, DC: Catholic University of America Press, 2010), 232–50.
    4. See Yves M.-J. Congar, OP, "'Civitas Dei' et 'Ecclesia' chez saint Augustin," Revue des
études augustiniennes 3 (1957): 1–14.
    5. Augustine, City of God 1, Preface, p. 1. In addition to Bettenson, I will also use the fol-
lowing translation: Augustine, City of God, trans. Marcus Dods, in Nicene and Post-Nicene
Fathers, 1st. ser., vol. 2 (Peabody, MA: Hendrickson, 1995). For the link with Virgil, see O'Daly,
Augustine's City of God, 75–76.
    6. Against supposing that this is the main point of the City of God, see Mary T. Clark, RSCJ,
Augustine (London: Continuum, 1994), 96.

the pagan gods were not able to protect the cities that worshiped them; nor were pagan gods able to prevent even their most fervent adherents from being slaughtered in gruesome ways. Although Augustine remarks that Alaric's soldiers spared those who took refuge in Christian basilicas, he grants that the living God allows us to suffer in history. He does so for the twin purposes of punishing the wicked and training the good to persevere. Augustine does not turn a blind eye to the terrible nature of the sufferings that we undergo; for example, he devotes significant attention to the plight of women raped by marauding soldiers. The key is to recognize that spiritual goods, not temporal goods, are the true gift of divine providence. Even death should not "be judged an evil which is the end of a good life; for death becomes evil only by the retribution which follows it."[7] This perspective, it is clear, requires affirming that meaning in this life is joined to one's relationship with God, which goes beyond this life. On this basis Augustine rules out suicide, although he understands the emotions of shame that can lead violated human beings to this action. Furthermore, the living God not only rewards the just but also punishes the unrepentant wicked in the life to come.

Having set forth a Christian understanding of innocent suffering, Augustine then turns to the history of Rome's calamities and wars. He argues that Rome's degraded worship reflects the immoral character of its gods and its own disastrous enslavement to temporal goods.[8] For example, propitiatory rites were offered annually to the Mother of the Gods in "terms so gross and immodest, that if [an estimable woman] had heard the like while alive upon earth, and had listened without stopping her ears and hurrying from the spot, her relatives, her husband, and her children would have blushed for her."[9] The Mother of the Gods was celebrated for her trickery. Thus both the goddess and her worshipers were known for lust and manipulation. The Romans constructed gods in their own worst image, and then they used those gods to justify their vicious behavior while at the same time openly mocking the behavior of the gods. Indeed, as Augustine shows, the gods and their worshipers behaved in the same fashion, rejecting virtue out of disordered desire for temporal pleasure and power. The gods regularly were depicted as fighting, cheating, lying, committing adultery, murdering their children, playing favorites, refusing to punish crimes, and so forth. As for Rome, Augustine shows that far from embodying the justice requisite for a true commonwealth, it too engaged in these practices and lived under a cloud of almost constant warfare rather than peace.[10]

7. Augustine, *City of God* 1.11, trans. Dods, p. 9.

8. See Robert Dodaro, OSA, "*Christus sacerdos*: Augustine's Polemic Against Roman Pagan Priesthoods in *De ciuitate Dei*," *Augustinianum* 33 (1993): 101–35.

9. Augustine, *City of God* 2.5, trans. Dods, p. 25.

10. See O'Daly, *Augustine's* City of God, 84; Robert Dodaro, *Christ and the Just Society in the Thought of Augustine* (Cambridge: Cambridge University Press, 2004), chap. 1.

Augustine also observes that the number of the gods worshiped by the Romans quickly became ludicrous. As in a human city, a god was needed for every task, so that even the growth of corn required, by Augustine's count, the overseeing labor of eight gods and goddesses. Greater gods such as Jupiter, Juno, Neptune, and Pluto supposedly occupied different realms of the spatial universe. The point is that all such gods are no more than a reflection of the spatiotemporal realm, which they transcend no more than we do. This remains the case even if one supposes that all the gods are simply instantiations or modes of the one god, Jupiter. The very fact that the Romans consider many gods to be needed indicates that their imagination understands divinity in a spatiotemporal manner, and therefore merely as a mirror of human beings. Otherwise, as Augustine notes, they could simply worship the one God.

Augustine goes on to critique the supposition that Jupiter requires to be worshiped under many instantiations and that worshiping only Jupiter would offend the other parts of Jupiter. Why would not worshiping Jupiter alone necessarily mean worshiping his parts? And how could one succeed in worshiping all his parts adequately (for example, the stars)? Similarly, the view that Jupiter is the world-soul runs into the problem that everything is therefore part of God, with the result that killing an ant would mean killing a part of God—or if not an ant, then at least when one spanks a child, one spanks God. If Jupiter is the world-soul and rational beings have Jupiter as their soul, then it also follows that Jupiter's parts "can become lustful, unjust, irreligious, and utterly worthy of condemnation."[11] Jupiter can hardly be angry when his own parts do not worship him. Rather than accept such conclusions, it is better to accept the worship of the gods on its own terms and assume that numerous gods exist, with their distinct realms and responsibilities.

As an example of the utterly anthropomorphic character of the gods, Augustine observes that the Romans have made Victory into a goddess. If Victory favors Rome, he asks, what need to propitiate Jupiter? The presence of Victory in the pantheon leads to the question, Why should increase in the size of the empire necessarily be celebrated? After all, even when a just war increases the empire's size, this war arises from the injustice of the people against whom the war was waged. The injustice of others causes no celebration. Does not the goddess Victory depend upon the prior work of injustice, in which case why should not Rome worship Injustice as a goddess? The making of goddesses included ones named Virtue, Faith, Modesty, and Felicity. As interior characteristics of good persons, these "goddesses" undermine the very notion of goddesses and instead direct us to seek God's gifts. Augustine imagines what might have happened had the Romans sought to worship Felicity alone and thereby learned how truly to seek happiness from the one God who alone can make us happy. Yet even the great Roman historian Varro supposes that

---

11. Augustine, *City of God* 4.13, p. 153.

he does the Romans a favor by listing all the gods and goddesses, with their specific functions.

Augustine's view is that the gods, insofar as they have any existence at all, must be demons. This would explain why the worship of the gods seems to encourage every vice and act of impiety. Philosophically erudite Romans such as Cicero sought to worship, in Stoic fashion, "the order of nature which is organized under the rule and government of the one true God."[12] Varro, who decried the introduction of images into Roman worship, believed God to be the world-soul. As Augustine points out, such worship still falls short of the mark, since only the transcendent God deserves worship. But even such worship failed to sway the great majority of the population, who continued to embrace the rites of many gods and goddesses. Only the living God, through the humility of Christ who reveals the eternal meaning of God's promises to Israel, could overcome both the superstitions of the Roman populace and the nature-worship of the philosophers.

If God is one and transcends the temporal order, then God governs the universe. Why then did God permit idolatrous worship to run rampant in Rome, and why did God allow the Roman Empire to flourish? Augustine observes that, within the Roman understanding of the gods as spatiotemporal agents, the common answers to questions about why certain things happen in history were either chance or astrological destiny. Augustine dismisses chance, because it denies that rational causality governs the universe and therefore denies the place of divinity altogether. What about the view, held by Stoic philosophers and others, that God deputizes the stars to determine sublunar events? Augustine points out that this determinism would mean that the stars "decreed the commission of crimes so abominable that if any earthly state had decreed them, its own destruction would have been decreed by the whole of humanity."[13] Against those who hold simply that the stars predict rather than cause events, he asks how twins, conceived at the same moment, can have such dissimilar fates.

Pressing further into the notion of destiny, Augustine takes up the Stoic view that God (Jupiter) wills an inexorable chain of causes. Cicero opposed this view and denied divine foreknowledge of events.[14] Given his understanding of God as an agent within the cosmic order, Cicero rightly held that divine foreknowledge would destroy human freedom and necessitate fatalism. Augustine argues that we do not need to choose between divine foreknowledge and human freedom. Nothing happens by fate, and yet the will of God governs the entirety of history. The transcendent God creates the order of finite causes, in which he includes the creation of free, rational agents. As eternal, God embraces and

12. Augustine, *City of God* 4.29, p. 172.
13. Augustine, *City of God* 5.1, p. 180.
14. See O'Daly, *Augustine's* City of God, 96–97.

knows all time, which is his creature. Augustine insists that our wills are true causes. Yet it is by God's will that we have free will, and it is by God's will that our freedom is perfected in choosing the good: "it is with his help that we are, or shall be, free."[15] Participation in the will of a finite god would indeed destroy our freedom, as Cicero recognizes, because the two wills would be on the same ontological plane. Participation in the will of the transcendent God, by contrast, makes possible our freedom, because he wills it.

Augustine moves from the notion of fate to the question of the greatness of Rome. This greatness was due not to fate but to the moral character of the Romans, especially at the outset of Rome's rise to power. The early Romans focused entirely on acquiring glory. At first they sought to gain glory in liberty; later they sought to gain glory by exercising dominion over other peoples. During the period in which they established their greatness, their thirst for glory prevented them from falling into pleasure-seeking or greed. Their greatness consisted in their devotion to personal and communal honor. Desiring to be honored, the leaders of Rome had sufficient personal virtue to enable Rome to thrive.[16]

Certainly Augustine considers love of praise to be a deadly vice. But when people worship temporal gods, people cannot conceive of a transcendent God in whom they participate and from whom they receive eternal happiness. Their worship ruled out truly divine agency, and so Roman heroes "were in an earthly city, and had before them, as the end of all the offices undertaken in its behalf, its safety, and a kingdom, not in heaven, but in earth."[17] Since they could not hope for a glorious eternal reward, it was hardly blameworthy that they hoped for a glorious earthly reward. Augustine comments sympathetically, "What else but glory should they love, by which they wished even after death to live in the mouths of admirers?"[18] If one can only pursue temporal goods, glory and honor are the least debasing goods that one can pursue. Having shown their worship of temporally bound gods, Augustine thus demonstrates that their greatness arose from choosing the best possible good available given

15. Augustine, *City of God* 5.10, p. 195. See David C. Schindler, "Freedom Beyond Our Choosing: Augustine on the Will and Its Objects," in *Augustine and Politics*, ed. John Doody, Kevin L. Hughes, and Kim Paffenroth (Lanham, MD: Lexington Books, 2005), 67–96; Mary T. Clark, *Augustine: Philosopher of Freedom* (New York: Desclee, 1958).

16. See Dodaro, *Christ and the Just Society*, 183–86; John von Heyking, *Augustine and Politics as Longing in the World* (Columbia: University of Missouri Press, 2001), 25–28, 38–40, 150–71. For Augustine's use of the Roman historian Sallust here and elsewhere in *City of God*, see Paul C. Burns, "Augustine's Use of Sallust in the *City of God*: The Role of the Grammatical Tradition," in *History, Apocalypse, and the Secular Imagination*, 105–14; O'Daly, *Augustine's City of God*, 240–46; Peter Busch, "On the Use and Disadvantage of History for the Afterlife," in *Augustine and History*, ed. Christopher T. Daly, John Doody, and Kim Paffenroth (Lanham, MD: Lexington Books, 2008), 3–30, at 21–23.

17. Augustine, *City of God* 5.14, trans. Dods, p. 97.

18. Augustine, *City of God* 5.14, trans. Dods, p. 97.

a conception of history as lacking a participation in the eternal. Seeking an earthly reward, the Romans received what they sought.

The tragedy of Rome is that its understanding of history, and of the divine, was faulty and cut many Romans off from true happiness, which comes only from God. Augustine draws two lessons: God's providence justly allowed the Roman Empire to increase, and God intended that those who seek a heavenly reward within the heavenly city should be inspired to an increase of fervor, humility, and endurance by seeing how devotedly these citizens of the earthly city pursued a merely earthly reward. Even the Christian martyrs cannot boast in their deeds, for they do for an eternal reward what many Romans did for an incomparably lesser earthly reward. Indeed, Christians should be ashamed if we do not outdo the Romans in great deeds. Before moving on, Augustine carefully distinguishes desire for glory from desire for domination; the latter does not require real honor from others, and so it is selfish and cruel. Augustine also remarks that it is unseemly that the virtues be put to the service of earthly glory, since such glory is ultimately no more than "empty conceit."[19] Lastly, he notes that God's governance has included upholding Christian Rome as well as allowing it to suffer, and he names Constantine and Theodosius as examples of praiseworthy Christian emperors. Theodosius, who submitted to public penance for having approved a massacre in Thessalonica, rightly valued being a member of the Church more than he valued being ruler of the world.[20]

Books 6–10

Augustine recognizes that he needs to treat in more detail the philosophers who, despite rejecting popular stories about the gods and attaining to some true insights about God, nonetheless advocate the worship of the gods as conducive to everlasting life. He respects the erudition of Marcus Varro, a friend of Cicero, and Varro is among those who encourage the worship of the gods. More important, Augustine has profound admiration for the writings

19. Augustine, *City of God* 5.21, p. 215. See Catherine Conybeare, "*Terrarum Orbi Documentum*: Augustine, Camillus, and Learning from History," in *History, Apocalypse, and the Secular Imagination*, 59–74, at 72–73; Thomas W. Smith, "The Glory and Tragedy of Politics," in *Augustine and Politics*, 187–213, at 193–97.

20. For discussion see Robert Dodaro, OSA, "Eloquent Lies, Just Wars and the Politics of Persuasion: Reading Augustine's *City of God* in a 'Postmodern' World," *Augustinian Studies* 25 (1994): 77–138, at 92–94; Dodaro, "Augustine's Revision of the Heroic Ideal," *Augustinian Studies* 36 (2005): 141–57; Robert A. Markus, "'Tempora Christiana' Revisited," in *Augustine and His Critics*, 201–13. See also Eric Gregory, *Politics and the Order of Love: An Augustinian Ethic of Democratic Citizenship* (Chicago: University of Chicago Press, 2008), chap. 2; Robert A. Markus, *Saeculum: History and Society in the Theology of St. Augustine*, 2nd ed. (Cambridge: Cambridge University Press, 1988); Markus, *Christianity and the Secular* (Notre Dame, IN: University of Notre Dame Press, 2006).

of the neo-Platonists, despite his equally deep critique of their position. He also wishes to comment in passing on Hermetic religion and on Stoic doctrine in general, although his focus is on the neo-Platonists. The second five books of the *City of God*, in short, discuss the approaches from within pagan philosophy that are closest to understanding history as not solely temporal but as participating in the transcendent and eternal.

Discussing Varro's theological writings, Augustine first notes that Varro treats human institutions prior to divine matters, with the resulting implication that the gods are human constructs (according to Augustine, Varro suggests that this is the case). Varro criticizes the popular stories about the gods, examines the role of the gods in the life of the city, and treats various theories about the nature of the gods proposed by Heraclitus, Pythagoras, Epicurus, and so forth. Augustine argues that Varro intends only the philosophers' theories about the nature of the gods to be taken seriously as theology, but even so Varro affirms the importance of the gods for the city (and thus also the importance of the stories, which Varro interprets as symbolizing natural phenomena, that undergird popular devotion).[21] Augustine finds the same support of natural theology, and a much stronger criticism of the city's encouragement of the stories about the gods, in the Stoic philosopher Seneca's *Against Superstitions*. Yet Seneca continued to worship the gods and attacked the religious practices of the Jews. In Varro's natural theology, sometimes Janus or Tellus is the world and Jupiter is the one who brings the world to fulfillment; in other places Varro identifies Jupiter as the world-soul. Varro discusses numerous other "select" gods, who seem to be either the world or parts of the world. Thus Varro firmly believed that the "vast structure of nature is ruled and directed by some invisible force," but he has no idea what that force might be, and his defense of the gods simply perpetuates the superstitions that the city deemed necessary for deluding and manipulating the populace.[22]

A better path, Augustine says, is to give up such gods and instead to worship the true Creator God. God's transcendence enables him to act freely in the world and to accomplish those things that Varro attributes to gods bound by spatiotemporal limitations. Augustine describes "the one true God who is active and operative in all those things, but always acting as God, that is, present everywhere in his totality, free from all spatial confinement, completely untrammeled, absolutely indivisible, utterly unchangeable, and filling heaven and earth with his ubiquitous power."[23] All things participate in the one true God, and some creatures participate freely: God "governs all things in such a manner as to allow them to perform and exercise their own proper movements. For although they can be nothing without him, they are not what he is."[24]

21. On Varro, see O'Daly, *Augustine's* City of God, 101–9, 236–38.
22. Augustine, *City of God* 7.17, p. 275.
23. Augustine, *City of God* 7.30, p. 292.
24. Augustine, *City of God* 7.30, trans. Dods, p. 140.

Only this Creator God, who sends us his Word when we were blinded by sin, gives eternal life. This gift is made known by progressive revelation, first through angels, then through the calling of Israel and the giving of the law and the prophecies that Christ fulfills. The humility of Christ frees humankind from the pride of worshiping creatures rather than the Creator. Augustine here presents a fully participatory understanding of history as the solution to Varro's insistence upon worship of the gods as necessary (even to the point of intentionally deluding the populace) for the flourishing of the human city. True human flourishing requires a theological account of time and eternity, of the Creator God's reaching out to blinded humans and inviting us to share in his very life. God desires to free us from superstitious delusions and to enable us to affirm the true religion.

Varro's theology allows that we participate in the world-soul, but the neo-Platonists go much further. Although they too encourage the worship of the gods, they teach a profoundly participatory vision of reality. Augustine inquires at length into whether their theology suffices. As we will see, he argues that their theology is insufficiently rooted in temporal history. They fail to recognize the intersection of participatory and linear-temporal history, as revealed preeminently by Israel's Messiah.

Augustine observes that the neo-Platonists "acknowledge God as existing above all that is of the nature of soul, and as the Creator not only of this visible world, which is often called heaven and earth, but also of every soul whatsoever, and as him who gives blessedness to the rational soul . . . by participation in his own unchangeable and incorporeal light."[25] How did this understanding of human life arise in the pagan world? Augustine begins with Pythagoras and Thales, and after tracing Thales's successors he arrives at Socrates, whose concern was morality rather than natural science.[26] Augustine considers that Socrates was motivated by the necessity of purifying one's life before prying into the causes of the universe (ultimately God). As Augustine puts it, Socrates intended that the soul, "delivered from the depressing weight of lusts, might raise itself upward by its native vigor to eternal things, and might, with purified understanding, contemplate that nature which is incorporeal and unchangeable light, where live the causes of all created natures."[27]

Socrates's followers, says Augustine, focused on the problem of identifying the highest good, that which makes us happy. Among his followers, Plato and his successors (whom Augustine calls "Platonists") united practical and contemplative inquiry, with the result that the Platonists were able to identify God as the transcendent "author of the universe, the source of the light of truth, and the bestower of happiness."[28] Arguing that the Platonists supersede the earlier

25. Augustine, *City of God* 8.1, trans. Dods, p. 144.
26. For the sources of Augustine's account of Socrates and Plato, see O'Daly, *Augustine's* City of God, 111–15.
27. Augustine, *City of God* 8.3, trans. Dods, p. 146.
28. Augustine, *City of God* 8.5, p. 306.

thinkers (Varro, the Stoics, and so forth) whose conceptions were bound to the spatiotemporal framework, Augustine applauds this breakthrough to an understanding of reality in which everything finite participates in God without being God. Through an intellectual ascent, beginning with material things and rising to God, the Platonists arrive at the doctrines of the transcendent God, the participation of all finite things in God, and the enjoyment of God as the highest good (the happiness) of the rational creature.

Augustine explains the existence of such good philosophy by reference to Paul's statement in Romans 1:19–20, "For what can be known about God is plain to them, because God has shown it to them. Ever since the creation of the world his invisible nature, namely, his eternal power and deity, has been clearly perceived in the things that have been made."[29] He also quotes Paul's statement in Acts 17:28, "'In him we live and move and have our being'; as even some of your poets have said." Yet in both cases, as Augustine notes, Paul goes on to urge repentance. The apostle to the gentiles underscores that the gentiles have offered false worship and have fallen into the sin of pride. Augustine states that the Platonists, and any other philosophers who share their views, share with Christians in the true knowledge of God. Regarding Plato himself, Augustine thinks it possible that he was acquainted with the contents of the books of Moses, at least so far as to understand God as "I AM" (Exod. 3:14). Although Plato knows truth about God and rejects degrading stories about the gods, however, not only Plato but also his followers such as Plotinus, Iamblichus, and Porphyry worship the gods. Debating especially with Apuleius of Madaura and the *Hermetica*, Augustine argues that the worship of gods amounts to demon worship, whereas the nobler impulses of such worship are reflected in the honor (not worship) that Christians pay to holy angels and martyrs.

Augustine also devotes some energy to arguing against Apuleius that there are no good "demons," *pace* Socrates's testimony that he was influenced by a good "demon" who mediated between him and the gods (in this regard, Plotinus agrees with Augustine). Augustine's purpose here is to lay the groundwork for discussion of the mediation of Christ, the one mediator between humans and God. He states that although Christ is mediator in his humanity, nonetheless "that Mediator in whom we can participate, and by participation reach our felicity, is the uncreated Word of God, by whom all things were created."[30] By taking on human nature, the divine Word enables us to partake in his own divine nature. The blessed in heaven participate not in the angels but in the "Trinity, in which the angels participate, and so achieve their felicity."[31] Augustine rejects the Platonic notion that divinity would be defiled by contact

29. For this natural but insufficient knowledge of the Creator, see Carol Harrison, *Beauty and Revelation in the Thought of Saint Augustine* (Oxford: Clarendon, 1992), 112–16, 195–96.
30. Augustine, *City of God* 9.15, p. 361.
31. Augustine, *City of God* 9.15, p. 361.

with humanity. Yet he grants that fallen humanity cannot draw close to God without being purified of sinful cleaving to creatures rather than to God.

For this reason the divine Word becomes man, but without sin. His holy actions establish the righteous and beautiful path upon which we can be united to God, who gives us happiness by giving us, in and through Christ and the Holy Spirit, "a share in his own being."[32] Augustine praises Christ's sacrifice and explains that in the Eucharist "the whole redeemed city, that is to say, the congregation or community of the saints, is offered to God as our sacrifice through the great High Priest, who offered himself to God in his passion for us, that we might be members of this glorious head."[33] This worship is offered solely to God, not to angels. Augustine here argues at length with Porphyry, especially Porphyry's approval of theurgic rites aimed at communion with angels and gods.[34] The angels themselves, Augustine observes, direct our worship toward God alone, according to Scripture. He treats the angels' role in the giving of the Torah and in the miracles by which God confirms his promises. The Old Testament sacrifices symbolize the efficacious sacrifice of Christ, in which the Church participates through the Eucharist. No other sacrifice, including those erroneously offered by the theurgists, is needed.

Augustine also takes up the neo-Platonist teachings on the "principles": the One, the Intellect, and the world-soul. Augustine states that there is in fact only one "principle," God, who is Father, Son, and Holy Spirit. For Porphyry, purification comes only from the "principles," but Porphyry rejected faith in Christ. Attributing Porphyry's position to a disdain for the flesh, Augustine emphasizes that only sin, not incarnation, is unworthy of God. The "principle," the Word, takes on sinless flesh in order to purify all those who are in the flesh; his death pays the penalty of sin for all of us because he does not owe the penalty. By faith, which is God's gift, humans—including a number who lived before Christ—receive this purification and are sanctified unto eternal life. The holy angels invite us to become their "fellow-citizens" in the "most glorious City of God, which knows and worships one God."[35]

As Augustine goes on to say, Porphyry also imagines that as a philosopher he does not need the purification supposedly offered by the theurgic rites; they are only for lesser minds. This pride indicates how badly Porphyry has miscalculated his situation: "Would that you had known him [Christ], and would that you had committed yourself for healing to him rather than to your

32. Augustine, *City of God* 9.23, p. 370.
33. Augustine, *City of God* 10.6, trans. Dods, p. 184.
34. See Robert Dodaro, OSA, "*Christus sacerdos*: Augustine's Preaching Against Pagan Priests in the Light of *S. Dolbeau* 26 and 23," in *Augustin prédicateur (395–411)*, ed. Goulven Madec (Paris: Études augustiniennes, 1998), 377–93; Eugene TeSelle, *Augustine the Theologian* (New York: Herder and Herder, 1970), 237–41.
35. Augustine, *City of God* 10.25, p. 408.

own frail and infirm human virtue, or to pernicious and curious arts!"[36] It is no wonder, says Augustine, that so many persons flock to Christ, whereas Porphyry's theurgy has almost no adherents. What would cure Porphyry is to recognize the humility of Christ as the true path, the path of divine grace, by which proud humans are purified. The wisdom of Christ leads to true worship and eternal life, whereas the erudition of Porphyry leads to boasting and theurgic communion with demons. Augustine adds that Porphyry errs by supposing that happiness requires escape from the body, despite Porphyry's own view that the stars are eternally blessed beings living in corporeal forms. Similarly Porphyry errs in accepting the doctrine of reincarnation and at the same time imagining that the purpose of the soul's embodiment is to teach the soul to flee forever from the evils of the material world, rather than to do good. Again, Porphyry errs about the soul's beginning and end, for he thinks that the soul is coeternal with God and the gods, and he denies that God has shown the way for the liberation of souls. Christ Jesus, fulfilling God's covenants and promises, is the way.

Indeed, the fundamental error that Porphyry, like other Platonists, makes is to neglect God's action in history.[37] Augustine lauds the Platonists for their discovery of the participation of every finite reality, and especially rational creatures, in the transcendent and eternal God. Pagan worship of spatiotemporal gods (or at best the world-soul) left them solely with this-worldly ends. This understanding of human life produced Rome, the greatest earthly city, because Roman citizens at their best devoted themselves at great personal cost to gaining honor and glory in the eyes of their compatriots and of future

36. Augustine, *City of God* 10.27, trans. Dods, p. 197.
37. Phillip Cary argues that Augustine himself denigrates this reality. See Cary, *Outward Signs: The Powerlessness of External Things in Augustine's Thought* (Oxford: Oxford University Press, 2008); Cary, *Augustine's Invention of the Inner Self: The Legacy of a Christian Platonist* (Oxford: Oxford University Press, 2000). For related views, see Stephen Menn, *Descartes and Augustine* (Cambridge: Cambridge University Press, 1998); Charles Taylor, *Sources of the Self* (Cambridge, MA: Harvard University Press, 1989); Olivier du Roy, *L'Intelligence de la foi en la Trinité selon saint Augustin* (Paris: Études augustiniennes, 1966). Against views such as these, see John C. Cavadini, "The Darkest Enigma: Reconsidering the Self in Augustine's Thought," *Augustinian Studies* 38 (2007): 119–32; Studer, *Grace of Christ*, 14–65; Lewis Ayres, "The Christological Context of the *De Trinitate* XIII: Toward Relocating Books VIII–XV," *Augustinian Studies* 29 (1998): 111–39; Robert Dodaro, OSA, "'Omnes haeretici negant Christum in carne venisse' (Aug., serm. 183.9.13): Augustine on the Incarnation as Criterion for Orthodoxy," *Augustinian Studies* 38 (2007): 163–74; Luigi Gioia, OSB, *The Theological Epistemology of Augustine's* De Trinitate (Oxford: Oxford University Press, 2008), especially chaps. 3–4; David V. Meconi, SJ, "The Incarnation and the Role of Participation in St. Augustine's *Confessions*," *Augustinian Studies* 29 (1998): 61–75; Michael Hanby, *Augustine and Modernity* (London: Routledge, 2003), chap. 2; Calvin L. Troup, *Temporality, Eternity, and Wisdom: The Rhetoric of Augustine's Confessions* (Columbia: University of South Carolina Press, 1999), 74–77, 176–78. For background to the longstanding debate about neo-Platonism in Augustine's theology, see Robert Crouse, "*Paucis mutatis verbis*: St Augustine's Platonism," in *Augustine and His Critics: Essays in Honour of Gerald Bonner*, ed. Robert Dodaro and George Lawless (London: Routledge, 2000), 37–50.

generations. The Platonists radically changed the understanding of history available to pagans: the primary meaning of human words and deeds now became their relationship to the eternal and transcendent God. Yet the Platonists erred by going too far in the other extreme and neglecting history's role in human salvation.

Scripture records a history in which God acts to reveal himself and to establish a community of holy worship—the City of God.[38] Augustine therefore ends his discussion of pagan worship and pagan philosophy with a summary of this biblical history: Abraham "was by birth a Chaldaean; but, that he might receive these great promises, and that there might be propagated from him a seed 'disposed by angels in the hand of a Mediator,' in whom this universal way, thrown open to all nations for the deliverance of the soul, might be found, he was ordered to leave his country, and kindred, and father's house."[39] This history involves the formation of the Jewish people, the tabernacle/temple and the priesthood/sacrifices, the "mystic symbolism" and the miraculous coming of the mediator in the flesh, Christ's Pasch and the apostolic preaching.[40] It will proceed to the resurrection of the dead, the last judgment, and the everlasting dwelling of the saints in beatific communion with the Holy Trinity.

Porphyry's esteem of the soul but neglect of the body, Augustine suggests, is similar to Porphyry's esteem of our participation in God but neglect of the embodied history in which this participation has actually been accomplished. In response to Porphyry's view that "the universal way for the soul's liberation" has not been found, Augustine asks: "Yet what could be found more striking than this historical record, which has taken possession of the whole world by its towering authority; or what more worthy of belief, seeing that in this record the events of the past are so narrated as to be also prophecies of the future?"[41] Scripture provides the key to understanding history aright, thanks to God's reaching out to us in the humble humanity of Christ.

Books 11–14

Books 1–5 showed that the worship of anthropomorphic gods tragically constricted human ends, while Books 6–10 argued that the best pagan philosophy, that of Plato and his followers, recognized the eternal and transcendent God in whose wisdom and beauty everything participates but failed to appreciate

38. For the contrast between Augustine's theology of the two cities (differentiated by their love) and neo-Platonic and Eusebian hierarchical view of the ideal earthly city as foreshadowing the heavenly state, see Dominic J. O'Meara, *Platonopolis: Platonic Political Philosophy in Late Antiquity* (Oxford: Oxford University Press, 2003), 154–58.

39. Augustine, *City of God* 10.32, trans. Dods, p. 203.

40. Augustine, *City of God* 10.32, p. 423.

41. Augustine, *City of God* 10.32, p. 424.

the true path to participation in God—namely, the embodied path of Christ's humility. Books 11–14 turn to the roots of the Christian understanding of history, Scripture's teaching that God is the Creator. What is included in this biblical understanding of reality as created?

For Augustine, Scripture, while written by humans, "is manifestly due to the guiding power of God's supreme providence, and exercises sovereign authority over the literature of all mankind."[42] Scripture proclaims that God wills humans to enter into communion with him. Those who, by the grace of God, love God above all things compose his eternal City. Yet the human mind and heart have turned away from God, so that we are in desperate need of renewal. The path to the City of God is the humility that comes from the mediator who is the Word incarnate. Since God makes us in his image, humans can know by philosophical reasoning that God exists and that everything else is God's creation. But without renewal and elevation by grace, humans cannot know how God intends for us to be united to him. The mediator is the path, and God teaches us about this path through Scripture, which consists of "writings of outstanding authority in which we put our trust concerning those things which we need to know for our good, and yet are incapable of discovering for ourselves."[43] These things are the realities of creation and salvation.

The world has a temporal beginning. Augustine explains that time and space did not exist prior to the creation of the world; there was simply God's eternal presence. He tries to understand the nature of the "days" (morning/evening) prior to the creation of the sun, and he argues that they have to do with the relationship of the creature to the Creator (and perhaps also with the angels). Likewise he interprets God's Sabbath rest as having to do with creation's goal of eternal rest in God. He reflects upon the difference between God and creatures, including the attribute of simplicity and the distinction between divine begetting and divine creating. He asks about the original happiness of the angels and about the fall of some angels by their free will. He inquires into the vast diversity of beings found in creation. Only God can create, and he creates everything good. He "turns evil choices to good use," so that everything ultimately enhances the beauty of creation.[44] Since God is not temporal, he comprehends the entire course of history "in a stable and eternal present."[45] The reason for the coming forth of all created things is God's goodness. Plato too identifies God's goodness as the cause of things,

42. Augustine, *City of God* 11.1, p. 429.
43. Augustine, *City of God* 11.3, p. 431. For Augustine's interpretation of difficult passages, see also 11.33, p. 469; 15.23, p. 638. On the literal and spiritual senses, see 13.21, pp. 534–35; 15.2, p. 597; 17.3, p. 715.
44. Augustine, *City of God* 11.17, p. 449. See Rowan Williams, "Insubstantial Evil," in *Augustine and His Critics*, 105–23, at 114–16.
45. Augustine, *City of God* 11.21, p. 452.

and Augustine notes that Plato either gained this insight from Genesis or from reasoning about the created order, since the insight is available in both ways.

The conclusion that God made the world through the Word because God is good leads Augustine to reflection on the trinitarian character of creation. The City of God receives everything from God: "If we inquire whence it [the City] is, God created it; or whence its wisdom, God illumined it; or whence its blessedness, God is its bliss. It has its form by subsisting in him; its enlightenment by contemplating him; its joy by abiding in him. . . . In God's eternity is its life; in God's truth its light; in God's goodness its joy."[46] Human beings share in the Trinity as the image of God, even though this image now needs to be renewed. Here Augustine reflects upon our existence and our knowledge and love of our existence; we thus reflect the divine trinity of "eternity, truth, and love."[47]

The fall of some of the angels inaugurates the distinction between the two cities. Augustine emphasizes, however, that we should not think of the devil as God's opposite. Only nonexistence is contrary to God, who is infinite existence. Physical and moral defect in being lessens a finite being's participation in God without destroying such participation entirely. Moral evil, by which the creature falls away from its true good, is caused by the creature's free will rather than by God. Augustine holds that God created humans six thousand years ago, in accordance with his eternal plan of creation, and that prior to the creation of humans, innumerable ages passed. He rejects the view that history repeats itself in endless cycles or that heaven, once attained, can be lost. God creates the human race as a social species, but wills that all humans come from one individual so as to "teach mankind to preserve a harmonious unity in plurality."[48] From eternity God knows that humans will divide into the two cities established by the angels.

Augustine then explores human death, which he describes as following upon original sin as a punishment.[49] Death is an evil, not an advantageous escape from the body. Because Christ pays the penalty of death for all humans, Augustine can distinguish between first death and second death. The latter occurs when we die without being united to Christ in faith and love, a situation that deprives the person of everlasting life with the Triune God. As Augustine recognizes, fallen life is a continual journey toward death, a continual dying.

---

46. Augustine, *City of God* 11.24, trans. Dods, p. 219.

47. Augustine, *City of God* 11.28, p. 463. For discussion see Lewis Ayres, *Augustine and the Trinity* (Cambridge: Cambridge University Press, 2010), 277–80.

48. Augustine, *City of God* 12.28, p. 508; cf. 13.3, p. 512. For discussion see Rombs, *"Unum Deum . . . Mundi Conditorem,"* 248–50.

49. See John C. Cavadini, "Ambrose and Augustine *De bono mortis,*" in *The Limits of Ancient Christianity: Essays on Late Antique Thought and Culture in Honor of R. A. Markus,* ed. William E. Klingshirn and Mark Vessey (Ann Arbor: University of Michigan Press, 1999), 232–49. On original sin, see Burnell, *Augustinian Person,* 81–83.

What Augustine here treats is the dissolution, in part, of the relationship between humans and God. Sin wounds this relationship. Christ alone can heal this wound; we are all wounded by Adam's fall, because the original harmonious relationship was destroyed. Christ not only heals the wound but also raises the bodies of the just in a state of glory, so that our bodies fully share, in union with our souls, in the everlasting happiness of communion with the Trinity. The participation of the soul in God is not weighed down by the body per se; rather, such participation is weakened, as experience shows, only by "bodies which are corruptible, burdensome, oppressive, and in a dying state."[50] Augustine discusses at some length Paul's teaching that, for those in Christ, the risen body will be a "spiritual body" (1 Cor. 15:44). The key is the saints' participation in Christ. Christ breathes the Holy Spirit upon the disciples (see John 20:22), and by the grace of the Holy Spirit the bodies of those who are in Christ will, in the resurrection, "be spiritual and immortal in virtue of the presence of a life-giving spirit."[51]

Not all, however, receive this healing and deifying participation in Christ and his Spirit. Augustine reflects further upon sin, by which the human race loses its original harmonious participation in God. Against Platonic and Manichean views of the body, he emphasizes that the body cannot be blamed for causing the first sin. Indeed, the devil, who has no body, is the greatest sinner. Sin consists in a cleaving to self rather than cleaving to God, in living according to "man's standard" rather than God's.[52] Living according to God's standard means possessing a rightly ordered will, so that one desires and chooses the good that truly makes one happy, as Adam and Eve joyfully did before the fall. Against the Stoics, Augustine defends the passions, which are good when united with a good will.[53] He notes that sin does not entirely corrupt the sinner, who continues to participate in God ontologically and therefore to be lovable; but sin lessens the sinner's participation in God, and so sin is hateful and destructive. As Augustine says, "Man did not so fall away as to become absolutely nothing; but being turned towards himself, his being became more contracted than it was when he cleaved to him who supremely is."[54]

The first humans, prior to sin, were free to avoid sin. Once the "first evil will" arises—"a kind of falling away from the work of God to its own works"—the human will becomes "the slave of vices and sins" and is not fully free.[55] True

---

50. Augustine, *City of God* 13.17, p. 528. Augustine does not hold that embodiment was caused by an original fall of souls. See Ronnie J. Rombs, *Saint Augustine and the Fall of the Soul: Beyond O'Connell and His Critics* (Washington, DC: Catholic University of America Press, 2006), especially 203–5.

51. Augustine, *City of God* 13.24, p. 545. See O'Daly, *Augustine's* City of God, 153.

52. Augustine, *City of God* 14.4, p. 553.

53. See O'Daly, *Augustine's* City of God, 154–58.

54. Augustine, *City of God* 14.13, trans. Dods, p. 273.

55. Augustine, *City of God* 14.11, trans. Dods, pp. 271–72.

freedom depends upon right relationship with God, because freedom is for attaining the good that makes us happy. When we turn away from divine love, we lose the freedom fully to give ourselves to others in love. Our fallen wills cannot restore us to relationship with God. Rather, we need God to heal our fallen wills. A bad will is "against nature," unnatural; we need God to heal our nature.[56] Here Augustine reflects on humility, which (paradoxically) exalts the soul by subjecting it to God in love. Pride is a rejection of the participatory character of human existence. Augustine concludes, "This then is the original evil: man regards himself as his own light, and turns away from that light which would make man himself a light if he would set his heart on it."[57] The just punishment of this sin is the weakening of human participation in God: "he who in his pride had pleased himself was by God's justice handed over to himself."[58]

To be handed over to oneself means to be handed over to interior rebellion, with death as the ultimate result. As examples of how the body dangerously becomes its own law after the fall, Augustine examines sexual lust and sexual shame (the covering of the sexual organs and the desire for privacy in sexual intercourse). He makes clear, however, that marriage and procreation are not the result of the fall.[59] Furthermore, the resulting situation of rampant sin does not overcome God's providential plan for bringing about the City of God, the communion of rational creatures in the trinitarian life. Augustine remarks that "evils are so thoroughly overcome by good, that though they are permitted to exist, for the sake of demonstrating how the most righteous foresight of God can make a good use even of them, yet good can exist without evil."[60] By no means does the post-Manichean Augustine think that good and evil are two opposing principles on the same ontological level. Evil is parasitic on good, and God permits evil not due to powerlessness but due to his providential plan for the saints.

In short, Augustine's analysis of creation and fall shows that the earthly city, which was created "by the love of self, even to the contempt of God,"[61] turns away from participation in God and seeks happiness strictly in the linear

56. Augustine, *City of God* 14.13, p. 572.

57. Augustine, *City of God* 14.13, p. 573. For discussion see Studer, *Grace of Christ*, 50–52; William S. Babcock, "The Human and the Angelic Fall: Will and Moral Agency in Augustine's *City of God*," in *Augustine: From Rhetor to Theologian*, ed. Joanne McWilliam (Waterloo, Ontario: Wilfrid Laurier University Press, 1992), 133–49.

58. Augustine, *City of God* 14.15, p. 575.

59. See John Cavadini, "Feeling Right: Augustine on the Passions and Sexual Desire," *Augustinian Studies* 36 (2005): 195–217; Jana Bennett, *Water Is Thicker Than Blood: An Augustinian Theology of Marriage and Singleness* (Oxford: Oxford University Press, 2008), 37–38, 59–65; David G. Hunter, "Augustinian Pessimism? A New Look at Augustine's Teaching on Sex, Marriage and Celibacy," *Augustinian Studies* 25 (1994): 153–77.

60. Augustine, *City of God* 14.11, trans. Dods, p. 272.

61. Augustine, *City of God* 14.28, trans. Dods, p. 282.

or horizontal dimension of history. The heavenly city, rooted by the gift of faith in the "love of God, even to the contempt of self," endures suffering and performs works of love in history, whose goal is eternal sharing in the trinitarian life "in the society of the saints, of holy angels as well as holy men, 'that God may be all in all.'"[62]

Books 15–18

In the previous section, Augustine examined the biblical accounts of creation and fall. He showed that human existence is radically participatory, even more than the Platonists supposed, and that humans have rebelled against this participation in God by claiming history as an autonomous realm, as happened in the Roman worship of spatiotemporal gods and corresponding pursuit of worldly glory. In Books 15–18, Augustine treats the biblical account of human history from the children of Adam and Eve through Christ Jesus. This section applies to the course of human history what Augustine has said about creation and fall. Here Augustine portrays history in a way that sharply differs both from the strictly linear understanding of history that pagan worship allowed, and from the otherworldliness that neo-Platonist philosophy encouraged. Biblical worship requires an understanding of history in which the linear is shot through with the participatory. Following Christ is not an otherworldly effort to escape from the body, but neither does following Christ have primarily this-worldly goals. Happiness—the City of God—begins here and now as the life of self-giving love by the grace of the Holy Spirit, a life that is ordered to everlasting embodied communion with the Trinity and that already participates, even if not yet fully, in this communion. History works itself out, in God's providence, in the conflict between those who love self over God (denying the participatory character of human existence) and those who love God over self (affirming that the self finds its happiness in participation in God). This conflict goes on within persons and within societies, and manifests itself in sinful acts and in acts of love.

On the basis of Scripture, Augustine undertakes to describe "the development of these two societies," the City of God and the earthly city, "throughout this whole stretch of time, or era, in which the dying yield place to the newly-born who succeed them."[63] He begins with Cain and Abel, who inaugurate the two cities. Cain shows himself to be a citizen of the earthly city, and indeed he not only murders his brother but also founds a city. Abel shows himself to be, by grace, a citizen of the heavenly city. After Abel dies, the line of the heavenly city descends from Seth, whose line continues after the flood through Noah. Augustine underscores that in this life there is conflict not only between good

---

62. Augustine, *City of God* 14.28, trans. Dods, p. 283.
63. Augustine, *City of God* 15.1, pp. 595–96.

and wicked (and between the wicked) but also between the good. While the good are progressing toward perfection, their deficiencies may cause conflict, as every pastor knows. Augustine quotes Paul's exhortations to his communities to be patient with each other, along with Jesus's exhortations to forgive each other.

Regarding Cain, Augustine examines God's displeasure with Cain and Cain's envy of Abel, as well as the allegorical interpretation of the story as symbolizing Christ and his slayers.[64] Cain's story has ramifications that cannot be adduced through the causal chain of linear history alone: his story also signifies, in God's providence, Christ's Passion and the efforts of believers to avoid envying their brethren. Yet Augustine is also concerned to defend Cain's story as linear history, since it hardly seems possible "that one man built a city at a time in which there seem to have been but four men upon earth."[65] Augustine reasons that the sacred author mentions only those humans who directly pertain to the narrative's goal of tracing the heavenly city from Adam to Abraham to the people of God (and contrasting it with the earthly city). Augustine takes care not to underappreciate the embodied history of the human race, as the Platonists did.

On biblical grounds, therefore, he argues that the early humans were much bigger and lived much longer. He emphasizes that the biblical texts are reliable even though copyists appear to have introduced minor errors. He seeks to give historical reasons for why early humans could make marriages (for example with sisters) that would later be forbidden. He explains the decline of righteousness prior to the flood by arguing that the "sons of God" (Gen. 6:2) were members of the City of God who married "daughters of men" who belonged to the city of man, with the result that the generation that followed was wicked. At the same time, he interprets Enoch's being taken up into heaven as instructing us regarding our future resurrection. This participatory meaning is also reflected in the symbolic numbers (especially seven and twelve) that Augustine finds throughout Scripture.

Likewise, Noah's ark is "a figure of the city of God sojourning in this world."[66] The dimensions of the ark symbolize the human body of Christ, the door in the ark's side symbolizes the spear-wound through which flowed the sacramental blood and water, and the squared beams symbolize the stability of the life of the saints. For those who doubt the accuracy of these interpretations, Augustine has a simple answer: it does not matter whether his precise interpretation is correct, so long as "all that is said is referred to this city of God we speak of, which sojourns in this wicked world as in a deluge."[67] He is

---

64. On Cain and Abel, see O'Daly, *Augustine's* City of God, 161–64; Donald X. Burt, OSA, *Friendship and Society: An Introduction to Augustine's Practical Philosophy* (Grand Rapids: Eerdmans, 1999), 18–20.

65. Augustine, *City of God* 15.8, trans. Dods, p. 289.

66. Augustine, *City of God* 15.26, trans. Dods, p. 306.

67. Augustine, *City of God* 15.26, trans. Dods, p. 306 (altered).

guided in this pattern of interpretation, he goes on to say, by the rule of faith. The key point is that no interpreter should think that the flood story is solely "a reliable historical record without any allegorical meaning, or, conversely, that those events are unhistorical, and the language purely symbolical."[68] From the biblical standpoint, history is irreducibly linear *and* participatory. The primary meaning for Augustine is the allegorical, participatory one, but this meaning should not be separated from linear-historical reference.

For the period from Noah to Abraham, Augustine focuses on the prophetic or participatory meaning, although he also examines difficulties in the genealogical record. He argues that the etymologies of the names Shem, Japheth, and Ham can now be seen as pointers to Christ and his Passion. He explains that the sacred author does not mention holy people between Noah and Abraham because of the sacred author's primary concern with the prophetic meaning: if all holy people were mentioned, "the narrative would become tedious, and would be more notable for historical accuracy than for prophetic foresight."[69] The tower of Babel, he suggests, is the city of Babylon, and it represents self-exaltation by contrast to humility. God punishes Babylon's self-exaltation by confusing human sovereignty at its root—that is, the shared language (in this case Hebrew) by which subjects can know their ruler's commands. Among the linear-historical questions that he raises is how, after the flood, species of animals came to dwell on remote islands, as well as whether there are human beings living "on the other side of the earth, where the sun rises when it sets for us."[70] He holds that among the sons of Shem, Japheth, and even Ham, there were persons who worshiped the true God by grace; whereas there were many others who belonged to the earthly city.

The advent of Abraham makes clearer the development of the City of God: the promises to Abraham place the whole history that follows in a participatory light. Augustine compares the family of Abraham's father Terah to that of Noah. God promises to make Abraham a great nation in whom all nations will be blessed, and God promises the land of Canaan to Abraham.[71] Augustine briefly comments on Melchizedek, who prefigures the eucharistic sacrifice, and on Abraham's faith, which was accounted to him as righteousness prior to his circumcision. He examines the symbolism of the sacrificial rite by which God confirms the covenant, and he notes the prophecy about Egyptian slavery. He records the birth of Ishmael and God's promise of Isaac, who symbolizes grace and brings about the renewal of his

68. Augustine, *City of God* 15.27, p. 645. See Curtis W. Freeman, "Figure and History: A Contemporary Reassessment of Augustine's Hermeneutic," in *Augustine: Presbyter Factus Sum*, ed. Joseph T. Lienhard, SJ, Earl C. Muller, SJ, and Roland J. Teske, SJ (New York: Peter Lang, 1993), 319–29.

69. Augustine, *City of God* 16.2, p. 652; cf. p. 653.

70. Augustine, *City of God* 16.9, p. 664.

71. On Abraham, see O'Daly, *Augustine's* City of God, 174–78.

parents (including their change of name). Baptismal grace is symbolized by God's commanding circumcision.

Augustine follows the Letter to the Hebrews in holding that after Isaac's birth, Abraham obeys God's command to lead Isaac out to be sacrificed in faith that Isaac would rise again. The ram caught in the thicket, which God provides in place of Isaac, symbolizes Jesus Christ. Augustine frequently quotes the promises that Abraham's descendants would be a blessing to all nations (Gen. 22:18 and elsewhere). Keturah, the wife whom Abraham takes after Sarah's death and with whom he has a number of children, symbolizes "the carnal people who suppose themselves to belong to the new covenant."[72] Isaac's blessing of Jacob rather than Esau also has christological meaning. As Augustine sums up his view of biblical history: "Historical events, these, but events with prophetic meaning! Events on earth, but directed from heaven! The actions of men, but the operation of God!"[73]

As one would expect, Augustine also finds christological meaning in the key events of Jacob's life. Jesus describes himself as Jacob's ladder in John 1:51. Jacob's wrestling with an angel leaves Jacob both blessed and crippled, blessed in his descendants who believe in Christ and crippled in those who do not. Jacob's deathbed blessing of Judah has to do with Christ's dying and rising, and with the eucharistic Church. Regarding Moses and the exodus from Egyptian slavery, Augustine focuses on the Paschal lamb as a marvelous symbol of Christ. He also shows that God's promises about descendants and land are fulfilled, both in terms of the earthly Jerusalem and in terms of the heavenly Jerusalem (the fullness of the City of God). The changes in priesthood from Eli to Samuel, and in kingship from Saul to David, symbolize the change from the old covenant to the new. Hannah's song of thanksgiving, which Augustine interprets in detail, prefigures the Church's fruitfulness by grace. Again, the promises that God gives to David about the kingship and the temple find their fulfillment in Christ, although Solomon's building of the temple and reign of peace prefigure Christ.

In the same vein Augustine comments on various psalms, emphasizing that God proposes to build not an earthly city but the City of God. Indeed, "Christ, who is God, before he became man through Mary in that city, himself founded it by the patriarchs and prophets."[74] The blessings that God promises are so great as to go entirely beyond what is possible in this world. Augustine identifies Psalms 110 and 22 as particularly significant in their reference to Christ, but he treats many other psalms as well. He also identifies references to Christ and the Church in Wisdom of Solomon, Sirach, Proverbs, Ecclesiastes, and the Song of Songs, but by this stage he admits that "we pass over many things in silence, in our desire to finish this work."[75]

72. Augustine, *City of God* 16.34, p. 696.
73. Augustine, *City of God* 16.37, p. 701.
74. Augustine, *City of God* 17.16, trans. Dods, p. 354.
75. Augustine, *City of God* 17.20, trans. Dods, p. 358.

Discussing the division of the kingdom after Solomon, Augustine describes how Jeroboam established idolatrous worship in Israel and how Judah too suffered from bad kings. During this period, which ended with the exile of both Israel and Judah, God sent numerous prophets. Before treating their prophecies, however, Augustine sketches the historical development of the earthly city since the time of Abraham. As before, he relies especially on the Roman historian Marcus Varro. Augustine here shows how history would appear if it were imagined to be strictly linear rather than participating in God's gracious providence. He states that human society is "for the most part divided against itself, and the strongest oppress the others, because all follow after their own interests and lusts."[76] History, on this view, is largely the record of empire and oppression, as it is in the modern study of history. Following the historical timeline, he treats the rulers and cults of Assyria, Greece, Babylon, and Rome (which "is like a second Babylon").[77] He pays special attention to the emergence of cults that worship dead humans as gods and to developments within the cults of the established gods.

During the time of Moses and Joshua, cults to various gods arose in Greece, and Hercules was renowned in Syria; and during the period of the judges in Israel, superstitious stories multiplied exponentially: the Labyrinth, centaurs, Cerberus, the Gorgon, Pegasus, Daedalus and Icarus, Oedipus, Ganymede, and so forth. More famous humans, after their deaths, were added to the list of gods: Orpheus, Ino, Castor and Pollux, Diomede, Codrus, Aeneas. As regards humans alleged to have been transformed into animals (e.g., Arcadians changed into wolves), Augustine draws the conclusion that whether or not such things happen, the power of demons to lead human beings astray is significant. The founding of the city of Rome occurred in the time of Hezekiah. Augustine states that God willed this founding so as to constitute a "second Babylon" by which the world would be conquered, united, and pacified. The oracles of the Erythraean Sibyl, quoted by the Christian author Lactantius, prophesied Christ's Passion and resurrection. During the period of the Babylonian captivity, important philosophers arose in the Greek world.

After providing this synopsis of the earthly city, Augustine turns to the prophets who flourished in Israel during this time. He begins with Hosea and Amos, and then treats Isaiah, their contemporary. Isaiah is so significant that he can be called the fifth evangelist, but Augustine limits himself for reasons of space to the extraordinary prophecy of the Suffering Servant. Indeed, in his section on the prophets, Augustine devotes the most space to Habakkuk, to whom he attributes numerous insights from the New Testament. He pairs Jeremiah and Zephaniah as contemporaries, both writing during the reign of Josiah. He mentions briefly Jeremiah's prophecy of the new covenant, and

76. Augustine, *City of God* 18.2, trans. Dods, p. 361.
77. Augustine, *City of God* 18.2, trans. Dods, p. 362.

he cites Zephaniah on the righteous remnant (the Jews who accept Christ). He places Ezekiel and Daniel during the period of the Babylonian captivity. From Daniel he quotes the prophecy about the coming of the Son of Man to the throne of God, and from Ezekiel he quotes the passages about the coming of the Davidic king to restore Israel. He concludes his discussion of the prophets by treating the prophets who lived at the end of the Babylonian captivity, Haggai, Zechariah, and Malachi. Haggai prophesies Christ's coming, Zechariah Christ's entrance into Jerusalem and rescue of sinners, and Malachi the end of animal sacrifices, the new covenant of peace, and the day of judgment.

Augustine emphasizes that almost all the prophets lived before the great Greek philosophers, and that Moses lived well before the Greek philosophers, although Moses learned some things from Egyptian sages (who were predated by Abraham). Augustine also contrasts the agreement that he finds among the biblical authors with the disagreements present among the Greek philosophers. The latter have formed numerous schools of thought rooted in profound disagreements about the nature of human happiness, how to attain happiness, the nature of the world, and many other subjects. Far from denying the wisdom of the Greeks, Augustine affirms that some of these philosophers apprehended "that God had made this world, and himself most providently governs it, as well as the nobility of the virtues, love of country, fidelity in friendship, and good works and everything pertaining to virtuous manners."[78] But even the wisest Greeks did not understand the end or goal of human life, and therefore they could not rightly weigh what they did understand. God revealed these things prophetically to the Israelites in an authoritative fashion, so that the simple Jews had an advantage even over the best Greek philosophers (let alone over the competing schools of thought).

Rather than leave the gentiles bereft, however, God inspired the Septuagint translation of the Hebrew Bible. On the grounds that "the same Spirit who was in the prophets when they spoke these things was also in the seventy men when they translated them," Augustine defends this translation against criticisms made of it by Jerome and others.[79] In Augustine's view, the Holy Spirit inspired even the Septuagint's errors of translation, including omissions and augmentations. The translators too were prophets. For this reason, Augustine is not worried when the Hebrew version and the Septuagint differ on matters of historical fact. The Holy Spirit thereby prompts readers "to rise above the level of mere historical fact and to search for meanings which the historical

78. Augustine, *City of God* 18.41, trans. Dods, p. 385 (altered).
79. Augustine, *City of God* 18.43, trans. Dods, p. 386. See Anne-Marie La Bonnardière, "Did Augustine Use Jerome's Vulgate?," in *Augustine and the Bible*, ed. and trans. Pamela Bright (Notre Dame, IN: University of Notre Dame Press, 1999), 42–51. For the view that *On Christian Doctrine* was at least partly a response to Jerome's Letter 53, see Mark Vessey, "The Great Conference: Augustine and His Fellow Readers," in *Augustine and the Bible*, 52–73, at 56–59.

record itself was intended to convey."[80] In linear history at least as found in Scripture, one must look primarily for the participatory meaning.

Augustine gives some attention to the situation of the Jewish people after the rebuilding of the temple, a period that lacked both prophets and kings. The Maccabean purification of the temple did not last long. Pompey conquered Judea for Rome in the first century before Christ. Herod was the first foreigner to rule Judea directly, and Augustine considers it fitting, therefore, that during Herod's reign Christ, the true Davidic king, was born. Although he did many miracles (from his incarnation to his ascension), many of his own people did not believe in him. The Roman destruction of the temple led to an even greater dispersion of the Jewish people, which Augustine considers to be providentially ordered to bear witness among the gentiles to the truthfulness of the prophecies about Christ. Augustine quotes Psalm 59:11 as a prophecy that commands the protection of the Jewish people in gentile lands. Augustine also inquires into the situation of the gentiles before the coming of Christ. He argues that some of them belonged to the City of God, as attested by the figure of Job. Yet no one belonged to the City of God other than through faith in Christ, the one mediator, and so such gentiles would have had to have received some knowledge, however implicit, of the future Savior.

Finally, Augustine inquires into the Church, the people of the new covenant. The Church contains not only those who are being saved but also those who bear the name Christian without the reality. The Church was spread by the "fire of love" by the apostles and their successors. The lives of the martyrs, who were filled with the Holy Spirit, bore such witness to the truth of the gospel that many gentiles rejected their false gods and accepted Christ. Even false teachers within the Church serve God's purpose in strengthening the Church's wisdom, patient endurance, and love of enemy. At all times, says Augustine, followers of Christ will endure persecution, whether from enemies outside the Church or from the actions of those who are Christian in name only. Although Augustine grieves that dissensions among Christians make Christ less persuasive to non-Christians and provide an opportunity for those who wish to slander the Church, he insists that God permits such trials in order to build up love and that God also provides great consolations. As Augustine concludes, "Not only from the time of the bodily presence of Christ and his apostles, but even from that of Abel, whom first his wicked brother slew because he was righteous, and thenceforth even to the end of this world, the Church has gone forward on pilgrimage amid the persecutions of the world and the consolations of God."[81] He adds that the time of the last persecution, that of the antichrist, cannot be predicted.

80. Augustine, *City of God* 18.44, p. 823.
81. Augustine, *City of God* 18.51, trans. Dods, p. 392. See O'Daly, *Augustine's* City of God, 193.

Augustine summarizes this section by remarking that the earthly and heavenly cities both enjoy good things and undergo afflictions in this world, but they do so "with a different faith, a different hope, a different love, until they are separated by the final judgment, and each receives her own end."[82] Viewed in terms of linear history, the two cities do not appear all that different. Both endure afflictions from enemies; both experience dissensions from within; both contain people who are more virtuous and people who are less so. But viewed in terms of the participatory dimension of history, the two cities are polar opposites. The earthly city recognizes no Creator, no transcendent God from whom all things come and in whom all things live, move, and have their being. As a result, the earthly city loves only this-worldly ends. The logic of the earthly city places the love of self above all else, with the resulting sovereignty of fallen human beings' lust for domination. This is Augustine's critique of the gods and those who worship them. Even the best pagan philosophers, Augustine argues, fail to recognize the centrality of humility, of receptivity and grace, in the relationship of creature to Creator.

By contrast, the heavenly city has faith in the transcendent Creator and hopes to enjoy him forever. The heavenly city loves the Triune God as its end. The love of God above all things is made possible by the grace of the Holy Spirit, and this love enables believers to be configured to Christ's life of self-giving humility. Desire for a heavenly kingdom, whose center is God, thus conquers desire for an earthly kingdom, whose center is the self. The difference can be seen in the pagan cultures' worship of powerful humans as gods, contrasted with Israel's worship of the God who becomes incarnate so as to save us through the humility of the cross. When read according to its prophetic meaning, as fulfilled in Christ, Scripture bears witness to the participatory blessings that God bestows on his people—the City of God—in the midst of linear history.

Books 19–22

The last section of Augustine's *City of God* treats the fullness of human participation in God—namely, resurrection and eternal life. It does so, however, in view of the fact that not all people will attain to this end. God permits some angels and humans to reject him permanently, to choose themselves over him. Those angels and humans who do attain to the end of eternal communion in the Trinity do so because the Triune God graciously draws them into his life. The goal of supreme participation in God is not something that rational creatures can accomplish on the basis of their own resources. This would be the case even had humans not fallen. The end or goal of history, its consummation, therefore consists in a liturgical communion that transcends

82. Augustine, *City of God* 18.54, p. 842 (altered).

(without negating) history. Only the Triune God can bring about this end or goal. History's significance consists in the fact that God is bringing about this goal in and through history. Because of history's participatory dimension, linear history contains the seeds of the new creation. Yet linear history also contains the beginnings of the everlasting rebellion and condemnation that is the "end" of the earthly city.

Augustine begins by discussing happiness.[83] In order to apprehend what makes a human being truly happy, one must inquire into particular goods. Our "final good," Augustine says, "is that for the sake of which other things are to be desired, while it is to be desired for its own sake." Our "final evil," likewise, "is that on account of which other things are to be shunned, while it is avoided on its own account."[84] Are there a "final good" and "final evil," and if so what might they be?

Augustine observes that this question led Marcus Varro to distinguish between 288 possible philosophical schools, based on diverse possible answers to the question.[85] For example, pleasure might be considered the final or supreme good, but then pleasure itself can be subdivided: Is it stimulation of the bodily senses, or suffering no pain, or enjoying all the natural bodily blessings, or enjoying all the natural spiritual blessings, or some combination of the above in which certain pleasures take precedence over others? Varro distinguishes the contemplative and active life, and he argues that only the supreme good can make a person happy, because otherwise the person would desire yet another good and would be unhappy until that further good were attained (and the supreme evil is simply the opposite of the supreme good). In order to identify the supreme good, Varro first inquires into human nature: Are humans bodies, souls, or a combination of the two? Concluding that humans are body-soul combinations, he reasons that the supreme good must fulfill the highest desires of both body and soul. What then are the goods that fulfill these desires? Varro arrives at the position that the supreme good must combine life, friendship with gods and humans, virtue, and bodily health.

Augustine notes that for the City of God, rooted in Scripture, the answer is easy: eternal life is the supreme good, and eternal death the supreme evil. Virtue enables us to obtain the former and avoid the latter. He expresses amazement that any philosopher could have supposed that it is possible "to be happy here on earth and to achieve bliss by their own efforts."[86] Is not our hold on the blessings of nature radically contingent in this life? Bodily ailments and spiritual ailments continually threaten to drag us down. Friends, family, and society often let us down and add to our cares and woes. Ignorance and

83. See Burt, *Friendship and Society*, 35–40.
84. Augustine, *City of God* 19.1, trans. Dods, p. 397.
85. See O'Daly, *Augustine's* City of God, 197–200.
86. Augustine, *City of God* 19.4, p. 852.

war, even a just war,[87] make us wretched. Friendship with angels is impaired by attacks of demons (often personating "gods"). Even if we have a modicum of peace at the present moment, we are always in danger of losing it. If life on earth is all there is, there is no happiness.

Augustine conceives eternal life in terms of peace. All humans, he observes, are in search of peace, both with our fellows and with ourselves, in spiritual and bodily well-being. Even those who lust for domination, whose pride rebels against God's rule, nonetheless desire to impose their peace on others. Unjust peace is a perversion of the true peace that is right order. Indeed, were there no order in the universe, there could be no rebellion. Evil is a privation of good, rather than an equal and competing principle. He defines peace as follows:

> The peace of body and soul is the well-ordered and harmonious life and health of the living creature. Peace between man and God is the well-ordered obedience of faith to eternal law. Peace between man and man is well-ordered concord. Domestic peace is the well-ordered concord between those of the family who rule and those who obey. Civil peace is a similar concord among the citizens. The peace of the celestial city is the perfectly ordered and harmonious enjoyment of God, and of one another in God. The peace of all things is the tranquillity of order.[88]

Augustine holds that God created all things in peace and bestowed upon humans the goods necessary not only for peace in this life but also for the glory of eternal peace. By using temporal goods well, we can attain to eternal peace, which we forfeit if we use temporal goods badly. We use temporal goods well when we use them as ordered, in a participatory manner, to enjoy God in eternal life. Humans need bodily health and temperance so as to pursue knowledge about how to live, and obtaining this knowledge requires God's direction and assistance. Similarly, in order to have peace, we must rightly order our loves, so that we truly love God, self, and neighbor.[89] He describes our temporal life as a pilgrimage toward our homeland, the Triune God, a pilgrimage that requires faith because we cannot see our end. Since true peace consists in our eternal enjoyment of God, all other forms of peace participate in this highest form.

Acutely aware of the effects in human life of the lust for domination, Augustine inquires into the forms of human dominion. Here he treats institutions

---

87. See David Lenihan, "The Just War Theory in the Work of Saint Augustine," *Augustinian Studies* 19 (1988): 37–70.

88. Augustine, *City of God* 19.13, trans. Dods, p. 409. On peace and order, see Burnell, *Augustinian Person*, 136–40; A. N. Williams, *The Divine Sense: The Intellect in Patristic Theology* (Cambridge: Cambridge University Press, 2007), 143–44, 151; Peter Slater, "Goodness as Order and Harmony in Augustine," in *Augustine: From Rhetor to Theologian*, ed. Joanne McWilliam (Waterloo, Ontario: Wilfrid Laurier University Press, 1992), 151–59.

89. See Burnell, *Augustinian Person*, 141–42.

such as the household, slavery, and the city.[90] Before sin, he argues, humans possessed dominion only over irrational animals. The subordination of wives to husbands and children to parents would have existed in the household before sin, but without coercive dominion. After sin, order requires the dominion of humans over other humans. Political and economic dominion is the punishment that comes upon humans due to the original rebellion, but since it is a just punishment—one necessary for maintaining human community insofar as it can be maintained after sin—Christians can exercise and obey authority so long as they recall that "even those who give orders are the servants of those whom they appear to command" and so long as they worship God alone rather than accepting laws requiring the worship of the gods.[91] The Church's role consists not in undermining authority but in using earthly peace, upheld by authority, for the purpose of guiding humans to eternal peace. By faith, the Church already participates in this eternal peace and "lives a life of righteousness, based on this faith, having the attainment of that peace in view in every good action it performs in relation to God, and in relation to a neighbour, since the life of a city is inevitably a social life."[92] Nonetheless, the peace enjoyed by Christians is imperfect in this life. Far from being perfect in virtue, Christians have peace through the forgiveness of sins rather than already enjoying blessedness.

Against the philosophical school called Academics, Augustine defends the ability of the human mind to know truth with certitude, and he similarly defends the trustworthiness of the senses. Faith is not erected upon an edifice of skepticism. He argues that Christians should combine the active life and contemplative life. Both action and contemplation should arise from and be guided by love. Action in service to neighbor must not be allowed to displace contemplative delight in truth. Living in this manner, the Christian will already be happy, even if this happiness is grounded in hope. The Christian is the truly wise person, "since no wisdom is true wisdom if it does not direct its attention, in all its prudent decisions, its resolute actions, its self-control and its just dealings with others, towards that ultimate state in which God will

90. See Burnell, *Augustinian Person*, 162–66; Harrison, *Augustine*, 213–16; John M. Rist, *Augustine: Ancient Thought Baptized* (Cambridge: Cambridge University Press, 1994), 236–39.
91. Augustine, *City of God* 19.14, p. 874; cf. 19.17, p. 878. For discussion see Robert Dodaro, OSA, "Between the Two Cities: Political Action in Augustine of Hippo," in *Augustine and Politics*, 99–115; Rowan Williams, "Politics and the Soul: A Reading of the *City of God*," *Milltown Studies* 19 (1987): 55–72; Burnell, *Augustinian Person*, 144–58; Rist, *Augustine*, 225–28; Charles T. Mathewes, *Evil and the Augustinian Tradition* (Cambridge: Cambridge University Press, 2001), 220–36; Oliver O'Donovan, "The Political Thought of *City of God* 19," in Oliver O'Donovan and Joan Lockwood O'Donovan, *Bonds of Imperfection: Christian Politics, Past and Present* (Grand Rapids: Eerdmans, 2004), 48–72; John von Heyking, *Augustine and Politics as Longing in the World* (Columbia: University of Missouri Press, 2001), 5–8.
92. Augustine, *City of God* 19.17, pp. 878–79. See O'Donovan, "Political Thought," 51–52; Smith, "Glory and Tragedy," 197–202.

be all in all, in the assurance of eternity and the perfection of peace."[93] Not knowing this peace or how to get there, the philosophers could not be fully wise. Nor could Rome, rooted in the worship of the gods (or demons), be fully just, and "where there is no justice there is no commonwealth."[94] Service to the true God is the common good of the city.

As an example of a deluded philosopher, Augustine turns to that great critic of Christianity, Porphyry. A defender of worshiping the gods, Porphyry nonetheless grants the greatness of Israel's God and imagines (on the basis of an oracle of Hecate) that Christ's soul is among the immortal souls of wise men. Had Porphyry realized that sacrifice can only rightly be offered to Israel's God, he would have been on the path of true wisdom.[95] Augustine also develops a definition of a commonwealth that includes Rome. Yet Rome has centered its love on temporal glory and has thereby turned aside from true justice. Without participation in the transcendent God, virtue stands as an end in itself and becomes its opposite, pride. Augustine underscores that "it is not something that comes from man, but something above man, that makes his life blessed."[96] We cannot have the peace we seek outside of relationship with the living God. Even so, the modicum of peace that the earthly city upholds can be used by Christians, as pilgrims, to spread the worship of God and to advance along the way to the heavenly city. The peace of eternal communion with this God is what we seek. Lacking this peace, the war of rebellion within ourselves will proceed everlastingly, as the just punishment of our free rebellion.

If God is just, however, why is there such a wide diversity of human experience? Among good persons, some suffer and some thrive, and the same holds for wicked persons. It is generally true that wicked actions lead to bad consequences and good actions are eventually rewarded, but in individual cases, justice cannot be counted on to prevail. Augustine reasons that only at the final judgment will we understand the justice of this diversity. At present, we can know only that God is just and that he conceals his reasons for a just purpose. We can also take heed of Ecclesiastes, which warns us that there are only two paths, that of vanity and that of keeping God's commandments. God sees and judges all our actions, even our hidden ones. In this regard Augustine surveys the numerous New Testament passages that speak of the final judgment at the resurrection of the dead. We can be dead in two ways: dead in sin or physically dead. The forgiveness of sins in Christ Jesus brings about a first resurrection for those who, having been dead in sin, receive Christ in faith. These will not

93. Augustine, *City of God* 19.20, p. 881.

94. Augustine, *City of God* 19.21, p. 882. In addition to works cited above, see Jean Bethke Elshtain, *Augustine and the Limits of Politics* (Notre Dame, IN: University of Notre Dame Press, 1995), chap. 5.

95. For Porphyry's historical critique of Scripture, see W. Den Boer, "A Pagan Historian and His Enemies: Porphyry against the Christians," *Classical Philology* 69 (1974): 198–208.

96. Augustine, *City of God* 19.25, p. 891.

be condemned at the second resurrection at the end of the world, when all the physically dead will rise, some to life and some to judgment.

Augustine pauses to critique the millenarian interpretation of the book of Revelation, which misunderstands the reference to two resurrections and supposes that the symbolic "thousand years" is not the time of the Church prior to the end of the world.[97] He presents the Church as "even now" being "the kingdom of Christ and the kingdom of heaven," but not in the way that will come about at the final judgment.[98] At present, the wheat and the tares grow together in the Church: there are some in the Church who do not love God and neighbor, and these will be exposed at the final judgment. Truly to be in the Church means to seek "the interests of Jesus Christ" rather than seeking one's own interests through the Church.[99] The "beast" of the book of Revelation symbolizes the earthly city, with its worship of creatures and its goal of temporal goods. The saints and martyrs are those who, by God's grace, have not joined themselves to the "beast." The final persecution, that of the antichrist, will last a short time and then all will be raised, the final judgment will take place, and the new heaven and new earth (the glorious City of God) will be inaugurated.

Augustine draws here not only on the book of Revelation but also on Peter and Paul. He also engages texts from the Old Testament, including Isaiah 26:19 and 66:12–24; Daniel 7 and 12; Psalms 50 and 102; Malachi 3–4; and Zechariah 12. He argues that while the wicked will not know what the blessed are experiencing, the blessed will know everything, including the punishment of the wicked, because they will rejoice in all God does. Malachi provides evidence that some of the dead will receive purifying punishments rather than condemnation. Although these Old Testament prophecies about the resurrection of the dead and the final judgment mention the Lord God rather than Christ, Augustine argues that passages such as Zechariah 12:10, about the mourning of the people on that day when they look upon the one whom they have pierced, indicate that Christ is intended. He states that "although the Father will judge, it is through the coming of the Son of Man that he will execute judgement."[100] The Son of Man will do so as the one possessed of the Holy Spirit, the one who endured the punishment of all sins and whose mercy for sinners shines forth with supreme love. Rejected by almost all humans in his crucifixion, he is now believed in by a countless multitude who trust in his cross for salvation. The rejected one will judge those who rejected his love.

97. See O'Daly, *Augustine's* City of God, 211–13; Pamela Bright, "Augustine and the Thousand Year Reign of Saints," in *Augustine: Presbyter Factus Sum*, 447–53; Paula Fredriksen, "Apocalypse and Redemption in Early Christianity: From John of Patmos to Augustine of Hippo," *Vigiliae Christianae* 45 (1991): 151–83, at 160–63.

98. Augustine, *City of God* 20.9, p. 915.

99. Augustine, *City of God* 20.9, p. 915.

100. Augustine, *City of God* 20.30, p. 961.

Do the bodies of the damned undergo everlasting corporeal punishment, and if so, how can they avoid disintegrating? Can a body that is capable of pain be incapable of death? Augustine gives various examples of material substances that hold up under intense force, for example diamonds. He also appeals to God's power as the Creator of all substances, and he observes that bodies before sin were incorruptible, so by God's power they could be made incorruptible again while still being capable of pain. On the bodily suffering of the damned, he quotes both Isaiah and Jesus (in the Gospel of Mark). Can material fire harm immaterial demons? He argues that this is possible, since humans themselves display how spirit and matter can be in contact. The point is that damnation, in its material fire and bodily pain, is indeed a continuation of the linear history on which the damned have staked their lives. During their lifetimes, the damned rejected the participatory relationship into which God called them. Hell continues the suffering that marks linear history and permits the damned their choice of rejection of participatory relationship.[101]

Yet should humans be everlastingly punished for sins committed during a brief duration of time? To this objection, Augustine replies that the temporal length of the punishment, even on earth, rarely matches the temporal length of the crime. A murder committed in a moment can bring about a lifetime's punishment. In Augustine's view, the rejection of the doctrine of everlasting punishment arises from a failure to appreciate the gravity of rebellion against God. To rebel against God is to destroy in oneself what could have been an eternal good. Rejecting an eternal good brings about an everlasting punishment, although God's merciful grace saves some. Punishment after death is purifying and temporary only for those who die in union with God but with some venial sins yet to be forgiven. For those whose rebellion is total and permanent, there awaits an everlasting fire that will be more or less intense depending on the degree of depravity of the unrepentant sinner.

Due to original sin, Augustine argues, the experience of punishment begins in infancy and continues throughout one's life. Even those few persons who for many years escape bodily illness have to contend with such punishments as ignorance, folly, the difficulty of learning, and so forth. Yet this suffering cannot prevent those whom God draws to himself from coming to God. God uses afflictions to recall us to the reality that our true peace is found only in him. Above all, God sends his Son to suffer for us in the flesh: so that we might come to share in his divinity, he came to share in our weakness. Augustine explains, "He became partaker of our infirmity, that we, being changed into some better thing, might, by participating in his righteousness and immortality, lose our own properties of sin and mortality, and preserve whatever good quality he had implanted in our nature, perfected now by sharing in the goodness

101. See Burnell, *Augustinian Person*, 79–81.

of his nature."[102] In this life, we cannot attain perfect peace; even those who
are in Christ must continually struggle against vices, the most insidious of
which is pride. This unremitting interior war against vices, however, is made
hopeful by Christ's victory, in which we participate sacramentally. Christ's
love inspires our longing to conquer with him and to enter into the perfect
peace of heaven, where we will be untroubled by bodily and spiritual threats
and where we will be holy, filled by "the fire of divine love."[103]

Augustine knows that many Christians have difficulty accepting the doctrine
of everlasting punishment and instead hold that God will set a limit to the
punishment of rational creatures. While valuing the compassion that motivates
this view, he argues that the punishment is indeed everlasting. He notes that
the argument from compassion requires logically that God eventually release
the fallen angels, including the devil, from punishment. Origen held that the
devil would indeed be redeemed, but most Christians have not wished to go
so far, because Scripture does not sanction it.[104] The logic of divine compassion
runs up against the express statements of divine revelation.

Even so, will not the saints, filled with love for their enemies, intercede for
their rebellious fellows? Will not God in his mercy grant their prayer, since
it will be rooted in love? On this view the biblical passages about everlasting damnation should be interpreted along the same lines as God's promise
to destroy Nineveh. God remains free to give way to the prayers of his holy
people. Indeed, with respect to Nineveh, God foreknew that he would have
mercy. The same will happen, then, at the final judgment. Those who hold this
view "suppose that the reason for the silence of holy Scripture on this point
is to ensure that many people should amend their lives for fear of lengthy or
even everlasting pains, and that thus there should be people capable of praying
for those who have not amended."[105] Augustine recognizes that some biblical
passages seem to point in this direction, including Romans 11:32.

Augustine asks why those who hold this view about the salvation of all humans nonetheless continue to suppose that the fallen angels will be everlastingly
condemned. He argues that there is a self-serving tendency in the positing of
exceptions to Christ's explicit words about everlasting damnation. As he points
out, others limit the exceptions to all baptized persons who have received the
Eucharist (see John 6:51) or to all Catholics who have received baptism and
the Eucharist (see 1 Cor. 3:11–15) or to all unrepentant sinners who performed

102. Augustine, *City of God* 21.15, trans. Dods, p. 465 (altered).
103. Augustine, *City of God* 21.15, p. 993.
104. See O'Daly, *Augustine's* City of God, 261–62; Caroline P. Bammel, "Augustine, Origen
and the Exegesis of St. Paul," *Augustinianum* 32 (1992): 341–68; Giulia Sfameni Gasparro,
"Agostino di fronte alla 'eterodossia' di Origene: un aspetto della origeniana in Occidente," in
Collectanea Augustiniana: Mélanges T. J. van Bavel, ed. B. Bruning, M. Lamberigts, and J. van
Houtem (Leuven: Leuven University Press, 1990), 219–43.
105. Augustine, *City of God* 21.18, p. 997.

works of mercy (see James 2:13 and Matt. 6:14). Responding to this quest for exceptions, Augustine begins with the case of the fallen angels. The Church has rejected the view that the devil will be saved. Yet, as Augustine says, "It was not that all those holy men, learned in the Scriptures of both testaments, grudged to angels, of whatever kind or in whatever numbers, the attainment of cleansing and of bliss in the Kingdom of Heaven, after chastisements of whatever kind and of whatever magnitude."[106] Instead, the Church rejected the view that the devil would eventually be saved on the ground of the words of Jesus Christ, as well as numerous other biblical passages.

These biblical passages make clear that humans too have a choice between everlasting punishment and eternal life. This choice consists in trusting in one's own resources—which after the fall means leading a life of sin (see Gal. 5:19–21)—or trusting in God's. As Augustine puts it, "This righteousness of God, which is the gift of grace without merits, is not known by those who go about to establish their own righteousness, and are therefore not subject to the righteousness of God, which is Christ."[107] We must pray for our enemies while they can amend their lives (as the Ninevites did); once their lives are over, they enter into the justice and mercy of God. The prayer of the saints accords with God's judgment, just as we do not pray for the fallen angels. We can affirm, however, that for all those who are damned (angels and humans), God in his mercy will ensure that "their sufferings are milder and lighter than their deserts."[108] In his mercy too God ensures that all those whom he draws to himself will be saved. Our merciful actions toward others must be rooted in faith and love; otherwise these actions will not be part of God's overcoming our vices. Acts of charity, such as financial support for the Church, do not provide a license to sin, and we must struggle against even venial sins in case they become mortal sins without our noticing.

The key point is that what we do in time carries forward into life after death. We must accept the relationship that is offered to us now, if we wish to be left with anything but a continuation of linear-historical troubles. Thus Augustine observes that "in vain, after this life, does a man seek for what he has neglected to provide while in this life."[109] Although some compassionate Christians seek to extend the choosing that occurs in this life into the next life, biblical revelation—the revelation of divine mercy—suggests that the life to come is in fact something quite different: an eternal fulfillment of participation or an everlasting experience of linear suffering (a much reduced participation in God's being, justice, and mercy). Life after death is not a continuation of history as we know it.

Augustine begins the final book of the *City of God* by surveying briefly God's creation of the universe, especially of rational creatures, and of God's

106. Augustine, *City of God* 21.23, p. 1000.
107. Augustine, *City of God* 21.24, trans. Dods, p. 471.
108. Augustine, *City of God* 21.24, p. 1005. See Burnell, *Augustinian Person*, 131–35.
109. Augustine, *City of God* 21.24, trans. Dods, p. 471.

permission of the introduction of moral evil. Rational creatures are wretched unless and until they enjoy God, which shows that God created rational creatures for himself. In history, God's purpose is to gather a people to himself, so as to bring together the full number of humans and angels in his fellowship. Our sin does not frustrate God's will, even though the holy will of human beings can often be frustrated, as when we pray that a tyrant will not decimate his populace. The difference is that God's will is transcendent and has in view God's whole plan, whereas our will is on the same ontological level as the tyrant's and so our holy prayers for temporal events are not always answered. God wills not the sin but the good that he has in view, which he can draw even out of sin.

God's will is that all nations shall be blessed through Abraham, and this has come to pass. God has also promised to establish his people in an ever-lasting kingdom. Against the possibility of this coming to pass, some have argued that earthly bodies can dwell only on earth. Augustine points out in reply that the union of body and soul[110] is a greater miracle than the dwell-ing of a risen body in a corporeal heavenly abode, where Christ's body now dwells. God is not prohibited from raising the earthly body and spiritualizing it so that it can exist without the limitations of earthly bodiliness and be "a spiritual body, clothed in incorruptibility and immortality," flesh subject to spirit.[111] Likewise, the restoration of bodies from the dust, and their rising in a condition of perfect maturity and beautiful splendor rather than of disease or advanced age, lies within the power of the God who can create from nothing. The distinction of gender will remain in the resurrection, since "a woman's sex is not a defect."[112] The complementarity of man and woman symbolizes the union of Christ and the Church, both now and forever.

Many learned men confess that Jesus Christ has risen from the dead; why then imagine the resurrection of all humans to be impossible? The power of the apostles' witness, Augustine argues, could have come only from God (with the confirmation of miracles), not from their own abilities. Here he compares the apostles' proclamation of Christ with the Romans' turning Romulus into a god—the key differences being that few ever believed in Romulus's divinity and that Rome had been built well before proclaiming Romulus a god, whereas the Church was built on the apostolic testimony that Christ is God. Faith in Christ's divinity is the foundation, not the result, of the Church's growth. This faith is rooted in prophecies given to Israel long ago, now fulfilled. Rome's power and fear of Rome supported worship of Romulus, whereas the humility of martyrs and fear of God supported worship of Christ.

110. On the union of body and soul, see Burnell, *Augustinian Person*, 18–44; George Lawless, OSA, "Augustine and Human Embodiment," in *Collectanea Augustiniana*, 167–86.

111. Augustine, *City of God* 22.21, p. 1064. See O'Daly, *Augustine's* City of God, 225–26.

112. Augustine, *City of God* 22.17, p. 1057. See Burnell, *Augustinian Person*, 44–50; E. Ann Matter, "Christ, God and Woman in the Thought of St Augustine," in *Augustine and His Critics*, 164–75.

Augustine also gives a number of examples of contemporary miracles, which are "even now . . . being performed in Christ's name either by his sacrament, or by the prayers and memorials of his saints."[113] He contrasts these miracles, performed by the intercession of the martyrs, with those allegedly performed by pagan gods. Again his point is that the Christian faith has to do with participation in God rather than with temporal power. The martyrs are not worshiped as gods. They serve God rather than serving themselves. Their goal is the same as God's: the building up of the Body, the Church, in union with her Head, Jesus Christ. Every member of the Body has an irreplaceable role in its harmonious perfection. This perfection flows from Christ's wounds, and so his wounds remain in glory, as may also the wounds of the martyrs.

To attain this perfection, humans must be radically transformed in this life, as Augustine shows by calling to mind the extent of human ignorance, lust, and violence. Just as children are trained by discipline, so too humans experience God's commandments as hard discipline. In our fallen condition, even profitable labor is distasteful to us. We are beset by numerous threats to our physical and spiritual health, so that exile, disease, sudden death, demonic attacks, and famine are not uncommon. At the same time, Augustine contemplates the extraordinary blessings that God gives humans, including existence, fitting bodies (hands, erect posture, voice, internal organs, and so forth), procreation, rationality, the arts, agricultural and technological development, poetry and philosophy, and above all the ability to attain eternal life by grace. The beauty and diversity of the natural creation likewise manifest God's bounty. Augustine expresses amazement and delight in light, stars, woods, the sea, birds, ants, bees, and many other natural blessings.[114]

The abundance of God's gifts does not mitigate the reality that our fallen condition, due to sin, is precarious and marked by violence and lust. Indeed, Augustine describes our condition as "a kind of hell on earth."[115] Liberation from the hellish aspects of linear history requires deepening our participation in God through the grace of Jesus Christ. Sharing in Christ's Spirit, we can begin even now to overcome the spiritual threats to our health and we can look forward to overcoming, forever, the physical threats. Absent Christ's Spirit, we can look forward only to a continuation of these hellish threats that characterize history. Life in Christ here and now consists in spiritual warfare in which we must strive with all our might to be holy, while repenting daily of our sins and depending entirely upon the grace of the Holy Spirit for our strength. We should take solace in this spiritual warfare by calling to mind all the blessings that God bestows on his creation. If the creation even after sin is so beautiful, the beauty of the sinless new creation, to which

---

113. Augustine, *City of God* 22.8, p. 1034.
114. See Harrison, *Beauty and Revelation*, 131–33, 160–62, and elsewhere.
115. Augustine, *City of God* 22.22, p. 1068.

our spiritual warfare leads, will be infinitely glorious. Augustine comments, "How complete, how lovely, how certain will be the knowledge of all things, a knowledge without error, entailing no toil! For there we shall drink of God's Wisdom at its very source, with supreme felicity and without any difficulty. How wonderful will be that body which will be completely subdued to the spirit."[116] In Christ Jesus and the Scriptures, God has promised that this will come about, and he cannot lie.

Augustine argues that even Plato has an inkling of the wondrous work that God will do in making us immortal: the soul will have its yearning for the body fulfilled through the restoration of the body in which it suffered on earth, a body now made glorious. Had their best insights been combined, Plato, Porphyry, and even Varro would have taught the resurrection of the body. In this light, at the end of his final book, Augustine turns to the vision of God enjoyed by the glorified soul. The glory of this vision cannot be conceived. Augustine says that "we, in our measure, are made partakers of his peace," because we belong to Christ's kingdom, but we know God through faith rather than through vision.[117] When we see God through vision, will our bodily eyes see him? Augustine answers that the saints will see God even when their eyes are closed.

Yet bodily eyes will retain a purpose in the new creation. Indeed, Augustine thinks that it is probable that glorified bodily eyes will in heaven be able to see immaterial realities, so that our bodily eyes will "see the material forms of the new heavens and the new earth in such a way that we shall most distinctly recognize God everywhere present and governing all things, material as well as spiritual."[118] In this life we have some small knowledge of God through his material creation; in the next life we will see him not only spiritually but even with our bodily eyes, as befits the most knowable reality who shines forth in everything. Spiritually, the whole City of God will know each other's thoughts, and all will rejoice together in the wisdom, love, and beauty of the Holy Trinity. We will be united in the praise of God.

Augustine goes on to say that our bodies will be beautiful and will move fully in accord with our souls. We will be filled with true glory, true honor, and true peace. Our reward will be God himself: all our longings will be fulfilled in him. Although there will be degrees of beatitude rather than a strict equality, no saint shall feel either pride or envy. The Body of Christ will be harmonious, with each member offering his or her contribution to the whole.[119] Freed from all sin and all possibility of sinning, the blessed will be far freer

116. Augustine, *City of God* 22.24, p. 1076.
117. Augustine, *City of God* 22.29, p. 1082.
118. Augustine, *City of God* 22.29, trans. Dods, p. 509. By contrast, Phillip Cary assumes that the vision of God negates the body; see Cary, "United Inwardly by Love: Augustine's Social Ontology," in *Augustine and Politics*, 3–33, at 26–27.
119. See Burnell, *Augustinian Person*, 166–72.

than we are now.[120] This freedom will be freedom for perfect love, for perfect joy. The suffering that we experience due to remembering evil will be no more, although our memories will retain knowledge of evil so as to enable us to rejoice more fully in the grace of Christ that glorified us.[121] We will participate in the very Sabbath of God himself. As Augustine puts it, "We ourselves shall become that seventh day, when we have been replenished and restored by his blessing and sanctification."[122] No more shall we wish to be God by grasping, for we will rejoice in partaking in God by his gift, since he is the cause of even the good works that unite us to him. Augustine divides human history into six epochs: from Adam to Noah, from Noah to Abraham, from Abraham to David, from David to the Babylonian exile, from the exile to Christ, and from Christ to the present day. All will culminate at the final judgment, followed by an "eighth day," eternal life.[123] How to describe this eternal day? "There we shall be still and see; we shall see and we shall love; we shall love and we shall praise. Behold what will be, in the end, without end! For what is our end but to reach that kingdom which has no end?"[124]

Conclusion

The *City of God* contrasts the power of Rome (and the god Romulus) with the power of the apostolic Church (and the God Jesus Christ). Rome builds the city first and then justifies it by deifying its purported founder, and Rome relies on political power to spread the worship of Romulus. The apostles have no worldly glory, erudition, or power. They are martyred for their efforts. Their proclamation that Jesus Christ is Lord of all does not have the backing of an already built, powerful Church. Their miracles are not self-serving, as are those of pagan gods, but instead point away from themselves to the living God who alone is worshiped. In short, the power of their witness comes from their participation in God through Christ and the Holy Spirit. Their witness is powerful too in calling others to share in this relationship that reverses the slavery to sin and death that we humans brought upon ourselves by turning away from God and striving to "be like God" in power through our own resources (Gen. 3:5).

In reflecting on historical existence, Augustine avoids both shallow pessimism and shallow optimism. His contemplation of the extraordinary blessings that God bestows on the world shows a keen appreciation of the beauty and fecundity of the world of nature, from stars and woods to ants and bees, as

120. See Burnell, *Augustinian Person*, 88–89.
121. See Burnell, *Augustinian Person*, 90–93, 131.
122. Augustine, *City of God* 22.30, p. 1090.
123. Augustine, *City of God* 22.30, p. 1091.
124. Augustine, *City of God* 22.30, p. 1091.

well as of the richness of human life, from existence and procreation to poetry, philosophy, the arts, technological developments, and the supreme goal of rationality (union with God). Yet he does not take this appreciation in a romantic direction by ignoring the horrific sin and suffering that characterizes human life both individually and socially. Rather, he squarely faces this horror and makes clear that to develop one's relationship with God requires a demanding life of spiritual warfare. Rome sought to acquire glory by self-sacrifice and military warfare; Christians must seek true glory by self-sacrifice and spiritual warfare. The goal is peace: the harmony of one's bodily passions rightly participating in one's spiritual acts, and of one's spiritual acts rightly participating in God's acts. Unlike Rome's warfare, which depended entirely on the strength of Rome, Christian spiritual warfare depends entirely on the power of God. Embracing the participatory dimension of history means learning to rely on God's power—that is, learning the power of humility and receptivity.

Finally, as an account of the vision of God, our adoption as children of God who share through the Holy Spirit in the Son's inheritance from the Father, Augustine's *City of God* identifies history as shaped by our Sabbath rest, our worship.[125] In eternal life, we will share in God's own "rest," because we have been created by God so that we might rejoice in him. In the state of glory our bodies will remain fleshly bodies even while being glorified so that we can see, with our bodily eyes, the God whose creative presence is proclaimed by every visible thing.

125. The priority of worship in our lives does not diminish the importance of our working, our daily tasks by which we work out our salvation through love of God and neighbor. On this point, see Robert Dodaro, OSA, "Augustine of Hippo Between the Secular City and the City of God," in *Augustinus Afer: Saint Augustin: Africanité et universalité*, ed. Pierre-Yves Fux, Jean-Michel Roessli, and Otto Wermelinger (Fribourg: Éditions universitaires, 2003), 287–305.

7

On the Trinity

In the prefatory letter to Bishop Aurelius of Carthage that Augustine appended to the final version of *On the Trinity* (399–419),[1] he remarks that he was upset that some of the books of *On the Trinity* had been published earlier without his consent. The widespread circulation of some of the early books bothered Augustine partly because he had not had a proper chance to revise them. But it also bothered him because he conceived of the fifteen books of *On the Trinity* as a unity. As he says of the fifteen books, "The inquiry proceeds in a closely-knit development from the first of them to the last."[2]

In the fifteen books of *On the Trinity*, however, the sheer variety of themes and the constant movement from historical revelation to philosophical speculation (and back again) hardly gives the appearance of the tightly organized argument that Augustine thought he had produced. Augustine moves freely from antisubordinationist arguments regarding Christ's "form of God" and "form of a servant," to the manifestations of the Son and Holy Spirit in the Old Testament theophanies (often read allegorically), to the work of the

1. For background in Augustine's early writings, with particular attention to his appropriation of neo-Platonic and pro-Nicene sources, see Lewis Ayres, *Augustine and the Trinity* (Cambridge: Cambridge University Press, 2010), chaps. 1–3; Nello Cipriani, "La presenza di Mario Victorino nella riflessione trinitaria di Agostino," *Augustinianum* 42 (2002): 261–313; D. W. Johnson, "*Verbum* in the Early Augustine (386–397)," *Recherches Augustiniennes* 8 (1972): 25–53. See also Ayres, "'Remember That You Are Catholic' (serm. 52.2): Augustine on the Unity of the Triune God," *Journal of Early Christian Studies* 8 (2000): 39–82; Michel René Barnes, "De Régnon Reconsidered," *Augustinian Studies* 26 (1995): 51–79.

2. Saint Augustine, *The Trinity*, Prefatory Letter, ed. John E. Rotelle, OSA, trans. Edmund Hill, OP (Brooklyn: New City, 1991), 63.

angels, to Christ's death and resurrection as the one mediator, to the pride of the neo-Platonists, to why the Father is not sent, to the distinction between names of God that refer to substance and names that refer to intra-divine relations, to divine simplicity and the appropriation of particular names to particular persons, to the value of the term "person," to our love for justice, to the mental word and the triad of the mind and its knowledge and love of itself, to the mental acts of memory, understanding, and will, to an allegorical reading of Genesis 1–3, to happiness and God's justice in Christ, to the perfection of the image of God in remembering, knowing, and loving God, to the inadequacy of the image.

What then are we to make of Augustine's claim to have written a work characterized by "closely-knit development" from the first book to the last?[3] As this chapter will suggest, Augustine organizes the work with a view to human ascent to intimate participation in God the Trinity. I divide my presentation of *On the Trinity* into four sections. Books 1–4 set forth the basis of our participatory ascent—namely, the truth that Jesus Christ and the Holy Spirit, as manifested in the Old Testament (with the assistance of the angels) and in the New Testament, are coequal with the Father. Books 5–7 contemplate how the New Testament names divine unity and distinction. If we do not understand this naming, we will not be able to gain insight into the God who is named or participate in him through Christ and the Spirit. Books 8–11 begin with the significance of justice and truth as indications of our participation in the divine light, and then identify created images through which to contemplate the divine unity and distinction that the previous section described. Through the image that is found in mental acts, we participate in the divine triune reality that is imaged. Lastly, Books 12–15 unite the image with the reflection on the missions of the Son and Holy Spirit found in the first section. Books 12–15 expose the highest possible participation in God the Trinity available in this life—namely, contemplation of the Triune God in and through the created image purified by the missions. Book 15 includes reflection on the weakness of the image, not to show that we do not participate in the Trinity through the created image purified by the missions, but to show that our participation in this life should be ever-increasing but cannot attain anything near the vision that will be given to us in eternal life.

---

3. For discussion of the structure of *On the Trinity*, see Nathan Crawford, "The Sapiential Structure of Augustine's *De Trinitate*," *Pro Ecclesia* 19 (2010): 434–52; Carol Harrison, *Augustine: Christian Truth and Fractured Humanity* (Oxford: Oxford University Press, 2000), 40–45; Lewis Ayres, "The Christological Context of the *De Trinitate* XIII: Toward Relocating Books VIII–XV," *Augustinian Studies* 29 (1998): 111–39; Luigi Gioia, OSB, *The Theological Epistemology of Augustine's* De Trinitate (Oxford: Oxford University Press, 2008), especially chap. 2; John C. Cavadini, "The Structure and Intention of Augustine's *De trinitate*," *Augustinian Studies* 23 (1992): 103–23; Earl Muller, SJ, "Rhetorical and Theological Issues in the Structuring of Augustine's *De trinitate*," *Studia Patristica* 27 (1994): 356–63; Edmund Hill, OP, "Karl Rahner's 'Remarks on the Dogmatic Treatise *De Trinitate* and St. Augustine,'" *Augustinian Studies* 2 (1971): 67–80.

In short, *On the Trinity* seeks to understand and to model what Christian life is all about. For Christians, the ascent to participation in God begins now: through the grace of the Holy Spirit, in faith and love, we are being conformed to the image of Jesus Christ, perfect wisdom and perfect love.

Books 1–4

Those who seek to come to know God, Augustine observes, err not only when they conceive of God in material terms. They err even more deeply when, while properly conceiving of God as spirit, they attribute to him capacities that he does not have and that they have invented without a natural analogue, such as the view that God causes himself to come into existence. It might seem that the Christian profession that God is triune is just such an invention. The biblical witness to the missions in history of the Son and the Holy Spirit provides an antidote to this view and to other errors about God. Augustine announces that his purpose in writing *On the Trinity* is to show the reasonableness of the doctrine of the Trinity to those imbued with the eyes of faith. The first step is to establish the biblical foundation for faith in the Triune God. He does so first through a creedal confession of faith, in which he notes that "the purpose of all the Catholic commentators I have been able to read on the divine books of both testaments, who have written before me on the trinity which God is," has been to teach that the Father, Son, and Holy Spirit are one God, although only the Son becomes incarnate and only the Spirit comes down upon the gathered community at Pentecost.[4] If the Father, Son, and Holy Spirit are one God, distinct only in relation to each other, how is it that in history the Son does things that the Father and the Holy Spirit do not do? Augustine seeks to contemplate this question not in order to satisfy curiosity but to grow in knowledge and love for God and to share what he learns with others.

Augustine first counters the view that the Son is not fully divine by means of John 1 and other biblical texts.[5] He also reviews the biblical argument for the divinity of the Holy Spirit. Since Jesus himself says that the Father is greater than he, Augustine explains that Philippians 2:6–7, which states that Jesus is in both the "form of God" and the "form of a servant," gives the rule for interpreting such passages.[6] He applies this rule to 1 Corinthians 15:24,

---

4. Augustine, *On the Trinity* 1.7, p. 69. On this confession of faith, see Ayres, *Augustine and the Trinity*, 96–105.

5. See Michel René Barnes, "Exegesis and Polemic in Augustine's *De Trinitate* I," *Augustinian Studies* 30 (1999): 43–59; Barnes, "The Visible Christ and the Invisible Trinity: Mt. 5:8 in Augustine's Trinitarian Theology of 400," *Modern Theology* 19 (2003): 329–55.

6. On this use of Philippians 2:6–7, see Ayres, *Augustine and the Trinity*, 146–59. See also Carol Harrison, *Beauty and Revelation in the Thought of Saint Augustine* (Oxford: Clarendon, 1992), 214–16, 235–38; Albert Verwilghen, "Jesus Christ: Source of Christian Humility," in *Augustine and the Bible*, ed. and trans. Pamela Bright (Notre Dame, IN: University of Notre

which states that Christ will deliver "the kingdom to God the Father," and to a number of other biblical passages. Augustine argues that Christ speaks according to the "form of a servant" so as to turn "our attention to the godhead and [point] the minds of men upward, since to raise them up was the reason why he himself had come down."[7] Throughout this discussion, he highlights the gift of the vision of Father, Son, and Holy Spirit, a gift that goes far beyond any ascent that we could achieve by our own resources. Why, however, does the New Testament contain such potentially confusing passages, and why is God difficult to discern? He suggests that the biblical diversity aims to wear down our pride and bring us to rely on the grace of Christ. He notes also that God intends for us to seek him both through studying his creatures and through studying his Scriptures.

Augustine goes on to discuss the New Testament's teaching that the Son is from the Father. Such derivation does not imply inequality. The Holy Spirit too does not speak on his own, but instead speaks what he receives. Again, this derivation need not mean inequality.[8] With this in mind, he explores the sending of the Son and Holy Spirit in history.[9] He explains that there was a time at which the Word should be incarnated in history, "and the time at which this should happen was timelessly contained within the Word."[10] The change referred to by the sending of the Son occurs in history, not in God. In the incarnation, the Word (the "form of God") does not change into a creature, but rather takes a human nature (the "form of a servant") as his own. The whole Trinity knows and wills this change in history, even though it is the Son who is sent as the incarnate Word, Jesus Christ. The sending of the Son and Holy Spirit occurs in their perceptible manifestation, which draws humans into communion with their invisible divine reality. Yet the Holy Spirit, although manifested by the dove descending on Jesus and by the tongues of fire, does not become incarnate in these physical symbols. Nor should perceptible manifestation be taken to mean that only the Father is immortal and unchangeable.

In light of these insights into the missions of the Son and Holy Spirit, Augustine asks whether the Father is sent in the Old Testament, as for example in the burning bush and in the pillar of cloud. At least the full sending of the Son and Holy Spirit, in its proper sense, awaits the incarnation and mysteries

---

Dame Press, 1999), 301–12; Jaroslav Pelikan, "*Canonica Regula*: The Trinitarian Hermeneutics of Augustine," in *Proceedings of the PMR Conference* 12–13 (1987–88): 17–29.

7. Augustine, *On the Trinity* 1.27, p. 86. On these arguments in Book 1 as characteristic of pro-Nicene theology, see Michel René Barnes, "Rereading Augustine's Theology of the Trinity," in *The Trinity: An Interdisciplinary Symposium on the Trinity*, ed. Stephen T. Davis, Daniel Kendall, SJ, and Gerald O'Collins, SJ (Oxford: Oxford University Press, 1999), 145–76, at 167–74.

8. See Ayres, *Augustine and the Trinity*, 178–81.

9. See Ayres, *Augustine and the Trinity*, 181–88; Basil Studer, OSB, *Augustins De Trinitate. Eine Einführung* (Paderborn: Schöningh, 2005), 171–79; Jean-Louis Maier, *Les Missions divines selon saint Augustin* (Fribourg: Éditions universitaires, 1960).

10. Augustine, *On the Trinity* 2.9, p. 103.

of Christ's life. Yet the burning bush and the pillar of cloud certainly reveal God through perceptible forms. Is the Father then "sent"? Do the Old Testament manifestations reveal the whole Trinity, or particular divine persons? In what way do the Old Testament manifestations anticipate the missions of the Son and Holy Spirit revealed in the New Testament?[11]

Seeking to address these questions in stages, Augustine begins with God's appearance to and speech with Adam and Abraham.[12] He finds that the manner of God's manifestation remains obscure. Adam may or may not have seen a form. If God manifested himself by vocal speech to Adam, then this could be the manifestation of God the Father, just as the Father speaks by a voice at Jesus's baptism and transfiguration, or it could have manifested the entire Trinity. The Lord appears to Abraham in the form of three men at the oak of Mamre, yet Abraham speaks to them as to one man. Again, this manifestation might have been of one divine person or all three. Regarding the two angels that Lot addresses as one Lord, Augustine considers it most likely that these two refer to the Son and Holy Spirit. The burning bush also involves the difficulty that the one speaking from the bush is first identified as an angel, and only then as the Lord God. The pillar of cloud likewise does not make clear whether it manifests the whole Trinity or one of the three persons. Nor do the theophanies at Mount Sinai make matters clear. On various grounds, he conjectures that the manifestation of God at Mount Sinai indicates the presence of the Holy Spirit more than the other two divine persons.

Central to Augustine's discussion are two points. First, although he makes clear that Scripture never states that the Father is sent, he emphasizes that we cannot say that the Old Testament theophanies did not include a manifestation of the Father. In Augustine's view the theophanies "contained enough likely hints and probabilities to make it impossible without rashness to say that God the Father never appeared to the patriarchs or prophets under visible forms."[13] The Ancient of Days (the Father) appears to the prophet Daniel, for example. Augustine emphasizes this point because some people held that only the Father was the invisible God described in 1 Timothy 1:17 and 6:16. Contrary to this view, not only the Son and the Holy Spirit but also the Father could manifest himself through a sensible form.

Second, Augustine seeks to refute those who claim that the Son of God is visible *as Son* and prior to his birth from the Virgin Mary. The Son makes

---

11. See L. Johan van der Lof, "L'exégèse exacte et objective des théophanies de l'Ancien Testament dans le 'De Trinitate,'" *Augustiniana* 14 (1964): 485–99.

12. Kari Kloos shows that the background to Augustine's approach here is his *Answer to Faustus, a Manichean*, not surprising given that Augustine began writing *On the Trinity* in 399. See Kloos, "History as Witness: Augustine's Interpretation of the History of Israel in *Contra Faustum* and *De trinitate*," in *Augustine and History*, ed. Christopher T. Daly, John Doody, and Kim Paffenroth (Lanham, MD: Lexington Books, 2008), 31–51, at 43–46.

13. Augustine, *On the Trinity* 2.32, p. 120.

himself manifest solely by created things; as Son, the senses cannot perceive him. Although Moses speaks with God (and perhaps in particular with the Son) through the Son's sensible manifestation, Moses nonetheless begs to see God (Exod. 33:13, 18) because God is invisible spirit. Prior to the incarnation, God does not have a bodily back. Even the incarnate Son does not possess a bodily divinity. Therefore when Exodus speaks of Moses seeing God's back at Mount Sinai, Augustine interprets this as referring allegorically to Jesus Christ. Believers in Christ, lodged in the Church (the "rock"), must be content with seeing Christ's humanity, even while we still lack perfect spiritual vision of his divinity. Like Moses, we yearn to rise from seeing Christ's "back" (his holy humanity) to seeing supremely his "face" (his divinity).[14] We rightly see Christ's "back" when we see him as risen. Sharing in the Church's faith in his humanity, we believe in his resurrection and receive forgiveness of our sins and union with God.

Augustine's exploration of the missions of the Son and Holy Spirit, and of the manifestations of God in the Old Testament, continues as he asks in what kind of forms God manifested himself in the Old Testament. Guided especially by the Letter to the Hebrews, Augustine focuses on the role of the angels. He first makes clear that God's will governs all things, even where God permits rebellion for the purpose of training his chosen ones in holiness. He describes God's will as manifesting itself in a pattern of participation: "From that lofty throne, set apart in holiness, the divine will spreads itself through all things in marvelous patterns of created movement, first spiritual then corporeal; and it uses all things to carry out the unchanging judgment of the divine decree."[15] Just as God wills the orderly events of the cosmos, so also he wills certain miraculous signs by which he manifests himself. God can enable angels to produce such signs, and he even gives demons the power to produce certain signs. Although God, the only Creator, is the ultimate cause of the miraculous sign, he causes it through the action of his creature. God also proclaims his words through angels, as well as through human prophets. At the burning bush, for instance, God speaks through an angel and, through the angel, God changes Moses's rod into a serpent (Exod. 3–4). The words and deeds are the Lord's, even though the vocal sounds and material changes are produced through the instrumentality of the angel.

Not only does Scripture frequently mention the angels' role in the Old Testament revelation, but also Augustine in this way defends God's invisible and unchanging nature.[16] When the Old Testament reports that Abraham and

---

14. For discussion see Ayres, *Augustine and the Trinity*, 159–62. See also Basil Studer, OSB, *Zur Theophanie-Exegese Augustins. Untersuchung zu einem Ambrosius-Zitat in der Schrift 'De videndo Deo' (ep. 147)* (Rome: I. B. C. Libreria Herder, 1971).

15. Augustine, *On the Trinity* 3.9, p. 132.

16. See Ayres, *Augustine and the Trinity*, 189–91.

Moses see God, this does not mean that they see "God in his own substance."[17] Rather, what they see is a visible form produced by an angel in obedience to God's will, a visible form that manifests God. Augustine also makes clear that the angels are not thereby mediators between God and humans; only Jesus Christ is the mediator. As Augustine states, "The law was given to that people as proclaimed by angels, but the coming of our Lord Jesus Christ was being prepared and foretold by means of it; and he, as God's Word, was present in a wonderful and inexpressible way in the angels through whose proclamation the law was given."[18] By speaking and acting on behalf of God, the angels prepare for the coming of the incarnate Son of God. The words and deeds of the angels point to Christ the mediator rather than displacing Christ the mediator. The Word guides the angels in their manifestation of his wisdom. By producing visible and audible forms, the angels represent either the whole Trinity or a distinct divine person, whether the Father, the Son, or the Holy Spirit. Their ministry allows us to understand how God appears in the Old Testament "by means of his creation and not in his own proper substance."[19]

These manifestations produced by God the Trinity through the angels are not yet divine missions. As Augustine suggests, however, even the New Testament missions—the incarnation of the Son and the descent of the Holy Spirit—do not reveal to our bodily senses the invisible and unchanging divine substance. What then differentiates the Old Testament manifestations from the New Testament missions?

Augustine speaks about the New Testament missions in terms of the Son and Holy Spirit being sent into the world for our redemption. The Father sends the Son in the incarnation, and, through the incarnate Son, the Father pours forth the Spirit into the world. The Old Testament divine manifestations, produced by the angels, prefigure these missions in a way that enables the people of the Old Testament to share by anticipation (faith) in the accomplishment of the missions.

To appreciate the mission of the Son, we must come to recognize our weakness. Augustine says that we must enter into our souls and see how far we have fallen away from God's goodness and love. The Old Testament manifestations of God, like the missions, recall us to our alienated condition and to our need for deeper participation in God.[20] Augustine states, "God sent us sights suited to our wandering state, to admonish us that what we seek is not here, and that we must turn back from the things around us to where our whole being springs from—if it did not, we would not even seek these things here."[21] God

---

17. Augustine, *On the Trinity* 3.25, p. 142.

18. Augustine, *On the Trinity* 3.26, p. 144.

19. Augustine, *On the Trinity* 3.26, p. 144.

20. See Robert Dodaro, OSA, *Christ and the Just Society in the Thought of Augustine* (Cambridge: Cambridge University Press, 2004), 143–44.

21. Augustine, *On the Trinity* 4.2, p. 153. See Ayres, *Augustine and the Trinity*, 166–68.

undermines our pride and reveals to us the path of humility, the path of dependence on God's gifting. We discover that our own resources move us further away from God, and that we only come closer to God when we trust in him in humility. In the Old Testament, God prepares through the ministry of the angels for the mission of the mediator, Christ Jesus. The manifestations of the Old Testament teach the people of God about their weakness and about God's future saving work, "in order that they too might be made weak through being humbled by the same faith as we and once weakened might be perfected."[22]

When the Word becomes incarnate, he cures our idolatrous foolishness with his divine truth, so that our souls become what they were made to be. Augustine comments, "Our enlightenment is to participate in the Word. . . . Yet we were absolutely incapable of such participation and quite unfit for it, so unclean were we through sin, so we had to be cleansed."[23] In God's harmonious plan, we are cleansed by sharing in God's justice through the humility of Christ, who takes on himself the penalty of our injustice and restores to us our proper humanity: "becoming a partaker of our mortality he made us partakers of his divinity."[24] The mission of the Son thus resurrects both our soul and our body by restoring us to spiritual and bodily life. Our restoration begins with repentance and faith and culminates in resurrection and eternal life.

We find our "sacrament" and "example" in Christ's cross and resurrection when we no longer cleave to temporal goods but instead love Christ in his rising and ascending to God the Father.[25] Augustine contrasts the discord and fragmentation of rebellion (cleaving as many individuals to the many created things) with the harmony and unity of body-soul restoration (cleaving as the one Body of Christ to the one God), which he connects with the number symbolism that he finds in Scripture. The Old Testament manifestations, in which all creation has some share, prepare for and prefigure this harmony achieved by the Son's mission from the Father: the many acclaim the one and are reconciled by the one. As Augustine says of this participatory unity, Christ the mediator "wants his disciples to be one in him, because they cannot be one in themselves, split as they are from each other by clashing wills and desires," and so he cleanses and unites his disciples "into one spirit in the furnace of charity," just as the Father and Son share one spirit and one love.[26]

22. Augustine, *On the Trinity* 4.2, p. 154. See Kloos, "History as Witness," 45.
23. Augustine, *On the Trinity* 4.4, pp. 154–55.
24. Augustine, *On the Trinity* 4.4, p. 155.
25. Augustine, *On the Trinity* 4.4, p. 156. See Basil Studer, OSB, "'Sacramentum et exemplum' chez Saint Augustin," *Recherches Augustiniennes* 10 (1975): 87–141; Dodaro, *Christ and the Just Society*, 147–59; Lewis Ayres, "Into the Poem of the Universe: *Exempla*, Conversion, and Church in Augustine's *Confessions*," *Zeitschrift für Antikes Christentum* 13 (2009): 263–81; Gioia, *Theological Epistemology*, 97–103.
26. Augustine, *On the Trinity* 4.12, p. 161.

Pride refuses to participate in God, refuses creaturely status. The devil fell for this reason, as did Adam and Eve. Seeking to lift themselves up, they cut themselves off from the source of life.[27] False worship belongs to this act of pride: Augustine describes "blasphemous symbols and godless curiosities and magical consecrations" as rooted in the desire for control, a desire that backfires in further fragmentation (to the point where, as Augustine says, few care about not sinning but almost all care about not dying).[28] By contrast, when God becomes a creature, his humility redeems creatures. The fragmentation of death is the penalty of sin, and Christ freely undergoes it for us out of love. The mission of Christ thereby conquers the devil's pretension to hold all humans in the just bond of the penalty of death. The devil's pride in his superiority to death contrasts with the Son's humility in his endurance of death for our sake. Here Augustine is at pains to contradict those whose rejection of Christ stems from their belief that no one worthy of worship would die. Those who reject Christ on these grounds do not understand his priestly sacrifice, by which he offers true worship.[29]

Without the mission of the Son of God, we could not purify ourselves for worship, and so we could not participate in God the Trinity as we were created to do. Augustine criticizes the neo-Platonic philosophers for their assumption that they can purify themselves by their own intellectual efforts. He also criticizes them for their ignorance of God's work in history. They take pride in knowing that God is eternal, but they fail to understand time.[30] Augustine contrasts these philosophers with the prophets who both knew of God's eternity and foretold the mission of the Son. This mission meets us where we are, enmeshed in temporal things, and leads us to eternal things. As Augustine puts it, "The eternal allied himself to us in our originated condition, and so provided us with a bridge to his eternity."[31] Christ has died and is risen; he has been sent so as to call us to follow him to everlasting life in truth. Before Christ, the manifestations of God proclaim that the Son will be sent; after Christ, the manifestations of God proclaim that the Son has been sent.

27. See Scott MacDonald, "Primal Sin," in *The Augustinian Tradition*, ed. Gareth B. Matthews (Berkeley: University of California Press, 1999), 110–39, at 114–20.

28. Augustine, *On the Trinity* 4.15, p. 163.

29. See Gioia, *Theological Epistemology*, 83–97; Earl C. Muller, SJ, "The Priesthood of Christ in Book IV of the *De trinitate*," in *Augustine: Presbyter Factus Sum*, ed. Joseph T. Lienhard, SJ, Earl C. Muller, SJ, and Roland J. Teske, SJ (New York: Peter Lang, 1993), 135–49.

30. On this point, see Roland J. Teske, SJ, "The Link between Faith and Time in St. Augustine," in *Augustine: Presbyter Factus Sum*, 195–206; Basil Studer, OSB, "History and Faith in Augustine's *De Trinitate*," *Augustinian Studies* 28 (1997): 7–50, at 12–16; John C. Cavadini, "The Darkest Enigma: Reconsidering the Self in Augustine's Thought," *Augustinian Studies* 38 (2007): 119–32.

31. Augustine, *On the Trinity* 4.24, p. 170. See Barnes, "Visible Christ and the Invisible Trinity," 344.

Augustine specifies that the Father sends the Son, not the man who the Son is. The temporal mission accords with the eternal procession. No inequality therefore arises from the temporal mission. The Wisdom of Solomon describes the entrance of wisdom into the holy soul. The mission of the Son makes this sanctification possible. Augustine states in this regard, "In this sacrament [the incarnation] that was prophesied for the future lay the salvation of those wise and holy men also who were born of women before he was born of the virgin; and in this sacrament now proclaimed as achieved lies the salvation of all who believe, hope, and love."[32] The Father sends the Son into the world in the incarnation, and we receive the one sent when we have faith in him. He can then be said to be "sent" to us. The Word or Wisdom of God is sent to us by the Father when our minds are enlightened by his truth. Thus the mission or sending has two senses: the Word's visible appearance in the world as Christ Jesus, and the Word's invisible indwelling in the minds of those who believe in him. The Father is the sender, and the Son the one sent.

What about the Holy Spirit? He is sent to us when we know him as proceeding from the Father and the Son. When Christ breathes the Holy Spirit on his disciples (John 20:22), he sends the Holy Spirit to enlighten their minds. He sends the Holy Spirit from the Father, and so again the temporal mission reflects the eternal procession. Yet had not the Holy Spirit already been sent to the prophets? Augustine holds that the Holy Spirit had been sent before, but not to the same degree. He grants that it is possible that the Holy Spirit had been manifested before by material things such as the dove or the tongues of fire, but he argues that the mission of the Son reveals not just another manifestation of the Spirit, but a mission of the Spirit that is joined to the Son's mission. Since the missions reflect the eternal processions, Augustine states that the Father could not be described as "sent" even if the Father chose to manifest himself through a creature. There is no one to send the Father; the Father is the source of all sending.[33] Augustine's theology of the missions thus begins with Jesus Christ and has its focus on our sanctification. The sending of the Son from the Father in the incarnation is the visible mission that provides the basis for the invisible mission of the Son and the Spirit. The distinction between mission and manifestation flows from the concrete humanity of Jesus.

With this, Augustine has laid the foundations for his theology of our ascent to God through Christ and the Spirit. The missions reveal how the Father's sending of the Son and the Spirit in time makes possible our coming to share in the eternal divine life of truth and love in which the Father begets the Son and the Father and the Son spirate the Spirit. The divine humility of the missions

32. Augustine, *On the Trinity* 4.27, p. 173. See Studer, "History and Faith," 35–39.
33. See Lewis Ayres, "*Sempiterne Spiritus Donum*: Augustine's Pneumatology and the Metaphysics of Spirit," in *Orthodox Readings of Augustine*, ed. George E. Demacopoulos and Aristotle Papanikolaou (Crestwood, NY: St. Vladimir's Seminary Press, 2008), 127–52, at 130–32.

overcomes our pride and invites us to participate, as creatures, in unity of the glorious processions.

Books 5–7

Augustine begins Book 5 with the warning, "From now on I will be attempting to say things that cannot altogether be said as they are thought by a man— or at least as they are thought by me."[34] Books 1–4 ground his ascent in the missions of the Son and the Holy Spirit, prepared for by the Old Testament manifestations. As we have seen, in Books 1–4 he insists that missions/processions do not indicate a lack of equality with the source, and he explains this further by means of the christological distinction between "form of God" and "form of a servant." Now in Books 5–7 he wishes to go further on the path of contemplation by which he seeks to participate in the truth that is God the Trinity. In particular, he seeks to understand what distinguishes the names for God that describe his oneness from the names for God that describe his threeness. Three biblical texts especially stimulate his inquiry: John 1:18 and 3:16, which describe the Son as only-begotten, thereby raising the question of whether a begotten Son can be the one unchanging God; and 1 Corinthians 1:24, "Christ the power of God and the wisdom of God," which raises the question of whether the Father is the one powerful and wise God or whether the Father lacks these attributes that he finds in the Son.[35]

Augustine's purpose is to better understand the reality in which he believes, not for mere factual understanding but rather for the sake of participating in the living divine truth. Unless he can understand the difference between names that describe the divine unity and names that (without compromising this unity) describe the divine threeness, he will not be able to proceed on his quest to participate more deeply in the divine truth that he believes and confesses. Distinguishing these names is made possible by the revelation of God's Trinity in and through the missions of Christ and the Holy Spirit, but the task now is to inquire into how the names that Scripture applies to the Trinity actually distinguish the divine persons while leaving conceptually intact the perfect unity of God. The goal throughout is to be lifted up into the wisdom of God.

Can this attempt to ascend to the Trinity avoid falling into philosophical pride because of its mode of sustained rational inquiry into God and its effort to understand mysteries that are infinitely beyond us? Augustine defends his attempt by noting that it arises from charity, which burns with the desire to

---

34. Augustine, *On the Trinity* 5.1, p. 189. See T. J. van Bavel, OSA, "God in between Affirmation and Negation According to Augustine," in *Augustine: Presbyter Factus Sum*, 73–97.

35. For background see Michel René Barnes, "One Nature, One Power: Consensus Doctrine in Pro-Nicene Polemic," in *Studia Patristica*, vol. 29, ed. Elizabeth A. Livingstone (Leuven: Peeters, 1997), 205–23.

know the beloved insofar as the beloved can be properly known by the creature. He emphasizes that God's revelation, not philosophy, measures his inquiry; the Trinity far surpasses reason and must not be reduced to what reason can demonstrate. At the same time, he points out that God should not be considered less than the greatest created power that we know—namely, intellectual power. When we observe our intellectual power, we do not find material quantity, color, parts, spatial movement, or other such things. God too should be recognized as immaterial, so that we can begin with the tremendous mystery of the one who is "good without quality, great without quantity, creative without need or necessity, presiding without position, holding all things together without possession, wholly everywhere without place, everlasting without time, without any change in himself making changeable things, and undergoing nothing."[36] If we think of God in this way, at least we will not attribute to God attributes that pertain only to creatures; we will at least be able to speak rightly about what God is not.

Citing Exodus 3:14, where God names himself "I am who I am" and simply "I am," Augustine argues that God's being is infinite. Anything that has being only partially can be changed. To have the potential to be more or less means that one has being in a limited manner. God *is* infinitely, and therefore he is not able to be less than he is. God's "substance," his infinite "to be," is unchanging not in a static way but as infinite existence. But if this is so, can God the Father, who is unbegotten, beget a Son? Does this not introduce a change into the substance of God?

The Arians, Augustine observes, press this question.[37] They point out that nothing said about God can rightly describe a change in God's substance, and they hold that everything said about God is said about God's substance. The divine substance is unbegotten. It follows, in their view, that the begotten Son is not of the same divine substance as the Father. Augustine answers by citing John 10:30, "I and the Father are one," which indicates unity of substance. How might the Arians get around this text? He suggests that the most plausible way would be to suppose that not all statements about God are predicated according to substance. But if so, the Arians would also need to admit that "unbegotten" and "begotten" might not have to do with the divine substance. There is no change in God's substance, but there can be relations in God that do not change the substance.[38]

36. Augustine, *On the Trinity* 5.2, p. 190.
37. For background to Augustine's critique of "Arians," see Michel René Barnes, "The Arians of Book V, and the Genre of *De Trinitate*," *Journal of Theological Studies* 44 (1993): 185–95; Barnes, "Rereading Augustine's Theology of the Trinity," 165–69; Gioia, *Theological Epistemology*, 148–51; Ayres, *Augustine and the Trinity*, 171–73; Brian E. Daley, SJ, "The Giant's Twin Substances: Ambrose and the Christology of Augustine's *Contra sermonem Arianorum*," in *Augustine: Presbyter Factus Sum*, 477–95.
38. For Augustine's sources and argument here, see Ayres, *Augustine and the Trinity*, 212–17.

The Father is eternally Father of the Son. As John 10:30 shows, they are of the same substance. It follows that begetting or fatherhood expresses an eternal relation in God rather than a change in the divine substance. The Son is "begotten" not with reference to his divine substance but with reference to the Father who begets. It is not the divine substance that is begotten, but the Son. The names "Father" and "Son" refer to relations in God, not to changes in God's substance. The Father is "unbegotten" because he is not the Son, rather than because his substance is different from the Son's. In making this distinction, Augustine draws profitably on Aristotle's categories: in creatures, the "accident" of relation does not change the substance. Whatever is said about God's substance pertains equally to the Father, Son, and Holy Spirit. The Father, Son, and Holy Spirit are distinct only in relation to each other. For lack of a better word, we name their distinction by calling them three "persons" of one substance. The Father, Son, and Holy Spirit do not participate in the divine substance (the one being, wisdom, goodness, greatness, eternity, etc.), as if there were three "beings" or "greatnesses." Far from being participations in God, the Father is God, the Son is God, and the Holy Spirit is God. The Father, Son, and Holy Spirit relate without changing the one divine substance, because they are the one God.

Augustine then inquires into the biblical names "Father," "Son," and "Holy Spirit." What does the New Testament teach us about these names? Jesus Christ reveals the Father. The Son is the Father's Word and image. Citing a variety of New Testament passages, Augustine describes the Holy Spirit as the "gift" of the Father and the Son.[39] The Holy Spirit is the communion of the Father and the Son, who proceeds from them as from one origin. The Holy Spirit is sent to us so that we can participate in this communion. The Father, Son, and Holy Spirit are the one Creator of all things. Augustine ascertains these truths from the missions of the Son and Holy Spirit revealed in the New Testament.

The biblical names "Lord" and "Creator" pose a different set of problems. Before creation existed, how could God have been Lord or Creator? If God is not eternally Lord and Creator, then are these proper names of God? Does God change himself when he creates, by adding to himself the attributes of Lord and Creator? Augustine explains that God is Creator with reference to the creation, so that the change occurs on the side of creation rather than on the side of God. God is infinite being; he does not become more so (or less so) when the creation comes to be. Creation has a relationship to God that does not change God. The God to which creation relates is the eternal, unchanging, infinite God. Likewise, when I accept God as my savior, he becomes my Lord, but the change is in me rather than in God. The names "Lord" and "Creator" are true names, because they describe our relation to God. They are not names that fill up what was previously a lack in God. Otherwise God would not be God, and "Lord" and "Creator" would name a limited, finite being among beings.

39. See Ayres, *"Sempiterne Spiritus Donum,"* in *Orthodox Readings of Augustine,* 140–44.

Continuing his exploration of the biblical names of God, Augustine turns to the questions arising from the anti-Arian use of 1 Corinthians 1:24.[40] Some fourth-century orthodox Christians used this verse to demonstrate that since God was never without his power and wisdom, the Son is coeternal with the Father. The problem with this way of putting it, however, is that it seems to commit orthodox Christians to the view that the Son is the Father's power and wisdom, so that without the Son the Father would lack power and wisdom. How can the Father beget power without being powerful, or beget wisdom without being wise? If the Son is the Father's power and wisdom, how can the Father and the Son be said to have one and the same substance? If only the Son were powerful and wise, then only the Son would be God. The Father would participate in the Son's power and wisdom, rather than being powerful and wise. Against such views, Augustine suggests that Paul has in view the Son's being begotten, so that the Son (as Son) is not merely power and wisdom, but power and wisdom from the Father, in relation to the Father. Augustine also employs the verse to observe that the Father cannot have more greatness than the Son, because the Son is the Father's greatness, in the sense that the Father begets his coequal Son. The same principle holds for the Holy Spirit, who is the gift and love of the Father and the Son. In order to pour out divine love upon us, the Holy Spirit must be this love—as must be the Father and the Son.

Can the New Testament's mix of names pertaining to the divine substance and names pertaining to the divine persons (distinct only in their relations of origin) retain the simplicity of God? There is no created analogue to the divine simplicity: both bodies and souls are multiple and changeable in themselves. God receives many names, but these names all refer to the simple divine reality, since God has no parts or components. But how can the three persons be the simple God? Despite the efforts Augustine has already made to deny it, does not the doctrine of the Trinity introduce multiplicity into God?

Augustine clarifies that the Father, Son, and Holy Spirit are unlike other triads in that they do not add anything to each other. The Father, Son, and Holy Spirit are not more than the Father. Since each person indwells the others (as follows from the relations of origin) they are inseparable. When we say that the Father alone is God, we mean that the Father is fully God, needing no augmentation, without denying that God is Father, Son, and Holy Spirit.[41] Even their unity as God is better described as simplicity, because God is not

---

40. For discussion see Ayres, *Augustine and the Trinity*, 221–27; Michel René Barnes, "*De Trinitate* VI and VII: Augustine and the Limits of Nicene Orthodoxy," *Augustinian Studies* 38 (2007): 189–202.

41. See Ayres, "*Sempiterne Spiritus Donum*," in *Orthodox Readings of Augustine*, 132–36. John Behr argues that Augustine differs from his predecessors in defining the one God in this way rather than conceiving of the one God as the Father. See Behr, "Calling upon God as Father: Augustine and the Legacy of Nicaea," in *Orthodox Readings of Augustine*, 153–65; Behr, "Response to Ayres: The Legacies of Nicaea, East and West," *Harvard Theological Review* 100 (2007): 145–52.

one among many other entities. The Father, Son, and Holy Spirit are the infinite God. They are not "one" if by this is meant the concrete dimensions that we associate with one entity set apart from others. The numbers three and one function differently with regard to the Triune God than with regard to creatures. Similarly, although we increase when we cleave to God, God does not increase by our participation in him. Since creatures are participations in God, the deepening of our participation augments us but not God.

At this stage Augustine briefly takes up seemingly subordinationist passages such as 1 Corinthians 3:23; 11:3; and John 14:28 by calling to mind once again the christological distinction between "form of God" and "form of a servant." He gently corrects Hilary's distinction of the divine persons according to eternity (Father), form/image (Son), and use/gift (Holy Spirit).[42] Although the Son and Holy Spirit are coeternal with the Father, Hilary's approach is not wrong if he means solely that the Father is the source. Hilary's approach also helps us to discern traces of the divine triad in the created order, as for instance in a creature's unity, form, and order.[43]

Circling back to 1 Corinthians 1:24, Augustine asks whether the Father, in speaking the Word, also speaks his own wisdom. Can the Father's wisdom be conceived outside the Father's speaking the Word, since the Father *is* this begetting? Is being the Father's Word the same as being the Father's wisdom? As has been the case throughout much of Books 5–7, Augustine is looking for a way of distinguishing, without separating, the person and the essence.[44] Begetting constitutes the Father as Father, and yet begetting does not constitute the godhead as godhead. If it did, then the distinct divine persons could not be the same God, since only one divine person begets. The distinct relations of origin cannot be understood without attending to what is common in God. Relational names do not take the place of substantial names, and vice versa. As Augustine remarks, "Every being that is called something by way of relationship is also something besides the relationship."[45] Indeed, if being were itself relation, there would be no relation. Augustine states that "if the Father is not also something with reference to himself, there is absolutely nothing there to be talked of with reference to something else."[46]

42. For correction of Augustine's understanding of Hilary, see Gioia, *Theological Epistemology*, 133. For Hilary's influence on Augustine's trinitarian theology, see also Ayres, *Augustine and the Trinity*, 90–91.

43. See John Edward Sullivan, OP, *The Image of God: The Doctrine of St. Augustine and Its Influence* (Dubuque, IA: Priory, 1963), 90.

44. Augustine prefers *"essentia"* to *"substantia"*: see *On the Trinity* 7.10, pp. 227–28. For discussion see Ayres, *Augustine and the Trinity*, 200–202, 207; and Roland Teske, SJ, "Augustine's Use of 'Substantia' in Speaking about God," *Modern Schoolman* 62 (1985): 147–63.

45. Augustine, *On the Trinity* 7.2, p. 219.

46. Augustine, *On the Trinity* 7.2, p. 220. See Mary T. Clark, RSCJ, "Augustine on Person: Divine and Human," in *Augustine: Presbyter Factus Sum*, 99–120, at 114–15; Peter Burnell, *The Augustinian Person* (Washington, DC: Catholic University of America Press, 2005), 187–93.

It follows that the Father does not become wise in begetting the Word. Rather, the Father and the Son have in common the attribute of wisdom (as with all of the substantial names of God). The Father and the Son are distinguished by the relation of origin in the communication of the divine substance, not by the substance itself. The divine substance must not be conflated with the relation: the Son relates to the Father, but wisdom in the Son does not relate to wisdom in the Father. The Son and the Father are distinct but their wisdom is in no way distinct. Only this preserves the unity and simplicity of God the Trinity.[47] Augustine comments that "the Father and the Son are together one being and one greatness and one truth and one wisdom. But the Father and the Son are not both together one Word, because they are not both together one Son."[48] The substance does not subsist outside the distinct relations, and yet the substance must be understood as common to the distinct persons rather than as relational in the way that the persons are.

Even so, Augustine appreciates that there is a biblical connection between "wisdom" and the Word. When we turn to the Word made flesh, we become wise. In the imitation of Christ's wisdom, the image of God in us becomes configured to the divine image.[49] The characteristics of wisdom give us some glimpse into the Word, although wisdom is common to all three divine persons.[50]

Augustine addresses the problems associated with using the term "persons" to describe the Father, Son, and Holy Spirit.[51] "Person" itself, like "essence," is a generic word; yet the Father, Son, and Holy Spirit are what they are because of distinct relations of origin. What they share in common belongs not to what is three in God, but to what is one. If they shared "personhood" in common, then this property would name what is one in God. Nor can we suppose that the one substance of God is diversified into three "persons": the divine essence is not the "stuff" of which the persons are made.[52] The Father is God, rather than being made out of God. The key to these problems is to realize that Scripture speaks about God in two ways: according to essence and according to relation.

47. For discussion see Lewis Ayres, "The Grammar of Augustine's Trinitarian Theology," in *Augustine and His Critics: Essays in Honour of Gerald Bonner*, ed. Robert Dodaro and George Lawless (London: Routledge, 2000), 51–76; Scott A. Dunham, *The Trinity and Creation in Augustine: An Ecological Analysis* (Albany: State University of New York Press, 2008), 39–40.

48. Augustine, *On the Trinity* 7.3, p. 221.

49. For discussion see Gioia, *Theological Epistemology*, 232–97, especially 238.

50. On Augustine's theology of trinitarian appropriation, see Ayres, *Augustine and the Trinity*, 228–29, 255–56.

51. See Ayres, *Augustine and the Trinity*, 217–20; Richard Cross, "*Quid tres?* On What Precisely Augustine Professes Not to Understand in *De Trinitate* 5 and 7," *Harvard Theological Review* 100 (2007): 215–32.

52. See Richard Cross, "On Generic and Derivation Views of God's Trinitarian Substance," *Scottish Journal of Theology* 56 (2003): 464–80.

Augustine recognizes that his discussion of the biblical names of God has been quite complex. For those whom the discussion confuses, he urges simple faith in the Father, Son, and Holy Spirit, the one God who is infinite perfection. Rather than weakening either the distinction of the persons or the unity of God by incautious speech, we should keep in mind that we are "talking about inexpressible matters, that we may somehow express what we are completely unable to express."[53]

In sum, the missions of the Son and the Holy Spirit provide the basis for the ascent. The God revealed by these missions is illumined through study of the biblical names for the divine oneness and threeness. Regarding the next step of the ascent, Augustine points out that his discussion of the divine names should assist in the interpretation of Genesis 1:26, "Then God said, 'Let us make man in our image, after our likeness.'" The reality to which the plural "our" refers is not gods, but the one God who is relationally distinguished as Father, Son, and Holy Spirit. If humans are in God's trinitarian image, then this implies that humans have a certain likeness to God, even if great unlikeness as well. The likeness offers the path for the next stage of the ascent. On the basis of Colossians 3:10, Augustine suggests that this likeness is in the mind, which makes sense since God is not material but spiritual (cf. John 4:24).

Books 8–11

On the basis of Books 1–7, Augustine turns to explore the revealed truth that humans are in the image of the Trinity. Although this is the main task of Books 8–11, he asks a preliminary question in Book 8: Is it possible truly to conceive of something that is not material? The danger is that one might find oneself, despite one's best efforts, thinking only "of masses and spaces, little or great, with images of bodies flitting around in [one's] mind like ghosts."[54] How can one "perceive the essence or being of truth without any mass, without any changeableness"?[55] If we cannot conceptualize spirit, we will inevitably assume that the Father and the Son together are greater than the Father, and we will imagine that the divine being relates to itself in the Father, Son, and Holy Spirit.

Augustine begins with a reflection on truth. God is truth. When we perceive truth, do we perceive God? We think of true things and find ourselves at the level of created realities. Truth itself we imagine as a bright light or as a spiritual form animating all things. Truth is good, and we can think of good air, a good house, and so forth. Certainly God is good, and created goodness participates in the infinite goodness that is God. Can we remove from our

---

53. Augustine, *On the Trinity* 7.7, p. 224.
54. Augustine, *On the Trinity* 7.11, p. 230.
55. Augustine, *On the Trinity* 8.1, p. 241. For discussion of Book 8, see Ayres, *Augustine and the Trinity*, 281–85.

thought "air" and "house," and simply see unrestricted "good"? Without this unchangeable good, no finite changeable good could exist. We love all the good things around us. Can we move from cleaving in love to these good things, to cleaving in love to goodness itself, in which the finite things participate?[56] Our goodness comes from the divine Creator: Augustine quotes Acts 17:28, "In him we live and move and have our being." In order to be truly good, our soul needs to love the creative source above the creatures.

A problem arises here: How can we love the good God if we do not know him? We need to love him in order to desire to know him, and we need to know him in order to love him. Augustine answers that we can know him by faith and on this basis rise to greater love. By faith too we know something about him: in his infinite humility, he became man and died and rose again for the forgiveness of our sins. Yet our faith in God the Trinity runs the risk of including false notions, in which case our failure to know the living God will result in an inability to love him. It seems that we cannot know what three-and-one means, especially since the transcendent God is not like a creature. In short, what do we love when, in faith, we love the Trinity?

Augustine tries to make this question more manageable by asking what we love when we love St. Paul. His answer is that we love his just mind, which is still alive although his body is dead. We know what a mind is because we too have a mind, and so we can love his mind. Yet how do we know what justice is, and can someone who lacks a just mind love (and desire to imitate) the just mind of another person? Augustine argues that even those who lack justice possess the form or idea of justice in their minds. Their minds are not just, yet their minds possess an accurate idea of justice. Even the unjust love this form, although they do not love it enough yet to imitate the just mind of another person.[57] Since the goodness of a person includes justice, we love a person rightly when we love the justice that we see in the person. Injustice lessens the goodness of the person, and so we cannot properly love injustice.

Speaking of love of God and love of neighbor, Augustine says, "True love then is that we should live justly by cleaving to the truth, and so for the love of men by which we wish them to live justly we should despise all mortal things. In this way we will be ready and able even to die for the good of our brethren, as the Lord Jesus Christ taught us by his example."[58] Love cannot

56. See Lewis Ayres, "The Discipline of Self-Knowledge in Augustine's *De trinitate* Book X," in *The Passionate Intellect: Essays on the Transformation of the Classical Traditions Presented to I. G. Kidd*, ed. Lewis Ayres (London: Transaction, 1995), 261–96, at 265.
57. See Gioia, *Theological Epistemology*, 203–4.
58. Augustine, *On the Trinity* 8.10, p. 252. On the relationship between love of God and love of neighbor, see Raymond Canning, *The Unity of Love for God and Neighbor in St. Augustine* (Heverlee, Belgium: Augustinian Historical Institute, 1993); Eric Gregory, *Politics and the Order of Love: An Augustinian Ethic of Democratic Citizenship* (Chicago: University of Chicago Press, 2008), 320–23 and elsewhere; Burnell, *Augustinian Person*, 101–35.

be separated from justice. We cannot love God or neighbor without loving justice. Furthermore, we cannot properly love our neighbor without loving love; if we hate love, then we will certainly not love our neighbor. When we love love, we love God: "God is love" (1 John 4:8). If we want to love God the Trinity, then, we need only to love our neighbor and to love the love with which we love our neighbor. When we love our neighbor and love this love, we "see" God.[59] From loving goodness and justice in our neighbor (that is, loving our neighbor's being, since evil is privation and cannot be loved), we rise to knowing and loving God. Augustine draws the conclusion that seeing supreme goodness and justice in the mind of St. Paul inspires us to greater love of God by inspiring a greater love for the "forms" of goodness and justice, which are God. Likewise, although God can be known and loved in some way without faith, faith in Christ Jesus inspires us to far greater love of God.

The act of love presents to us a triad: lover, beloved, love. Could this be the human mind's trinitarian image? Before proceeding, Augustine reminds us that even if we find a trinity that truly reflects God the Trinity, this understanding will be but the beginning of our quest to know the God who infinitely transcends and surpasses our minds. He also warns once more against the supreme danger inherent in his participatory ascent—namely, that of incautious reasoning that attributes to God the Trinity what does not belong to him and thereby arrives at a false god and a disordered love.

When one loves oneself, the lover and the beloved differ from the love. Only God is love; no human lover simply is love. When the mind loves itself, furthermore, the lover and the beloved are the same. Even so, Augustine finds himself on a promising track: lover/beloved and love are the same in the mind that loves itself fully, and they are also distinct with reference to each other. Can this dyad become a triad? Augustine observes that only the mind that knows itself can love itself. There are two dyads: mind and its love, and mind and its knowledge. These two dyads resolve into a triad: mind, its knowledge of itself, and its love of itself.[60] When the mind knows and loves itself fully, these three are equal. Mind is the same as mind fully knowing itself (or loving itself). They are the one mind, not parts of the mind or accidental qualities of the mind.[61] But they are clearly distinct according to relation of origin: mind generates knowledge, and mind and knowledge breathe forth love. In the mind that knows and loves itself, each of them is in the other; for example, the mind that knows itself knows its love of itself, and the mind that loves itself loves its knowledge of itself. Mind, knowledge, and love thus compose a triad or trinity that images the divine Trinity.

59. For a critique of Augustine's view, see Andrew Louth, "Love and the Trinity: Saint Augustine and the Greek Fathers," *Augustinian Studies* 33 (2002): 1–16.
60. See Ayres, *Augustine and the Trinity*, 285–90.
61. See Burnell, *Augustinian Person*, 65–67.

Or do they? Augustine notices that in knowing and loving itself, the mind does not love something eternal and unchanging. The human mind is not eternal truth, although it participates in this truth and therefore can make judgments of truth. The human mind possesses ideas of justice, goodness, and beauty, but the human mind itself is not these forms. The mind can be mistaken about someone else's justice. Yet the mind still rightly knows and loves the justice that it attributed to that person. When we conceive something in the mind, we formulate an inner word rooted in love primarily for the creature or primarily for the Creator. Only loved knowledge is a "word" in the sense of a concept about which we form a judgment.[62] Love unites the word to the mind by approving the concept that the mind has articulated. When the mind knows itself and approves what it knows, it generates a "word" that is loved. This word is the image of the mind. In this way Augustine further develops his triad as an image of the Trinity, by establishing how the mind's knowledge of itself is word and image, united to the mind by love.

But if the mind's knowledge of itself is describable as a begotten word or image, why cannot the same thing be said of the mind's love of itself? Augustine mentions that even Scripture sometimes seems unclear with regard to why the Holy Spirit is not another begotten Son. What distinguishes the Holy Spirit from the Son, since the Father is the source of both?

When it fully knows itself, the mind begets or generates a perfect knowledge of itself. This process can aptly be described as generation or begetting, because knowledge is brought forth or brought to light. The appetite or will to know—which is a love stimulated by partial knowledge rather than love for the unknown—then becomes love for what the mind has come to know. Thus love is not "brought forth" in the same way that knowledge is.[63] Rather, love embraces what is known and approvingly unites it to the mind. Augustine adds that no mind is ignorant of itself. The purpose of the mind seeking to know itself is to recollect itself and thereby rediscover, in its fallen condition, the immaterial substance that it truly is.[64] Augustine explores memory, understanding, and will in terms of whether the first two have the right objects and whether the third makes good use of what the memory and understanding possess; and he shows that each is fully in the other, so that each and all are equal to each and all, and the three are one.[65]

Augustine is not satisfied with solely identifying the triad of mind, knowledge, and love. He also wishes to find triads that model the Trinity in the

62. See Ayres, *Augustine and the Trinity*, 291–93; A. N. Williams, *The Divine Sense: The Intellect in Patristic Theology* (Cambridge: Cambridge University Press, 2007), 167–71.

63. See Ayres, *Augustine and the Trinity*, 293.

64. See Ayres, *Augustine and the Trinity*, 298–302. See also Rowan Williams, "The Paradoxes of Self-Knowledge in the *De trinitate*," in *Augustine: Presbyter Factus Sum*, 121–34, at 133.

65. For discussion of Book 10, see especially Ayres, "The Discipline of Self-Knowledge in Augustine's *De trinitate* Book X," 272–96. See also Ayres, *Augustine and the Trinity*, 303–5.

bodily powers of the human person. The ascent that he envisions ultimately attains to a union with God that involves not only beatific vision but also bodily resurrection. In eternal life, the soul and body of the human person unite in participating in the Trinity. Furthermore, in this life bodily triads are more apparent to us, and they can help us to understand the mental triad that is the image of God.

The first bodily triad that Augustine identifies has to do with the act of seeing. In the act of seeing, he finds the visible object, our vision of the object, and our intention to see the object. Comparing this triad to the image of mind, knowledge, and love, he observes that the visible object is like the mind, because the visible object at least partially brings forth or generates our vision of the object. Our vision of the object is sense knowledge, and our will to see the object is the desire or love that binds together the visible object and the vision of the object. These three, of which the last is the most spiritual, form a unity in the act of seeing. A second bodily triad consists in the act of recollection, which unites the mind's eye, the remembered image, and the intention to remember. The mind's eye in a certain sense brings forth or begets the image stored in the memory, and the intention to remember binds together the mind's eye and the remembered image.

These likenesses to the Trinity are what we should expect to find, given that the Trinity is the Creator. As presented by Augustine, these triads constitute a movement inward, an ascent from the material toward the spiritual, that leads toward the fully participatory image of the Trinity: mind, knowledge, and love. In living out this ascent, the key is to ensure that our diverse intentions or wills, which have their own particular ends, "are referred to the end of that wish or will by which we wish to live happily and to come to that life which is not to be referred to anything else but will be all-sufficient to the lover in itself."[66] Our desires form "a ladder for those who would climb to happiness."[67] In the relationship between memory (and imagination), sight, and the will Augustine finds another triad, that of Wisdom 11:20: measure, number, and weight.[68]

Books 12–15

The first seven books set forth the foundations of Augustine's ascent—that is, the missions of the Son and the Holy Spirit along with conceptual clarifications regarding the biblical naming of God. There would be no participation in God the Trinity without the missions of the Son and the Holy Spirit in history (prepared for in the Old Testament theophanies), and there would be

66. Augustine, *On the Trinity* 11.10, p. 312.
67. Augustine, *On the Trinity* 11.10, p. 312.
68. See Harrison, *Beauty and Revelation*, 101–10.

no participatory ascent toward greater understanding of God without the key rules for interpreting the biblical names of God, above all the christological distinction between "form of God" and "form of a servant" and the distinction between names that refer to the divine substance and names that refer to the distinct relations of origin. These seven books, of course, do not merely show the biblical and theological foundations for the ascent to participation in God the Trinity. They also compose in themselves a rigorous participatory ascent, because by their end we already find ourselves led by the true mediator and true image, Jesus Christ, into the intelligibility of the Father's only-begotten Word who with the Father spirates the Holy Spirit as gift and love.

Extending this biblical and theological path, Books 8–11 investigate whether, and if so how, intellectual participation in God the Trinity is possible. Can we truly raise our minds to perceive an immaterial, infinite reality, without being bound by the material images so fundamental to our act of understanding? When we love the Trinity whom we know in faith, what are we loving? Augustine helps us answer these questions by exploring our love of justice and the relationship of love of neighbor to love of God. As we have seen, he finds a triad in the act of love: lover, beloved, and love. Already at the end of Book 7, he noted the significance of Genesis 1:26, "Then God said, 'Let us make man in our image, after our likeness.'" If we are in the image of God, then by this image or likeness we must be able to know and love him. Books 8–11 develop Augustine's insight that the mind, when it knows and loves itself, leads us into the intelligible mystery of the three-and-one. The image of the Trinity found in mind, knowledge, and love is supported by Augustine's analysis of our mind's participation in the eternal "form" of truth and justice and by his account of the triads that lead us from bodily sensation to intellectual act.

Is our contemplation of the Trinity through the created image of mind, knowledge, and love as far as we can go with respect to participation in this life in the trinitarian wisdom and love? Augustine thinks that we can ascend further. While granting the weakness of the created image, Books 12–15 make the case that the participatory ascent to the Trinity can be enhanced by combining what we have learned about the image with the earlier reflections on the missions of the Son and the Holy Spirit. Our contemplation of the Trinity through his image thereby becomes a contemplation of the Trinity through the image as purified and elevated by the missions of the Son and the Holy Spirit. This is the highest degree of participation in God the Trinity possible in this life.

Augustine is aware, however, that contemplation of God retains our attention only with difficulty. We tend to focus instead upon the manifold beauty and operation of bodily creatures. Against this tendency to neglect divine things, he argues that our upright posture should suggest to us the need to raise our mind "toward what is highest in spiritual things—not of course by the elevation of pride but by the dutiful piety of justice."[69] We share sense memory with other animals, but the ability to make use of memory in thought and to make judgments of truth according to nonbodily standards does not appear in the other animals. We have the ability to contemplate eternal truth (*sapientia*), although we use our minds largely with regard to this-worldly things (*scientia*).[70] The mind is one entity, but it has two functions (cf. 1 Cor. 12:8).[71]

Augustine makes these observations in preparation for his discussion of two alternatives to his path of participatory ascent via the trinitarian image of mind, knowledge, and love. Both alternatives derive their intelligibility from bodiliness and appeal to Genesis 1 for support. The first alternative holds that the image of the Trinity is found in the union of man (Father), woman (Holy Spirit), and child (Son). This proposal focuses attention upon bodily relationships rather than upon spiritual relationships. Augustine grants that this proposal helpfully reminds us that human bodies, as created by God, manifest traces of the Trinity. The key concern that Augustine expresses, however, is that if the image of God were man, woman, and child, then individual humans would not be made in the image of God. Adam and Eve would not have been in the image of God prior to their having a son, Abel. Genesis 1:27 says that male and female are in the image of God, and neither this passage nor any other biblical text implies that they only became the image of God after having a child.

The second alternative consists in the view that only men are the image of God. On this view, the bodily difference between male and female suffices to make only the male human person the image of God. St. Paul seems to lend support to this position when he writes to the Corinthians about proper comportment in worship, "For a man ought not to cover his head, since he is the image and glory of God; but woman is the glory of man" (1 Cor. 11:7). To this passage, Augustine opposes Genesis 1:27, "So God created man in his own image, in the image of God he created him; male and female he created them." These passages seem to conflict, but Augustine holds that God intends to teach truth through both of them. Certainly, Genesis 1:27 is absolutely clear that men and women are created in the image of God. The bodily difference does not prevent women from being the image of God the Trinity. What then could Paul have meant?

Here Augustine returns to his reflections on the mind's two functions, *sapientia* and *scientia*. Suggesting that in 1 Corinthians 11:7 Paul has in view a symbolic understanding of male and female, Augustine conjectures that the symbolism at play has to do with the relationship of the two functions of the mind: wisdom is "male," and science "female."[72] Since he recognizes that this

69. Augustine, *On the Trinity* 12.1, p. 322. On contemplation see Williams, *Divine Sense*, 175–87.

70. See Dodaro, *Christ and the Just Society*, 165–68; Williams, *Divine Sense*, 172–73.

71. See Burnell, *Augustinian Person*, 29–30.

72. He goes on to note that earlier Catholic interpreters of Genesis 2–3 had symbolically interpreted the man as the mind and the woman as the bodily senses. Augustine disagrees with

interpretation may seem far-fetched, he gives other examples of Paul's statements about women that call for a symbolic interpretation. For instance, Paul says that women will be saved by bearing children and adds that charity and holiness will be the salvation of women. Augustine comments that certainly Paul could not mean that childless virgins could not be saved. Instead, Paul's mention of "children" may symbolically mean the good works that flow from charity and holiness. Also, if Paul thought that bodily form actually excluded women from being the image of God, then how is it that Paul writes that we become new creatures, with a new nature, when we are "renewed in the spirit of your minds" (Eph. 4:23)? Paul makes the same point to the Colossians: "You have put off the old nature with its practices and have put on the new nature, which is being renewed in knowledge after the image of its creator" (Col. 3:9–10). Can Paul have considered that women, because of their bodies, could not be renewed in their minds, renewed in the image of the Creator? Could this be the same Paul who writes to the Galatians that "there is neither male nor female; for you are all one in Christ Jesus" (Gal. 3:28)?

In 1 Corinthians 11:7, Paul is discussing the covering of the female head during Christian worship. This covering has no meaning in itself; it must therefore have "some hidden sacramental or symbolic meaning."[73] In light of Paul's other symbolic renderings of the male/female bodily difference—and given Paul's clear assertion that women are equal to men in Christ Jesus—Augustine argues that the supposition that only men are in the image of God has no purchase as an interpretation of Paul. As Augustine puts it, "The authority of the apostle as well as plain reason assures us that man was not made to the image of God as regards the shape of the body, but as regards his rational mind."[74] Since the image of God in humans does not consist in the shape of the body, the image of God must consist in the mind. Women and men both fully possess the rational mind, which is constitutive of human nature. The head covering of which Paul speaks can have to do with the image of God only if it relates somehow to the mind. In reasoning about divine things our heads are symbolically uncovered; in reasoning about things pertaining to creatures our heads are symbolically covered. Male and female here signify the two functions of the mind.

In the fallen human person, *scientia* usurps the place of *sapientia*. The fallen human person cleaves to the created things of this world rather than to the Creator. Stripped of the contemplation of eternal truth, the fallen person clothes himself or herself in mere rhetoric rather than in good works. Augustine offers here a spiritual interpretation of Genesis 3. The fall depicts the soul's

---

this interpretation on the grounds that Genesis 2:20 emphasizes how distant the woman is from other animals, and humans share the bodily senses with other animals. See Augustine, *On the Trinity* 12.20, p. 333.

73. Augustine, *On the Trinity* 12.11, p. 328.
74. Augustine, *On the Trinity* 12.12, pp. 328–29.

effort to cleave to a part as though it were more than the whole: this proud and greedy grasping means that the soul, which in God enjoyed the whole, cannot even enjoy the part. In cleaving to a part, the soul lives according to what it governs (the body) and thereby loses its governance of the body and falls into a life marked by the pursuit not of wisdom but of the satisfaction of curiosity, conceit, and bodily lust. Rather than possessing the divine things that are the common good of rational creatures, the soul chooses to live for the bodily things that are a private good. Since the human person's proper good or ultimate end is God, making bodily things into our proper good distorts everything we do.

This point leads Augustine to clarify his understanding of the image of God in us. The image of God is only fully itself when the mind's contemplation of God governs the mind's reasoning about this-worldly things. For the image of God to be what it should be, the mind must cleave to God by knowing and loving him, rather than cleaving to any creature. Although thinking about this-worldly things is not wrong in itself, it must not be allowed to distract us from our true end and our true good. Such distraction characterizes the fallen image of God. Augustine explains that "man's true honor is God's image and likeness in him, but it can only be preserved when facing him from whom its impression is received."[75] The first humans fell by loving themselves more than they loved God, but this descent did not leave unimpaired their humanity; rather, they fell all the way to the level of animals, seeking only this-worldly goods. The lesson is that the image of God, the mind, must put *sapientia* (knowledge of God) first in order to undertake fruitful *scientia* (knowledge of creatures). Possessed only of *scientia*, the human person falls into a ridiculous and deadly pride, in which the goods of this world are not referred to God.

Augustine observes that only the grace of God through the missions of the Son and the Holy Spirit can restore the fallen image of God. Without this grace, the fallen image of God devotes itself to thinking about, and acting on, selfish goals. The fault consists not in thinking about this-worldly things, which is necessary and good, but in failing to focus on divine things and thereby failing to be configured to God's "eternity, truth, and charity."[76] We must set our heart upon union with God, for which we were created. With divine things constantly in mind through *sapientia*, we can properly understand this-worldly things through *scientia*, which builds up the moral virtues and gives us helpful historical knowledge about past actions and their effects. Contemplation and action go together. Healed by grace, the image of God can relate to other created things without cleaving to them and without impeding the ascent to God the Trinity. In this life, the *sapientia* that we attain can never

75. Augustine, *On the Trinity* 12.16, p. 331. See Gioia, *Theological Epistemology*, 238–39, 279–80, 285–97.

76. Augustine, *On the Trinity* 12.21, p. 333.

be full, because our transitory thoughts cannot abide for long among eternal things. Yet we can return over and over again to incorporeal truth, which we retain in our memory. Augustine dissents, however, from Plato's view that all learning is recollection.

Augustine has thus shown the pattern of his intellectual ascent to the three-and-one: from the triad in sight, to the triad in recollection of sense images, to *scientia*, to *sapientia*. When the mind knows itself, this knowledge of a created thing is *scientia*. The image of the Trinity, therefore, attains perfection in the mind knowing God: *sapientia*. At this stage, Augustine brings in John 1:1–14, in order to show how contemplation of eternal things is rightly combined with knowledge of temporal things. John 1:1–5 involves contemplation; John 1:6–11 largely involves knowledge; and John 1:12–14 combines the two. Lacking an awareness of history (*scientia*), we could not have faith's contemplative knowledge of divine realities (*sapientia*). Knowledge of history does not simply serve this-worldly ends; rather, the ultimate purpose of knowledge of history is to assist in the purification of the image of God and its reclamation of *sapientia*.[77] Rooted in the graced contemplation of the eternal God, faith has a certitude that goes beyond that of historical knowledge; yet at the same time faith involves historical knowledge.

What is the content of this faith, and how does it perfect the image of the Trinity? Augustine suggests that the fact that all people seek happiness sheds light on why all people can find salvation in one faith. Everyone wants to be happy, but people seek happiness in different ways because they enjoy different things and place their happiness in those things. Surely, however, a life of crime (for example, murder and rape) cannot be a happy life, even if the criminal enjoys it. It is possible to enjoy something wrongly. Augustine defines the happy person as one "who has everything he wants, and wants nothing wrongly."[78] These conditions cannot be met except through faith in God, a faith that leads to sharing in God's own life. For one thing, to want to be happy means to want to be immortal.[79] If we are not alive, we certainly cannot be happy. The desire for happiness cannot include the desire not to be happy (by being dead). If we love the happy life, we certainly will not love its annihilation. Happiness also is not merely endurance, resignation, or hope. Rather, happiness is enjoying all the good that we were made for, and enjoying it without threat of losing it against our will. This is so because happiness describes the fulfillment of the human will, the human desire for the good. Death threatens to deprive us of all good against our will. The immortality that could make us happy is not just endless sensation. The fulfillment of rational creatures requires knowing and loving in the highest possible way, communion with the Trinity.

77. For discussion see John C. Cavadini, "The Quest for Truth in Augustine's *De Trinitate*," *Theological Studies* 58 (1997): 429–40.
78. Augustine, *On the Trinity* 13.8, p. 349.
79. See Burnell, *Augustinian Person*, 56–57.

Faith, then, promises exactly what the will to happiness requires. According to Christian faith, not only the soul but the whole person will be immortal. As John 1:1–14 teaches, this will come about through the Word made flesh, not through our own powers. Augustine recognizes, however, the difficulty that people have with faith's teaching that the incarnate Son of God died in order to reconcile us with God. Could not God have saved us without becoming man and dying? Why would the Father send his Son on such a gruesome mission? Augustine explains that God's love is the opposite of our pride, as God shows by coming to share our humanity and our mortal condition. From within our condition, he freely pays our penalty by his cross and opens the path of our immortality by his resurrection. God loves us so much that he shares what is ours so that we might share what is his. The risen Christ pours forth his Holy Spirit on us and unites us to himself in charity. He heals the image of God in us, without any preceding worthiness on our part for such a gift.

Augustine combats certain misunderstandings of the reconciliation enacted by Christ's dying on the cross. For instance, one might imagine that the loving Son freely became man so as to appease the wrathful Father, in which case the Father and the Son would be divided, one loving us, the other hating us. If, however, the Father loved us so much as to send the Son, then why bother sending the Son to his death? No reconciliation by the blood of the cross would seem to be needed, since Father and Son are already united in loving us. If the Father does not spare the Son (Rom. 8:32), does this mean that the Son did not freely go to his death, but rather was killed by his Father?

Against these misunderstandings, Augustine observes that the mission of the Son was fitted to the fallen human condition. Cleaving to created things in contempt of the Creator is an action that has consequences. It is a radically unjust action, and as such it changes the human relationship to God. Human pride renounces a relationship to the God who is infinite humility and love. Once this just relationship is broken by the first humans, succeeding generations of humans suffer under the same brokenness, since we cannot restore the relationship from our own wounded resources. We are justly punished with the demons who share our pride. Indeed, since we are bonded to the demons by pride, we are rightly said to be enslaved to Satan. God justly permits this enslavement, but at the same time he overcomes Satan, not by power and compulsion but by justice and love. The lust for domination rules Satan, who does not understand the power of self-giving love; humans "imitate him all the more thoroughly the more they neglect or even detest justice and studiously devote themselves to power."[80]

How then is the human image of God healed and transformed? Augustine answers that the healing occurs by Christ's overcoming of the lust for domination by means of the seeming weakness of justice. The chains of enslavement

80. Augustine, *On the Trinity* 13.17, p. 356.

to Satan are broken by the death of one who does not justly owe the penalty of death, and whose divinity means that he gives up his life entirely freely.[81] When Jesus Christ freely pays the penalty for all, human debtors are freed from the bond that would otherwise hold us in everlasting death. Although Augustine emphasizes that Christ achieves the forgiveness of our sins by his justice, Augustine also points out that Christ's power is manifested by his resurrection. If we share in his justice by faith and charity, we will share in his power through resurrection unto eternal life.

In Christ, the human image of God once more manifests the justice of humility before God. God's "wrath," Augustine notes, described our relationship to him—the fact that our sins alienated us from God—rather than an emotion in God. By freely paying the penalty for our sins, Christ reconciles us to God. Indeed, Christ makes bodily death itself into a path of power, as demonstrated by the martyrs. God permits death and suffering to continue after Christ, because these bodily sufferings correct our sins, test our justice, and stimulate our desire for the fullness of life with God. The path of the suffering Christ constitutes the path for perfecting the image of God in us.

By becoming incarnate, God also shows that the spiritual creatures, the demons, have no right to set themselves up as mediators simply because they are immaterial. The incarnation is also a supreme instance of God's bestowal of unmerited grace; and similarly, Christ's humility and obedience instruct us regarding the way of true happiness. In the man Christ Jesus, the conquered human race conquers without being able to boast, because Christ is God. Born without sin, virginally conceived rather than conceived through concupiscence, Christ enables us to be reborn in holiness.

Returning to his distinction between *scientia* and *sapientia* (knowledge of temporal things and knowledge of eternal things), Augustine notes that the grace of Christ, revealed in history, has to do with *scientia*. God informs our *scientia* so as to perfect our *sapientia*. As Augustine says, "Our knowledge therefore is Christ, and our wisdom is the same Christ. It is he who plants faith in us about temporal things, he who presents us with the truth about eternal things."[82] Lacking faith in Christ, even the best pagan philosophers worshiped false gods. Faith in Christ, by contrast, perfects the image of God by leading us through knowledge to wisdom. Wisdom does not supersede or negate knowledge, because both involve the same Christ.

In bringing the image of God to the wisdom of divine contemplation, God gives us faith so that we can see how the goal of happiness is to be reached.

<hr />

81. See J. Patout Burns, "How Christ Saves: Augustine's Multiple Explanations," in *Tradition and the Rule of Faith in the Early Church: Essays in Honor of Joseph T. Lienhard, S.J.*, ed. Ronnie J. Rombs and Alexander Y. Hwang (Washington, DC: Catholic University of America Press, 2010), 193–210.

82. Augustine, *On the Trinity* 13.24, p. 363. See Ayres, "The Christological Context of the *De Trinitate* XIII," 118–22.

Those who despair of eternal life live as if this-worldly goods were paramount, and they thereby fail to attain eternal life with God. Faith in Christ frees us from this error and enables us to live a truly virtuous life in hope and charity. In faith's knowledge, the temporal leads to the eternal. But the mind's knowing and loving of that which is known in faith—a triad that builds upon the triads of sensation and remembering—is not fully the image of God. This is the case because faith's knowledge will pass away when we attain the vision of God in eternal life. The image of God in us should consist in contemplating the eternal God himself, not our temporal conceptions of God. Can such wisdom be found in earthly life, where we walk by faith not sight? Augustine insists that the image of God "must be found in something that will always be, and not in the retention, contemplation, and love of faith, which will not always be."[83]

He argues that the mind's consciousness of itself, a consciousness that is always in our memory even if we have not brought it to thought, is an immortal triad.[84] The mind does not pass away. Thus as regards the mind's consciousness of itself, its memory, understanding, and will present an immortal image of the Trinity. This image exists so long as the mind exists, and does not change when we move from faith to sight. The mind remembering, understanding, and loving itself does not depend upon knowledge of temporal things. Faith and the virtues begin to be in the mind's consciousness, which was already present without them. Augustine reflects here on whether all the moral virtues, or only justice, will be present in eternal life. His central point, however, is that the mind's consciousness underlies all knowing and loving. From the moment the mind "began to be it never stopped remembering itself, never stopped understanding itself, never stopped loving itself."[85]

Augustine does not end with self-consciousness. The wisdom for which Christ purifies the image of God consists in the contemplation of God; if the mind were to stop at remembering, understanding, and loving itself, it would remain foolish. How then does the mind, in this life, remember, understand, and love God in a way that resolves Augustine's earlier concerns about a triad based on temporal faith? The answer is that the human mind, our self-consciousness, participates in the divine mind. Although fallen humans have turned away from God, forgotten him, and refused to love him, no human can so turn away from God as to entirely erase the memory and the love of God. For all humans are inclined to know truth and to love the good. Sin does not erase the mind's "natural memory, understanding, and love of itself."[86] The created light of the mind continues to participate in the divine light even when the created light has fallen and has not been healed by the missions of the Son

83. Augustine, *On the Trinity* 14.4, p. 372.
84. For background in Cicero, see Ayres, *Augustine and the Trinity*, 308–13.
85. Augustine, *On the Trinity* 14.13, p. 382.
86. Augustine, *On the Trinity* 14.19, p. 385.

and the Holy Spirit. As Augustine remarks, "It is in virtue of this light that even the godless can think about eternity, and rightly praise and blame many elements in the behavior of men."[87] The unchangeable standards of justice and truth persist as ideals even in unjust minds, because even unjust minds exist by participation in the divine mind.

The missions of the Son and the Holy Spirit restore the mind's ability to remember, know, and love itself as a participation in the eternal divine mind.[88] Although this reality is never utterly effaced by sin, nonetheless the image of God needs reforming, having "lost justice and the holiness of truth" (cf. Eph. 4:22–24).[89] This reformation of the image takes place by reclaiming the knowledge of God, as Augustine suggests in light of Colossians 3:9. Since the image is in the mind, its reformation requires "the renewal of your mind" (Rom. 12:2), or as Paul urges in Ephesians 4:23, "be renewed in the spirit of your minds." The reformation of the image does not occur once and for all at baptism, although baptism brings about the forgiveness of the sins that distorted the image. Rather, the image remains weak and so its reformation involves a gradual process. By God's grace, we advance toward a greater love for eternal realities, which we come to prefer over temporal realities.[90] As faith and charity unite us more and more strongly to God, we curb and overcome our greed and lust for temporal goods. We receive the perfect image of God only in the vision of God, when "we shall be like him [God], for we shall see him as he is" (1 John 3:2). Not only will the image of God in our minds perfectly reflect the Trinity, but also our resurrected bodies will image the risen body of the incarnate Son (cf. 1 Cor. 15:49). The specific perfection of the image of God, however, consists in contemplative wisdom: as Jesus says, "This is eternal life, that they know thee the only true God, and Jesus Christ whom thou hast sent" (John 17:3).

Such wisdom, which God makes possible for us through Christ and the Holy Spirit, consists in the perfect participation of our mind in the divine mind. This participation has already begun now. Even in this life, our minds already taste the immortality of the good and the true, and find here an immortal triad. Augustine urges us to focus our attention on developing this triad, so that the mind not only knows of the ideals of justice and truth but also shares in them consciously as sharing in God. Here Augustine is both inspired and repelled by Cicero, who teaches on the one hand that we should seek immortal wisdom and on the other hand that if we are destined to be annihilated, we should

87. Augustine, *On the Trinity* 14.21, p. 387.

88. See Rowan Williams, "*Sapientia* and the Trinity: Reflections on the *De Trinitate*," in *Collectanea Augustiniana: Mélanges T. J. van Bavel*, ed. B. Bruning, M. Lamberigts, and J. van Houtem (Leuven: Leuven University Press, 1990), 317–32, at 321.

89. Augustine, *On the Trinity* 14.22, p. 388. Augustine's reference to "justice and the holiness of truth" comes from his text of Ephesians 4:23.

90. See Ayres, *Augustine and the Trinity*, 305–8.

hope for a happy death. Since our mind already tastes the eternal goodness and truth, there can be no happy annihilation: we are made for communion with God. Yet neither can there be happiness or return to God's justice and truth without faith in the mediator, Jesus Christ, and imitation of his justice, humility, and obedience in death. Reason alone is a dead end, leading simply to pride. Augustine concludes that the wise participation in God for which God created his image comes about only through the incarnate image, the wisdom of God, Christ Jesus.

In his prologue to the fifteenth and final book of *On the Trinity*, Augustine states that the work's plan has been "to train the reader, *in the things that have been made* (Rom. 1:20), for getting to know him by whom they were made."[91] We have examined the pattern of this participatory ascent, which begins with God the Trinity's descent (the missions and theophanies) and then ascends through the divine names, the created image, and the image perfected by the missions. Book 15 addresses the limitations of the created image and encourages an ongoing effort to participate more deeply in the Trinity through faith in Christ the mediator and through the gift of the Holy Spirit. Much of Book 15 is devoted to the Holy Spirit, who is the gift that we need in order to be drawn into the divine life. Augustine takes as his guiding text Psalm 105:4, "seek his presence continually." The incomprehensible God "is sought in order to be found all the more delightfully, and . . . found in order to be sought all the more avidly."[92] Even the weakness of the image is an aid to ascent, since searching causes us to grow in communion with Father, Son, and Holy Spirit.

The argument of Book 15 begins by discussing the weaknesses of the image of God. First, Augustine points out that apprehending the triad of memory, understanding, and love does not constitute a proof that God is Trinity. We know God as Trinity only through revelation; the created image assists us in our effort, as Christians, to understand and love the divine three-and-one.[93] As Augustine shows, we cannot know that God is Trinity by analogy from any created perfection, since these perfections analogously name what is common in God. Another problem is that the created image is not man, whereas God's wisdom, knowledge of himself, and love of himself are all nothing other than God. In the created image, furthermore, the mind does not love without the movement of the will. By contrast, the Father is love in himself; to be love, he does not rely upon the Holy Spirit. The Holy Spirit is not the Father's love, just as the Father is not the Holy Spirit's memory.[94] In addition, whereas our mind reasons discursively and reflects upon past and future, God is infinite

91. Augustine, *On the Trinity* 15.1, p. 395.
92. Augustine, *On the Trinity* 15.2, p. 396.
93. See Studer, "History and Faith," 19–32.
94. See Ayres, *Augustine and the Trinity*, 232–33; Williams, "*Sapientia* and the Trinity," 330–31.

present, with no before or after. Indeed we cannot even comprehend how our memory and understanding operate, much less God's.

How then does the image of God in the mind illumine God the Trinity? Augustine draws upon St. Paul's suggestion that "now we see in a mirror dimly [or: in an enigma], but then face to face" (1 Cor. 13:12). When we look into a mirror, what we see is an image. According to Genesis 1, we are this image of God. We are not a static image; as Paul goes on to say, "we all, with unveiled face, beholding the glory of the Lord, are being changed into his likeness from one degree of glory to another" (2 Cor. 3:18). God is perfecting his image in us. By grace, God heals us of our sins and sanctifies us, so that we might reflect his wisdom and charity. When we move from faith to sight, we will be like God.[95] Augustine makes much of Paul's emphasis on the enigmatic character of what we see in the mirror. In Augustine's view, Paul means to describe the image as "an obscure allegory."[96] The image of God in us is an obscure one, not one that is easily known.

This obscurity, Augustine proposes, fits with what he has been saying about the image of God in the mind's consciousness of itself (and, more perfectly, of itself as a participation in the divine light). We all have self-consciousness, but we do not reflect on our self-consciousness. We think about various objects, but we do not often think about our own thinking. Augustine examines our inward thought as an inner word that reflects the Word: "When we utter [interiorly] something true, that is when we utter what we know, a word is necessarily born from the knowledge which we hold in the memory, a word which is absolutely the same kind of thing as the knowledge it is born from."[97] This inner word is prior to any vocal sound or written sign. Just as the Word of God is begotten of the Father and becomes incarnate, so also the inner word is begotten of the mind and becomes vocal sound. Every work too originates in an inner word, just as God creates through the Word. When our inner word is perfectly true and lovable, then the image of God in us will be perfect.

Our knowledge, however, is weak; indeed Augustine suggests that human knowledge has absolute certitude in only a few cases such as knowing that we are alive, although he has no doubt that the bodily senses and other people's testimony offer reliable witness as well. By contrast, God knows everything without learning it and with perfect truth. God's knowledge is his being, whereas our knowledge differs from our being. We generate our inner word in time, whereas God's Word is eternal. In the Trinity, the Son receives his knowledge from the Father, and he and the Father are this knowledge. Our inner word, therefore, is far from the Word begotten by God the Father. Even when the image of God in our mind is perfected by the vision of God, our inner word will still be creaturely.

95. See Gerald Bonner, "Augustine's Conception of Deification," *Journal of Theological Studies* 37 (1986): 369–86.

96. Augustine, *On the Trinity* 15.15, p. 407.

97. Augustine, *On the Trinity* 15.19, p. 409.

What about the Holy Spirit? Augustine asks whether, if God is love, the Holy Spirit can properly be named love.[98] In answer, he cites a number of biblical texts that associate the Holy Spirit with "love" and "gift." The Holy Spirit proceeds as gift of love from the Father and Son, and so the Holy Spirit is named by what they possess in common. Only when we receive this gift can we attain to eternal life. The mission of the Holy Spirit bestows upon us this gift. Augustine takes the opportunity to criticize the Eunomian heresy that held that the Son of God is the product of the Father's will: the Trinity is no more the product of will than the divine nature itself is. This heresy imagines the Trinity in creaturely terms, forgetting that the begetting and spiration are eternal and not the acts of a prior God who chose to become Father. Augustine concludes this discussion by urging believers to remember, know, and love the Trinity in their minds, and thereby to become more perfectly the image of God without imagining that the image can ever come close to equaling what it images.

When believers remember, know, and love, it is one person who is doing the remembering, knowing, and loving. By contrast, God is three persons. This difference is significant enough on its own, but it goes deeper than merely the contrast between three divine persons and one human mind. After all, the unity of Father, Son, and Holy Spirit is perfectly simple, whereas any human unity is a composite. The unity of the divine persons constitutes a far more inseparable unity than that of the one human mind. Still another difference presents itself: as the image of God, a human person has a mind that remembers, understands, and loves. As the Trinity, God does not possess the mind and its acts; rather, the triad *is* God. Similarly, a human person can have great memory and understanding but little love: the three hardly need be coequal, whereas in God the three are supremely coequal. Again, a person's memory, understanding, and will change, whereas the Father, Son, and Holy Spirit do not change. Thus without denying that some likeness exists between on the one hand memory of intelligible things, understanding as formulated in the inner word, and love that proceeds from and unites memory and understanding, and on the other hand the Father, Son, and Holy Spirit, nonetheless this likeness pales in comparison to the dissimilitude. Augustine adds that one should not suppose that the Father, Son, and Holy Spirit are less intelligible than our memory, understanding, and love. In eternal life, we will see the Father, Son, and Holy Spirit far more clearly than we now see our mind.

The purpose of the image, of course, does not consist in its ability to lead us to reflect upon our self-consciousness and to apprehend its operations. Rather,

98. See Ayres, *Augustine and the Trinity*, 251–54, 258–59; Gioia, *Theological Epistemology*, 135–39; Basil Studer, OSB, "Zur Pneumatologie des Augustinus von Hippo (*De Trinitate* 15,17,27 – 27,50)," *Augustinianum* 35 (1995): 567–83; Joseph Ratzinger, "The Holy Spirit as Communio: Concerning the Relationship of Pneumatology and Spirituality in Augustine," trans. Peter Casarella, *Communio* 25 (1998): 324–37, at 327–31.

when rightly seen, the image of God in us enables us to see our conscious operations as participations in the divine light, participations that reflect, however dimly, the three-and-one. Apprehending the mind is useless without recognizing the image of God by means of the purification achieved by faith.

At the end of this meditation Augustine returns to the Holy Spirit, not only to the difficulty of showing why he is not another Son from the Father (Augustine resolves this by observing that he proceeds from the Father and the Son), but also to the problem of the dual gift of the Holy Spirit, the first in the risen Christ's breathing the Spirit upon his disciples, the second at Pentecost. The gift of the Holy Spirit inspires in us love for God and for neighbor, and Augustine suggests that Christ's twice giving the Spirit expresses this twofold orientation of love. Augustine wonders that anyone knowledgeable in Scripture could have ever supposed that Christ was not God, since Christ breathes forth the Holy Spirit. Yet Christ, as man, received the Holy Spirit and was perfected in grace by the Holy Spirit. Although Christ fully possessed the Holy Spirit at his conception, as we find in Luke 1:15, nonetheless he also received the Holy Spirit (in the form of a dove) at his baptism so as to show the power of baptism in forming Christ's Body, the Church.

Augustine similarly inquires into the order of the trinitarian processions: Might the Holy Spirit have already proceeded from the Father so as to assist in the begetting of the Son? The trinitarian processions have no temporality. In begetting his Son (distinct from him only as Son), the Father gives the Son all that he is except his Fatherhood. The Son thus receives from the Father the power to spirate the Spirit with the Father, who is the source. Since the Son is begotten, there are not two Fathers in the Trinity, even though the Father enables the Son to spirate the Spirit with him. As Augustine puts it, "The Son is born of the Father and the Holy Spirit proceeds from the Father principally, and by the Father's wholly timeless gift from both of them jointly."[99] To this conclusion about the difference of generation and procession, Augustine adds a lengthy quotation from a sermon that he delivered on the subject. He is aware that believers will find his arguments about the image of God and about the trinitarian processions much more persuasive than will unbelievers, and so he encourages unbelievers first to be enlightened by faith in what the Scriptures attest and then to explore the mind as an image, rather than the other way around. Illumined by faith, the believer should turn to the mind, created spirit, in order to seek understanding of the mystery of uncreated Spirit, three-and-one.

In his concluding observations, Augustine makes clear that speculation about the Trinity is not the aim of his work. Rather, participation in the Trinity is

---

99. Augustine, *On the Trinity* 15.47, pp. 432–33. See Ayres, "*Sempiterne Spiritus Donum*," in *Orthodox Readings of Augustine*, 146–49; Gioia, *Theological Epistemology*, 139–46; Ayres, *Augustine and the Trinity*, 263–66.

what he seeks. He compares himself to the man, beaten and left on the side of the road, whom the good Samaritan has found half-dead.[100] In seeking truth about things, he has discerned the light of the mind, which participates in the divine light, eternal truth. In the divine light, he sees the Father and his Word and Gift, but he can see these distinct persons only dimly, in the image of his mind and its operations. He sees his own inner word begotten of his memory, and he sees the joining of this inner word to the memory by love, which is not another word or image. The book closes with a prayer, in which he begs to share more and more in God the Trinity and in which he looks forward to eternal life: "Let me remember you, let me understand you, let me love you. Increase these things in me until you refashion me entirely."[101]

Conclusion

Augustine's lengthy quotation from Cicero's *Hortensius* at the end of Book 14 is significant. Why does Augustine quote Cicero at the very moment that his ascent is reaching its pinnacle? In Augustine's *Confessions*, it is Cicero's *Hortensius* that first awakens him to what the life of wisdom can be. As Augustine says of *Hortensius*, "It altered my prayers, Lord, to be towards you yourself. It gave me different values and priorities [*vota ac desideria*]. Suddenly every vain hope became empty to me, and I longed for the immortality of wisdom with an incredible ardour in my heart. I began to rise up to return to you."[102] Cicero urges his readers to seek wisdom. Yet Cicero is ultimately agnostic about whether death is the portal to eternal life or to annihilation, and Cicero knew no commonwealth other than Rome.

In *On the Trinity*, therefore, Augustine offers a new *Hortensius*, completely revised on christological and trinitarian grounds.[103] The true wisdom is to enter into one's mind and recognize its operations as the image of the divine Trinity by whose light we remember, understand, and love. This path to wisdom requires faith in the mediator and the grace of the Holy Spirit, so as to be undertaken in charity rather than in pride. The missions of the Son and the Spirit, coequal with the Father, reveal the divine Trinity to us. We can then learn how to name the Father, Son, and Holy Spirit, one God, without detracting from the divine simplicity or blurring the distinction of divine persons. Speaking about God the Trinity leads us to ask about our mind, by which we

100. See Roland Teske, SJ, "The Good Samaritan (Luke 10:29–37) in Augustine's Exegesis," in *Augustine: Biblical Exegete*, ed. Frederick Van Fleteren and Joseph C. Schnaubelt, OSA (New York: Peter Lang, 2001), 347–67.
101. Augustine, *On the Trinity* 15.51, p. 436.
102. Augustine, *Confessions* 3.4.7, trans. Henry Chadwick (Oxford: Oxford University Press, 1991), 39. See Ryan N. S. Topping, *St. Augustine* (London: Continuum, 2010), 38.
103. See Gioia, *Theological Epistemology*, 227–31.

speak these truths. Enlightened by Christ and the Spirit, we find in our mind and its knowledge and love an image of the eternal Trinity, and we discover that even our sensation and recollection are pointing us toward this spiritual triad. The missions of the Son and the Holy Spirit purify and strengthen the image in us, despite its inevitable weakness.

At its height, this ascent provides us with a glimpse, in and through our renewed and reconfigured mind, of the Holy Trinity. This path of wisdom always stretches on before us in this life, because the mystery is infinite and inexhaustible. Only in eternal life will the reality of the Trinity become clear to our minds, but even now we can participate more and more in God. In Christ and his Spirit, we can live the theocentric life of wisdom, to which Cicero pointed in an inadequate but inspiring way. Augustine's *On the Trinity* is an invitation to this life of participatory ascent and a guide to its paths and pitfalls. Augustine invites the reader to move with him from the history of God's dealings with Israel and the missions of the Son and Spirit, revealing the coequal Trinity, to the inward ascent to contemplative embrace of the God who has revealed himself in history. As quoted by Augustine at the end of Book 14, Cicero teaches that the greatest philosophers consider that we have immortal souls and that if so the best thing we can do is to devote ourselves, in philosophical studies, to seeking the wisdom that fosters (in Cicero's words) "[the soul's] ascent and return to heaven."[104] This participatory ascent is Augustine's purpose in *On the Trinity*, from a perspective schooled by Christ the mediator in the commonwealth of the Church.

104. Quoted in Augustine, *On the Trinity* 14.26, p. 391.

Conclusion

The briefest of conclusions is appropriate. Lewis Ayres observes that for Augustine, "one of the functions of the incarnate and resurrected Christ is to lead our intelligence beyond an obsession with the material, to imagine the immaterial reality of the divine as the source of our material world."[1] The real is not limited to the empirical. Each of us, our communities, and indeed the entire cosmos points to a Creator who utterly transcends anything created. God is not another finite mode of being; God is not contingent upon the act of another. God is radically unlike us, and yet the perfections that we find in creatures all come from and participate in God, who is the source of all finite being and goodness. Humans have turned away from God, but this infinitely personal and infinitely present Creator reaches out to persons not simply individually but by forming a people, Israel, by whom he is known. With the extraordinary humility that is the mark of the true God who pours forth all things, he enters into history so intimately as to come to Israel as Savior and to heal the wound of sin from within our plight. Christ reveals his Father in the Holy Spirit, and invites us to share in the eternal glory of the infinite unity and communion that is the trinitarian life. This relationship of love is what we have been made for and what the Church is all about.

Augustine knows, however, that to many people it seems that God would not want to know us and that no transcendent God would bother to create a material realm filled with corruption and all sorts of sins. To think in this way, however, is to shield our eyes from the divine generosity and to ignore the mystery and depths of personal communion. The excitement of knowing and loving the infinitely gracious God infuses Augustine's work. He rejoices

---

1. Lewis Ayres, "The Fundamental Grammar of Augustine's Trinitarian Theology," in *Augustine and His Critics: Essays in Honour of Gerald Bonner*, ed. Robert Dodaro and George Lawless (London: Routledge, 2000), 51–76, at 70.

in the love and humility of God who frees us in Christ from the bonds of sin and death. This God is so generous, so lovable.

If we are asked in what way Augustine is most relevant today, therefore, the answer is that he is among the greatest theologians of the living God, the Triune God whose nature is first revealed in his covenants with the people of Israel and who is most fully revealed by Christ Jesus and the Holy Spirit. The "new atheists" of today would not be new to Augustine. Not only does he have responses to their questions about God, but also he perceives the way in which our lives are shaped by our loves—and the way in which Christian faith opens us to the greatest possible commitment of love.

The *Confessions* will always be relevant to people who struggle with the big questions about life, death, and God. In the story of his life, Augustine shows us why theology must not rest in any subject but God, and he also shows that the living God is found only in humility. Ultimately we must allow ourselves to be oriented by God. This is what God, in Christ, does for us. We inevitably imagine that we will find God in power, but instead we find him in love. Likewise, the *City of God* has an enduring relevance, especially in societies that have lost their collective apprehension of a transcendent end or goal for the human race. In such societies, it will easily seem that this-worldly things are the only real objects of worship and pursuit. We find however that living in this way proves futile and mires our lives in meaninglessness. The *City of God* examines how God, in Scripture, reveals to us a better way.

The task of being conformed in wisdom and love to Christ's better way means that academic learning cannot suffice. We want to get to the core of things, and to be enlivened by an enduring relationship. The labor of *On the Trinity* is to show that the Triune God's transcendence actually makes possible his profound presence to us. The wisdom of learning how to speak about God turns out to be an existential encounter of knowing and loving the Trinity whose image we are. The fact that he escapes the finitude of our modes of knowing is a sign that we have found the true Creator God.

On the Trinity is vibrantly alive within contemporary theological debates. Similarly, the *Confessions* and *City of God* continue to be influential in contemporary study of the human person and of the goals of politics. Whereas *On the Trinity* is a book for speculative theologians, *Confessions* and *City of God* attract all sorts of readers. Modern secular anthropology and political science neglect these works at their peril. Fortunately, there are readers such as Hannah Arendt, Charles Taylor, and Pierre Manent whose creative engagements with these works bear evident fruit today.

By contrast, *On Christian Doctrine* and *Answer to Faustus, a Manichean* are not frequently consulted by contemporary biblical scholars. For scholars who care about why it is that Christians read these diverse texts as one Bible, however, engagement with both *On Christian Doctrine* and *Answer to Faustus, a Manichean* is necessary. The great point of *On Christian Doctrine* consists in the view that all Scripture has to do with love of God and love of neighbor. Love unites both the texts and the persons and deeds to which the texts refer to the Triune God who is love. The challenge for readers informed by *On Christian Doctrine* consists largely, therefore, in how to teach and preach this love, given the evidence in the world and even in Scripture that tells against the priority of love. Recent debates over Christian "supersessionism," the view that the Church negates and displaces the people of Israel, have begun to recover the significance of *Answer to Faustus, a Manichean*. In this work, Augustine explains why the relationship of the two Testaments cannot be conceived either as strict continuity or strict discontinuity. Rather, because Jesus is the Messiah of Israel, the fulfillment he brings is neither a negation nor a linear extension. In *Answer to Faustus, a Manichean* Augustine shows why Christians embrace the Old Testament even while considering its covenants to be fulfilled in Christ. Everyone who seeks to understand what might be meant by messianic fulfillment, and why Christian Scripture has two Testaments, will benefit from Augustine's arguments in *Answer to Faustus, a Manichean*.

Augustine's *Homilies on the First Epistle of John* is now timelier than ever because of the ecumenical movement of the past century. As a Catholic bishop, Augustine sought a dialogue with the Donatists, but he also polemically critiqued them. He is thus a somewhat unlikely progenitor of contemporary ecumenical theology: not only did he view Donatists as schismatics who were in grave error on central points of faith and practice, but also he was wrongly willing to support the imperial decrees that persecuted Donatist Christianity. Yet Augustine recognized the difficulties of his position, and he attempted to face these difficulties by reflecting on what it means for believers to love both God and each other, given that the Church consists of sinful and weak people. This work of Augustine goes to the heart of Christian unity as Christ's Body and therefore stands as a fundamental work for all who care about the specific unity that should characterize Christians in faith and love.

Contemporary theologians and biblical exegetes often fear that a predestining God has to be arbitrary and deficient in love toward some of his rational creatures. Augustine's doctrine of predestination holds that God predestines some to eternal life but permits others, by their own free choice, to fall away permanently and suffer everlasting damnation. Despite the puzzles caused by this doctrine, *On the Predestination of the Saints* demonstrates that it is a biblical doctrine that has to do strictly with God's grace. Predestination bears witness to the Triune God's eternal plan to share his life with rational creatures. I do not suppose that Augustine has the last word on the topic, but he reminds us in a powerful way that everything good is God's gift.

Throughout his works, Augustine shows that "to praise you [God] is the desire of man, a little piece of your creation. You stir man to take pleasure in praising you, because you have made us for yourself, and our heart is restless until it rests in you."[2] We are made to love the Triune God and to participate in his life. This is the message of these seven works of Augustine. May the ongoing conversations about these seven works be a blessing for the Church and the world. May they help us learn to praise God so as to rest in him forever!

2. Augustine, *Confessions* 1.1.1, trans. Henry Chadwick (Oxford: Oxford University Press, 1991), 3.

For Further Reading

In the footnotes, I have provided a bibliographical introduction (largely of English-speaking research) to these seven central works of Augustine. If I were stranded on a desert island and could only have thirty items from the works I cited, these recent studies are the ones that I would choose first:

Ayres, Lewis. *Augustine and the Trinity*. Cambridge: Cambridge University Press, 2010.

———. "Augustine, Christology, and God as Love: An Introduction to the Homilies on 1 John." In *Nothing Greater, Nothing Better: Theological Essays on the Love of God*, edited by Kevin J. Vanhoozer, 67–93. Grand Rapids: Eerdmans, 2001.

———. "The Christological Context of the *De Trinitate* XIII: Toward Relocating Books VIII–XV." *Augustinian Studies* 29 (1998): 111–39.

———. "'Remember That You Are Catholic' (serm. 52.2): Augustine on the Unity of the Triune God." *Journal of Early Christian Studies* 8 (2000): 39–82.

Barnes, Michel René. "Exegesis and Polemic in Augustine's *De Trinitate* I." *Augustinian Studies* 30 (1999): 43–59.

———. "The Visible Christ and the Invisible Trinity: Mt. 5:8 in Augustine's Trinitarian Theology of 400." *Modern Theology* 19 (2003): 329–55.

Burnell, Peter. *The Augustinian Person*. Washington, DC: Catholic University of America Press, 2005.

Byassee, Jason. *Praise Seeking Understanding: Reading the Psalms with Augustine*. Grand Rapids: Eerdmans, 2007.

Cavadini, John C. "The Darkest Enigma: Reconsidering the Self in Augustine's Thought." *Augustinian Studies* 38 (2007): 119–32.

———. "Simplifying Augustine." In *Educating People of Faith: Exploring the History of Jewish and Christian Communities*, edited by John Van Engen, 63–84. Grand Rapids: Eerdmans, 2004.

————. "The Sweetness of the Word: Salvation and Rhetoric in Augustine's *De doctrina christiana*." In *De doctrina christiana: A Classic of Western Culture*, edited by Duane W. H. Arnold and Pamela Bright, 164–81. Notre Dame, IN: University of Notre Dame Press, 1995.

Crawford, Nathan. "The Sapiential Structure of Augustine's *De Trinitate*." *Pro Ecclesia* 19 (2010): 434–52.

Daley, Brian E., SJ. "A Humble Mediator: The Distinctive Elements of St. Augustine's Christology." *Word and Spirit* 9 (1987): 100–117.

Dodaro, Robert, OSA. *Christ and the Just Society in the Thought of Augustine*. Cambridge: Cambridge University Press, 2004.

Fitzgerald, Allan D., OSA, ed. *Augustine through the Ages*. Grand Rapids: Eerdmans, 1999.

Fredriksen, Paula. *Augustine and the Jews: A Christian Defense of Jews and Judaism*. New York: Doubleday, 2008.

Gioia, Luigi, OSB. *The Theological Epistemology of Augustine's* De Trinitate. Oxford: Oxford University Press, 2008.

Harrison, Carol. *Beauty and Revelation in the Thought of Saint Augustine*. Oxford: Clarendon, 1992.

————. *Rethinking Augustine's Early Theology: An Argument for Continuity*. Oxford: Oxford University Press, 2006.

Lienhard, Joseph T., SJ. "Augustine of Hippo, Basil of Caesarea, and Gregory Nazianzen." In *Orthodox Readings of Augustine*, edited by George E. Demacopoulos and Aristotle Papanikolaou, 81–99. Crestwood, NY: St. Vladimir's Seminary Press, 2008.

Martin, Thomas F., OSA. "Paul the Patient: *Christus Medicus* and the '*Stimulus Carnis*' (2 Cor. 12:7): A Consideration of Augustine's Medicinal Christology." *Augustinian Studies* 32 (2001): 219–56.

Meconi, David V., SJ. "The Incarnation and the Role of Participation in St. Augustine's *Confessions*." *Augustinian Studies* 29 (1998): 61–75.

O'Daly, Gerald. *Augustine's* City of God: *A Reader's Guide*. Oxford: Oxford University Press, 1999.

Paffenroth, Kim, and Robert P. Kennedy, eds. *A Reader's Companion to Augustine's* Confessions. Louisville: Westminster John Knox, 2003.

Rombs, Ronnie J. *Saint Augustine and the Fall of the Soul: Beyond O'Connell and His Critics*. Washington, DC: Catholic University of America Press, 2006.

Schlabach, Gerald W. *For the Joy Set before Us: Augustine and Self-Denying Love*. Notre Dame, IN: University of Notre Dame Press, 2001.

Studer, Basil, OSB. *The Grace of Christ and the Grace of God in Augustine of Hippo: Christocentrism or Theocentrism?* Translated by Matthew J. O'Connell. Collegeville, MN: Liturgical Press, 1997.

Wetzel, James. *Augustine and the Limits of Virtue*. Cambridge: Cambridge University Press, 1992.

Williams, Rowan. "Language, Reality and Desire in Augustine's *De doctrina*." *Literature & Theology* 3 (1989): 138–50.

―――. "Politics and the Soul: A Reading of the *City of God*." *Milltown Studies* 19 (1987): 55–72.

Subject Index

198

nature, 4, 43–44, 47, 75, 100–101, 117, 120–21,
    126, 129, 135, 143–44, 149, 156, 188
  divine, 82, 122, 183
  human, xvii, 5, 17, 25, 34, 82, 122, 138, 154, 174
  neo-Platonic, xvi, 89, 93, 99–102, 105, 110,
    120–21, 123, 130, 152, 159
Noah, 24, 130–32, 149

On Christian Doctrine, xi–xiii, xvii, 1, 16, 19,
    188–89
On the Predestination of the Saints, xii–xiv,
    xviii, 71–72, 74, 88, 189
On the Time of the Christian Religion, 79
On the Trinity, xii–xiii, xviii, 151–53, 181,
    185–86, 188

participation, xii, xviii, 22, 71–72, 82, 84,
    99–101, 106–7, 114, 118–19, 121–22, 141,
    156–58, 163, 165, 180–82, 184
  in Christ, 31, 83, 128
  in God, 77, 79, 89–90, 94, 125–30, 145, 147,
    149, 152–53, 157, 171–72, 181
  human, 97, 129, 137
Pasch, 45, 50, 99, 125, 133
Passion (Christ's), 131–32, 134
passions, 65, 94, 108, 123, 128, 150
peace, xiii, 10, 40–41, 49, 60, 63, 101, 108, 110,
    115, 133, 135, 139–41, 143–44, 148, 150
Pelagianism, xvii, 82
Pelagians, xiii, xvii, 82, 84
Pelagius, xvii, 73
persecution, xv, 25, 39, 136, 142
  and *traditores*, xv, 68
pilgrimage, 66, 108, 136, 139, 141
Plato, 11, 121–22, 125–27, 148, 176
Platonists, 113, 121–22, 124–25, 128, 130–31
preaching, xiii, xvi, 1, 15–16, 45, 53, 83, 86,
    109, 125
predestination, xii, xvii, 71, 74, 77n15, 80–84,
    86, 189
priesthood, 28, 125, 133
property, xiv, xvi, 23, 166
prophets, 6, 12, 21, 30–31, 134, 156, 159–60
  false, 60
  of Israel, 24–25, 29, 31, 35–36, 43–45, 135–36
  patriarchs and, 27, 35, 37, 42, 44, 46, 133, 155
  testimony of Christ, 1, 24–25, 27–29, 42

resurrection, xii, 21, 32, 35, 128, 131, 137, 142,
    146, 158, 177
  of the body, 40, 148, 171
  of Christ, 31, 39, 134, 156, 178

of the dead, 31, 125, 141–42
  See also cross; death
Retractions, 74–75, 89
revelation, 79, 90, 101, 121, 144–45, 151, 156
  of God, 39, 161–62, 181
rhetoric, 11, 15–16, 94, 94n19, 174
Rome, xiv–xvii, 96–98, 114–19, 124, 134–36,
    141, 146, 149–50, 185

sacrament, 12, 31–33, 45, 53–55, 60, 62, 108–11,
    147, 158, 160. *See also* baptism; Eucharist
sacramental signs, 31–33, 47
sacrifice, 6, 39, 58, 111, 123, 125, 132–33, 141,
    150, 159
  animal, 22, 28, 30–31, 35, 37, 40, 135
  of Christ, 22, 123
  See also Eucharist
saints, 8, 13, 36, 38, 52, 108–10, 123, 125, 128–
    31, 142, 144–45, 147–48
salvation, xi, xiii–xiv, 8, 12, 17, 32, 42, 53–55,
    59, 72, 79–80, 83, 92, 101, 103, 125–26, 142,
    144, 160, 174, 176
  instrument of, 2, 9, 76
  order of, 71
  way of, 37, 81, 85, 99, 150n125
  See also Church
sanctification, 75, 149, 160
Satan, 44, 177–78. *See also* devil
schism, xv, 55, 60
  between Catholics and Donatists, xiii–xiv,
    xvii, 55, 62, 189
Scripture, xiv–xv, xvii, 3, 9, 11–15, 23, 37–39,
    53, 55, 72, 87, 89, 99, 101, 106, 108, 123,
    125, 130–31, 136–38, 148, 154–56, 161, 166,
    170, 184, 188
  authority of, 10, 110, 126
  books of, 1, 8, 10
  Christian, xii–xiii, 189
  condemnation of, 41
  as holy/sacred, 16, 25–26, 144
  testaments of, 19, 27, 54, 145, 158
  theology of, xii, 20
  words of, 2, 109
  See also interpretation; signs
signs, xvii, 3, 8–10, 13, 15, 156, 188
  scriptural, 12, 17, 19
  See also sacrament
simplicity, xii, 126, 152, 164, 166, 185
sin, 5, 9, 14, 21, 30, 35–37, 40, 54–56, 59, 63,
    66–67, 72, 77, 82, 90, 93, 101, 104, 106, 110,
    121–22, 146, 149, 158, 179, 187

forgiveness of, 53, 61–62, 68, 83, 98, 140–41, 156, 168, 178, 180, 182
mortal, 145
original, 82, 92, 127–28, 143
and punishment, 108, 129, 142–43, 159
sinless, xvii, 51, 57–58, 123, 147
sinner, 27–28, 39, 41–42, 46, 52, 64–65, 78, 80, 91, 135, 144
venial, 143, 145
See also death
Son of God. *See* Jesus Christ
soul, 26, 65, 82, 92–93, 95–97, 99–100, 104, 125, 128–29, 148, 157–58, 160, 168, 174–75, 177, 186
body and, 138–39, 146, 164, 171
of Christ, 141
rational, 108–9, 121
world-soul, 116–17, 120–21, 123–24
symbols, 14, 20, 22–23, 31–33, 35–39, 41–43, 46, 125, 142, 154, 158–59, 173–74
of Christ, 24, 29–30, 45, 123, 131–33, 146
See also Church; sacrament

teachings, xvi, 17, 29, 45, 74, 123, 177
Catholic, 98, 100, 108
of Christ, xv, 6, 23, 34, 46–47, 111
false, 26, 42–43
in Scripture, xvii, 13, 15, 20, 72–73, 126, 128, 154
Theodosius, 119
time, xiii, 8, 14, 29, 34, 40, 42, 45, 53, 79–80, 90, 99, 104, 106–7, 114, 121, 126, 145, 159, 162, 182. *See also* eternity
Trinity, 9–10, 106–7, 109, 122, 125, 128, 130, 148, 154–55, 162, 180, 183–84
divine, xii, 127, 169, 185
doctrine of, 153, 164
eternal, xiii, 8, 186
God the, xviii, 69, 90, 152, 157, 159, 161, 166, 168–69, 175, 181–82
image of, 167, 170–73, 176, 179
Triune God, 79, 110, 137–39, 165, 188–90
truth, 9–10, 15, 24, 27, 37, 42, 47, 51, 72, 78–79, 86, 92–96, 107, 121–22, 127, 159–60

of Christ, 45, 55, 136, 140, 152, 163, 166–68, 172, 176, 178–80, 181 (*see also* charity; grace)
divine, 158, 161
eternal, 54, 99–100, 105, 170, 173–74, 185
of faith, 13
law of, 31
perfect, 182
of Scripture, 14, 46, 90
spirit of, 61
two cities, 113n2, 125n38, 127, 130, 137

unity, 5, 60, 93, 127, 152, 158, 161–62, 164–67, 171, 183, 187
in Christ, 103, 174, 189
of the Church, xii, xvii, 50, 53, 62, 66
in faith, 21, 32, 103, 127
of Old and New Testaments, xiv, 32

Varro, 116–17, 119–22, 134, 138, 148
victory, 72, 101, 116, 144
vision, 8, 57, 121, 148, 150, 152, 154, 156, 171, 179–80, 182

will, 7, 35, 42, 72, 74, 76–78, 86–87, 99–100, 127–29, 154, 158, 170–71, 176–77, 181
of Christ, 63, 84
of God, 9, 40, 53, 79–80, 82, 84–85, 109, 117–18, 126, 134, 146, 156–57, 183
wisdom, 36, 39, 42, 51, 75, 85, 94–95, 98, 103, 127, 140–41, 148, 153, 157, 163–64, 172–73, 175, 179, 185–86, 188
of Christ, 124, 166, 178, 180
of God, 83, 125, 148, 160–61, 165, 181–82
participation in, 99, 101, 106, 109
Word. *See* Jesus Christ
worship, xv–xvi, 12, 22, 26, 33, 37, 40, 81, 89, 95, 110, 123, 132, 140, 149–50, 150n125, 159, 173–74, 178
of Christ, 55, 146
idol, 11, 42, 134, 146
pagan, xiv, 30, 113, 115–22, 124–25, 130, 137, 141–42
See also Arian

Scripture Index